Venus in Hollywood

THE CONTINENTAL ENCHANTRESS
FROM GARBO TO LOREN

Some of the material in Chapter 4: *Vilma Banky, Queen of the Pleasure Domes* originally appeared in a series of articles, *The Rise and Fall of the Movie Pleasure Domes*, published in *Cue* Magazine.

Venus in Hollywood

*THE CONTINENTAL ENCHANTRESS
FROM GARBO TO LOREN*

by Michael Bruno

LYLE STUART, INC. ~ NEW YORK

Most of the photo illustrations are from the Cinemabilia *collection. Original sources include: Fox films, Metro Pictures, Famous Players-Lasky, Samuel Goldwyn, Metro-Goldwyn-Mayer, Paramount, United Artists, Columbia Pictures and 20th Century-Fox.*

Contents

Part I

P-s-s-st! When Does
the Orgy Begin?

Chapter 1

Track In, Track Back

They came from Sweden, like Garbo and Ingrid Bergman; they came from Germany, like Marlene Dietrich; they came from France, like Danielle Darrieux, Simone Simon, and Brigitte Bardot; they came from Italy, like Valli and Gina Lollobrigida and Sophia Loren; they came from Hungary, like Vilma Banky; from Poland, like Pola Negri; from Russia, like Nazimova and Anna Sten; from Austria, like Luise Rainer and Hedy Lamarr; from Greece, like Melina Mercouri.

They were the world's most beautiful women, and one of them, Garbo, was an actress without peer. Others, like Negri and Dietrich, were extraordinary personalities, with a magnetism that made itself felt in remote outposts of the Arctic or deep in the jungles of Africa. And others still, like Hedy Lamarr, were merely beautiful, in a way that one woman in fifty million is beautiful, in a way that makes men drop things and wander naked in the night and howl like wolves.

Through war and depression, amid flood and famine, they were worshiped in enormous picture palaces, designed to look like Gothic cathedrals or Arabian harems. There, in a hushed atmosphere in which the fading notes of the giant Wurlitzer still throbbed in one's ears, two-thirds of the nation paid homage to Venus while nibbling on popcorn, bodies swallowed in overstuffed parlor chairs, feet sunk in a sea of broadloom. Overhead a thousand lavender stars twinkled from the ceiling as Ronald Colman kissed Vilma Banky in *The Dark Angel*, to the strains of "Love's Old Sweet Song," which was performed tenderly by a live symphonic orchestra in the pit. Freshly scented air—it varied from the headiness of lily of the valley to the languor of crushed roses to the sweetness of lilac, depending on the picture—was swept through the vast recesses of the theater by gently purring fans, to add to the euphoria. No sense was left untouched, at prices that began at a quarter (before noon) and mounted to an astonishing one dollar and sixty-five cents as evening fell over the unreal cities of America.

Some of these love-goddesses, like Valli and Bergman, spoke an Oxford-accented English when they arrived in Hollywood; others, like Garbo and Anna Sten, spoke no English at all. Most of them would never overcome the hurdles of Anglo-Saxon consonants—v's became w's, s's became z's, and vowels were added to guttural words to soften them into dulcet Mediterranean music. Dietrich, whose English became impeccable over the years, held up production on her first American movie, *Morocco*, because she couldn't pronounce the word "help." The opening shot had her gazing into a typical von Sternberg smog, a lady of mystery and allure. Adolphe Menjou catches sight of her (he must have had the eyes of a cat), and asks if he can be of any help. The words from this exquisite lady emerged as, "I don't need any Hell-ubbh." While the expensive cast and crew cooled their heels for hours, von Sternberg coached her again and again. "HELP!" he shouted. "HELL-UBBH!" repeated the most exotic beauty in the Western world.

Garbo's dialogue, on the other hand, was tailored to circumvent these problems; and Anna Sten, in her first film, *Nana*, spoke her lines phonetically. Sound was to undo Vilma Banky, who retired, and Pola Negri, who returned to Germany. But, on the whole, Americans were fascinated with foreign accents; they made perfectly commonplace lines, like "I want to go home," sound curiously existential. As the vogue for the foreign film star swept Hollywood, an English actress faked a quite creditable continental accent and, as Sari Maritza, had a fleeting fame. After all, you could see the girl next door just by looking out the window; when you paid a quarter, you wanted something special for your money. To be foreign was "in."

Von Sternberg was one of a handful of directors whose name was linked with the great continental stars. Others were Ernst Lubitsch, who directed Negri, Dietrich, and Garbo; Rouben Mamoulian, who piloted Sten, Dietrich, and Garbo; and Clarence Brown, who took Garbo through the hurdles of her first talkie, *Anna Christie*, and led her to other high points in her career. These Venuses were made of fragile stuff, and they required a very special kind of handling. When they felt they could not go on any longer—could not face one more day of California sunshine, one more press interview with Louella Parsons or Jimmy Fidler, one more fatherly pat from Louis B. Mayer—the director-Pygmalions came to the rescue of their Galateas. "You muzzt go on, *cara mia*," Ernst Lubitsch would say, a sympathetic tear falling from the dark, tragic eyes in his round clown's face. He would fall to the floor, wringing his expressive hands, the hands that created the fabulous touch that brought Hollywood out of the Paleolithic stage, weeping, "You—just—muzzt."

"Ernst! Ernst!" cried the chastened Venus to the broken kewpie doll at her feet. And the show would go on.

Venus also required a very special kind of Adonis—he could be English like Cary Grant (who appeared with Dietrich and Bergman), French like Charles Boyer (Garbo, Bergman, Dietrich, Lamarr), or even American like Fredric March (Sten, Garbo) or John Gilbert (Garbo). But whatever he was, he was not of the "Oh, shucks, ma'am," school. He dressed well and his hair was smooth and sleek. He knew how to kiss a lady's hand while looking at her, smolderingly, in the eyes—an act of such great dexterity that only a few could master it. And he was smart enough never, never to upstage the star. Many tried, but few were chosen.

It was important that nothing go wrong, for the films in which Venus appeared were top-budgeted and required expensive personnel—very special photographers, like Lee Garmes; superb set designers, like Cedric Gibbons; accomplished couturiers, like Adrian. One false step and a Venus-vehicle was a shambles—insiders say that Constance Bennett may have precipitated the demise of Garbo by steering her toward an atrocious wardrobe in *Two-Faced Woman*. While Connie looked trim and chic in this picture, Garbo, in Carole Lombardish evening pajamas and Jean Harlowish cocktail dresses, looked like Miss Drag Queen of 1941. Her intuitive elegance was gone, and the illusion was destroyed. It was the false brush stroke that made Mona Lisa a parody of herself.

Because these films were so very well done, their production cost was rarely recouped by the United States rentals. But they more than made up for the deficit in their European distribution, and in rentals from all parts of the world. Between the two world wars Venus became Big Business on an international scale; and you will still stumble upon these films—*Shanghai Express, Angel, Ninotchka, Camille, Desire, Algiers*—in odd parts of the globe today. Note how simple the titles were—there was a point to that, also. They translated easily into foreign languages—never presenting the pesky problems of *A Streetcar Named Desire* or even of *Little Women*, which as *Les Pétites Femmes* in France had a meaning that Louisa May Alcott never intended.

The impact of Hollywood on these beauties who came from the great capitals of Europe—from Berlin, Rome, Vienna, Paris, Stockholm, Athens, and Budapest—was, inevitably, one of shock. In the premovie era, Hollywood was a sleepy hamlet, settled by Kansas prohibitionists with rather genteel pretensions to culture, their bean fields dotted with white frame houses that had something of the simple poetry of Grant Wood. At night, while the residents gathered to sing Bach cantatas, the coyotes howled, a grim reminder that this land of milk and honey was not yet tame.

By 1914, when the movie colony settled in, it hadn't changed very much. And even today, despite a heavier sprinkling of gray flannel suits and button-down collars, it is essentially a small town. Some of the winding roads off Laurel Canyon were, until lately, unpaved, and startled snakes still crawl from the underbrush. Social engagements are limited to those in one's own income group, and your last picture still determines your status.

It's much like any small town in America, only more truncated in its relationships and less generous in its division of geographical space and worldly wealth. When Garbo once found a chair for an aged extra, and led her to it, the movie colony buzzed for days. Such direct and spontaneous acts were unheard of. If she felt sorry for the old lady, she could have had an assistant director handle it. The kings and queens of Hollywood—ex-chorus girls, waitresses, lumberjacks, soda fountain attendants—should never stoop so low.

The lilting name, Hollywood, conjured up quite another kind of community to a European—handsome, Bauhaus-like movie studios, all within walking distance of one another, separated by rows of holly trees that flourished under a gentle, lemon-tinted California sun. But holly would not grow in Hollywood, as an English couple, who tried to plant it, soon learned. According to this story, which may be apocryphal, the sentimental pair had hoped that the holly seedlings they put in their front yard would take root in time for Christmas. A Christmas of sun instead of snow was more than they could bear, and they lavished their love on the plants. All day and all night they dreamed of those brilliant green leaves, with gentle thorns that pricked the fingers like kisses, and the rich redness of the holly berries, clustered like lovers on the stem. But, alas, the semitropical clime doomed the seedlings. Sadly they watched them wither away, and somehow they could never quite believe in anything again.

For the Stockholm and Berlin beauties, particularly, the shock of Christmas in Hollywood was sharp and severe. With tear-drenched eyes they remembered the streets of their northerly cities at that time of year—the sharp gusts of wind that swept off your hat as, laden with parcels, you went from shop to shop to buy presents for those you loved. After they became well established, both Garbo and Dietrich would try to arrange shooting schedules so they could spend their Christmases elsewhere.

But, of course, the real shock to a European, accustomed to neat, trim blocks linked together with a good transportation system, was the tremendous geographical distances they had to cover each day to get to and from their studios. Few studios were in Hollywood proper. Most of them spilled out over the surrounding hills, each a city within a city, each miles removed from the other. One could not hop from one's hotel in Beverly Hills to a tram that took one to Culver City. No; a chariot had to be dispatched for Venus, not, alas, one drawn by doves, but by a studio chauffeur who, one learned in time, reported all he saw and heard to a supervisor who reported all he heard by proxy to the secretary of a producer who reported all she heard to the producer. One got rid of the studio chauffeur as soon as one could, and hired one's own driver, only to discover that he was equally corrupt. By an intricate system of drumbeats, the accuracy of which would startle the natives of Nairobi, every intimacy of a star was reported all over town. When they stopped caring about what system of birth control you practiced, you were on the skids and might as well book passage on the *Bremen* and go home.

But that Hollywood sun, so unkind to holly, was a blessing to celluloid. It made the whites on film crisp and firm, and the blacks sharp and defined. In 1914, it was this sun which drew young Cecil B. DeMille to Hollywood. He arrived with a contract in his pocket to film *The Squaw Man* for Famous Players-Lasky—a considerable undertaking since it was the industry's first feature-length picture.

DeMille's original destination had been Arizona but, as if he were a playactor in one of his future epics, he just kept on going until he reached The Promised Land. He rented a barn and painted FAMOUS PLAYERS-LASKY on the façade in bold, white letters. Production on *The Squaw Man* then began, to the sound of whizzing bullets from rival film pioneers, trying to scare Cecil away. (Could these gunshots have emanated from D. W. Griffith, whose *The Birth of a Nation* was in an early production stage; or from Griffith's close crony, Mack Sennett, whose studios were then the largest in town? No one knew.)

But Cecil didn't scare easily, and he settled down in Hollywood with an enclave of DeMilles that included his brother William and his niece Agnes. They had something neither Griffith nor Sennett had—a solid bourgeois façade—that got them in with the First Hollywood Families. They gave the new industry respectability, which it needed badly; since, with the coming of the movies, the town was overrun with sweating, swearing cowhands, hoping to pick up an easy buck as a movie extra; with high-drinking stuntmen, willing to take any risk for a day's work; with not-quite-right-in-the-head innocents from tank towns all over the United States, lured to the blossoming film capital with advertisements that exhorted: "BE A MOVIE PLAYER! Join the silent army of film favorites! Be known in the palaces of the great and wealthy and in the cottages of the lowly!"

Needless to say, the original settlers were discomfited. They were interested in art—the refined art of Bach—but the movies, which some crazy poet called Vachel Lindsay said were *the* new art, weren't their idea of art. Art was a church choir singing in the sunset, a little off pitch, to be sure, but the spirit was there. Art was the lovely poetry of Henry Wadsworth Longfellow and John Greenleaf Whittier, so beautiful, so refined. Art was the poetic painting of Maxfield Parrish, in exquisite shades of purple, orange, and bottle green. Art was *Ramona* by Helen Hunt Jackson.

The movies—loud, raucous, tinny, illiterate, with misspellings on every title-card—were hardly their idea of art!

Most of the one- and two-reelers ground out in early Hollywood were, as late as 1914, still being shown in nickelodeons—vacant stores, filled with chairs rented from the undertaking parlor, with a barker advertising the wares out front. His spiel was fast and to the point for, once he had lured a sufficient number of paying customers inside, he would rush to the back of the theater, take off his shirt and derby, and project the films. When the show was over, he would clean up the mess left by the audience, put on his shirt and derby, go out front, and begin barking again: "Come on in, folks: Only a buffalo nickel, a half a dime, a fifth of a quart-ah, a tenth of a half-doll ah, a twentieth part of a doll-ah, folks, a twentieth part of a doll-ah, for an experience you'll never get over. . . . See the bee-oot-ee-fool Biograph Girl, laugh till your sides ache at Jack Bunny, thrill to the daring Pauline. . . . Only a buffalo nickel, folks, a twentieth part of a doll-ah. . . . What's that, lady? 'Little Mary?' I've got her tomorrow. . . . Come on in, folks, step right up, for an experience you'll never get over, only a buffalo nickel, folks, a twentieth. . . . What's that? 'Little Mary?' I've got her tomorrow. . . . The bee-oot-ee-fool Bio-graph girl. . . . Yessir, thank you, sir; remember, no spittin' inside the thee-ay-ter. . . . Come on, folks, step right up, for an experience you'll never get over. . . . What's that, lady? 'Little Mary!' Come back tomorrah. . . . All right, folks, step right up, folks, bust your sides laughin' with Jack Bunny. . . . Yes, ma'm, thank you, ma'm, that's a pretty hat, ma'm, but make sure you take it off inside the thee-ay-ter. . . . What's that, kid? 'Little Mary!!!' Now, what does a nice kid like you want to see 'Little Mary' for? Ain't you heard that beneath them golden curls she's a hoor? What's a hoor? Go away, kid, you bother me. . . . Well, thanks, kid, you want to come in anyway? Thanks. Make sure you don't have to make pee-pee before going into the thee-ay-ter. . . . Come on in, folks, only a buffalo nickel, a half a dime, a fifth of a quar-tah, a tenth of a half-doll-ah, a twentieth part of a doll-ah, only a twentieth part of a doll-ah. . . . 'Little Mary!' Ain't you heard she's dyin'? Yep, old demon rum done got her. . . . What's that, kid? You, again! Well, if you have to go, go to the saloon next door and tell the bartender Jake says you can use the Gent's Room, but hurry up now, show's startin' in five minutes, no tarryin' at the bar, kid, just go to the Gent's Room and come right back . . . tell the bartender Jake sent ya. . . . That's a good kid. . . . What's that? 'Little Mary!!!!!' No, don't show her pictures here. . . . This is a family-type thee-ay-ter. . . . O.K., folks, show in five minutes, folks, step right up, folks, only a buffalo nick. . . . 'Little Mary!' Are you kiddin'. . . . ."

Chapter 2

Little Mary and the Vamp

"Little Mary" was, of course, the dimpled blonde who was born plain Gladys Smith in Toronto, Canada, in 1893, a year that saw such other convulsions of nature as the dethroning of Queen Liliuokalani in Hawaii and the sinking of the British warship, *Victoria*. The entire world came to know her as Mary Pickford, a name conferred on her one day by the startled David Belasco, whose office she crashed, stating that unless he gave her a part in a Broadway play she would retire from the theater forever. She was then thirteen.

Belasco noted those dimples and that drive, and gave her a part at once. So did D. W. Griffith, when she stormed his Biograph Studios on East Fourteenth Street in New York. No one could know then that those studios, which occupied a handsome brownstone mansion, would one day be called "the cradle of genius," and that from them would also spring Lillian and Dorothy Gish, Lionel Barrymore, and Mack Sennett. If two such great showmen as Belasco and Griffith succumbed to Little Mary on sight, it was only inevitable that the rest of the world would too, and in no time at all this pint-sized terror held the universe in the palm of her hand. Even today, when her silent pictures are shown in Paris at gala festivals, riots are quelled and everyone, from students at the Sorbonne to the men who work in sewers, pauses to lift his hat to Little Mary.

Americans are more fickle. Today the name evokes an image of a pudgy half-pint, close to middle age, whose calculated look of juvenile demureness was framed in long sausagelike curls that were a bit too golden to be true. In this guise, or variations thereof, she played in *Daddy Long-Legs*, *Little Lord Fauntleroy*, *Rebecca of Sunnybrook Farm*, and *Little Annie Rooney*. But the fact remains, she was the first actress who knew how to play before the camera—when to throw an emotion away, when to milk one, when to state one simply. She knew that the screen was the most revealing of all mediums and that you could not afford to be insincere. She came across *real*. A childhood of poverty had given her an emotional depth beyond her years and it contrasted, interestingly, with those middle-class curls. She was a Duse in dimity.

To nickelodeon operators she was also a cause of bankruptcy. Audiences would come to see Little Mary, but hardly anyone else. They got a couple of Little Marys a month, but they were open seven days a week, three hundred and sixty-four days a year. Eventually, even the couple a month were cut down, when Little Mary bought up her early Biograph comedies and removed them from circulation. This was a shrewd move on her part, designed to prevent overexposure and to keep up a demand for her new products. In this manner, she stayed at the top for two golden decades—golden not only for audiences, but for Miss Pickford herself, who became the richest woman in Hollywood, the Hetty Green of the motion picture industry.

It was John P. Harris who had opened the nation's first nickelodeon in Pittsburgh in 1905, with Edwin J. Porter's *The Great Train Robbery*, the *Gone with the Wind* of its day, as the main feature. At the Pittsburgh premiere, screams from the audience warned the good guys that the bad guys were coming, and the sight of a train approaching them in rapid motion had something of the impact that Cinerama had on latter-day audiences. It was established with the first of the flickers that the screen had an extraordinary ability to take the audience right into the frame of the picture, establishing an immediacy and rapport that had never been seen before. Robert Flaherty noted this when he screened the walrus fight sequence from his *Nanook of the North* for the Eskimos: They projected themselves into the action, thinking it was all happening to them. They were *there*.

Harris's first nickelodeon brought in $22.50 in nickels on opening day. On the second day the receipts tripled. Everyone wanted to see the pictures that moved, that told a story, and that involved you in the action. Soon there would be one hundred nickelodeons in Pittsburgh alone, and in St. Louis a Greek waiter who saved $3,000 in tips (his name was Spyros Skouras) got into the act. He named his theater the Olympia, and personally threw out the bums who came in to snooze instead of to watch Little Mary—the love of drama being more important to a Greek than the need for sleep. As a matter of fact, as Skouras's chain of nickelodeons expanded, he got very little sleep himself—he worked around the clock, from morning to night, fighting to get the best available cinematographs. (The industry grew up so fast that no one knew what to call the product: At various times they were cinematographs, cinemas, photoplays, motion pictures, moving pictures, and, finally, just movies.) In Boston, Louis B. Mayer wasn't getting much sleep either; nor in New York were William Fox and Marcus Loew, who were battling for the big spoils; nor in Youngstown, Ohio, were the brothers Warner, who had abandoned the family butcher shop for nickelodeons.

But, by 1914, the nickelodeon era was nearing its close. The five-cent picture shows had put the nation's vaudeville houses out of business, and the new movie entrepreneurs were buying them up fast. After raising their prices to a dime, they began to show two-reelers around the clock, interspersing film with live entertainment. In Chicago, Barney Balaban announced the finest $25,000 theater in town, to replace a famous nickelodeon called the Kedzie. At this new theater, mothers could check their baby carriages in the lobby and, for ten cents, see Lillian and Dorothy Gish in *An Unseen Enemy* or Blanche Sweet in *The Goddess of Sagebrush Gulch* plus Sophie Tucker and the Marx Brothers *live*. Balaban was even then dreaming of a 1,000-seat "presentation house," with an orchestra pit large enough to hold a full symphony orchestra.

There were loud protests from Vachel Lindsay, writing in

the *Atlantic Monthly* and the *New Republic*, who didn't approve of the trend toward bigger theaters and longer pictures. To him, those old Biograph cinemas were poems which lovingly conveyed the everyday aspects of American life. What could be more moving than *The Italian*, which portrayed the metamorphosis of a Venetian gondolier into a New York bootblack? The power of a single visual image to tell an entire story was illustrated in this film when a group of immigrants, dewy-eyed with dreams of streets that were paved with gold, descended a separate gangplank from that of the bored first-class passengers. Such scenes could say in a split second what would take a spoken tragedy an entire evening.

But Lindsay's moving protest to the contrary, the industry was forging ahead. And the first problem the titans were going to tackle, was What to do about Little Mary.

Little Mary and The Little Fellow, Charles Chaplin, were the first stars to demand a million dollars a year, back in those days when a million dollars a year was really a million dollars a year. As they drove up production costs, it was difficult to keep theater admissions to a dime. Furthermore, audiences were becoming more selective—they knew that pictures could move by now, and they wanted to see a big star for their money.

It seemed the logical thing to do to bring in ready-made stars from the Broadway stage. A few years ago, those *grandes dames* wouldn't even have considered it—then, movies were way beneath their dignity and their artistry. But things were different now. Legitimate theaters were being converted into movie palaces. Fine old opera houses were closing down. Vaudeville had been dealt a sharp blow on the head.

And, besides, the terms were good. The movie people were offering the Broadway stars real money—as much as $50,000 a picture, more than they made in an entire year.

Jane Cowl, dark-eyed, regal, intelligent, made *The Garden of Lies* for Sam Goldfish (later Samuel Goldwyn) in 1915, the same year that satin-skinned Lillian Russell made her screen debut in *Wildfire*, that Fanny Ward starred in *The Cheat*, that Elsie Janis appeared in *Betty in Search of a Thrill*, that Mrs. Leslie Carter chewed the scenery in *DuBarry* and Lenore Ulric did everything but climb up a wall in *Kilmeny*. Even the very grand Maxine Elliott descended from J. P. Morgan's private railway car long enough to sign a move contract; and soon Laurette Taylor, the camera swathed in gauze to hide her years, would do *Peg O' My Heart*. Cecil B. DeMille, always eager to outdo his rivals, went them one better by bringing in a real opera star, Geraldine Farrar, and starring her as Carmen and Joan of Arc. The next year, Goldwyn topped that one by bringing in Mary Garden and starring her in *Thais*. Thus, a pattern of rivalry was established between DeMille and Goldwyn that would grow as the industry grew. They were birds of a feather who not only flocked but fought together.

Then Adolph Zukor and Sam Goldwyn and Cecil B. DeMille, the three moguls who brought in the big Broadway actresses, sat back to wait for the profits. They never came in. The people who paid two dollars to see Jane Cowl on Broadway or five dollars to hear Geraldine Farrar at the Met weren't the people who would pay a dime to see them in a photoplay. And, even if they were, the effect on the box office would have been negligible—the movies were a medium for the masses, not the upper classes. Furthermore, by the time these great actresses were recruited for the cameras, they were women well into their forties, to be kind about it. Soon, Goldwyn Pictures got a reputation in the trade as The Old Ladies' Home.

Goldwyn and Zukor foresaw imminent bankruptcy unless they changed their course of action. They decided to keep an eye trained on the doings of William Fox, whose balding head, said one biographer, Upton Sinclair, gave him the appearance of a bronze Buddha. Fox was indeed someone to keep an eye on—beginning his career as a vendor of penny lozenges, he bettered himself by becoming a cutter of suit linings, and then acquired a theater empire almost overnight. Now he was even producing successful motion pictures.

One of them, *A Fool There Was*, starred Theda Bara, whose father, said the press releases, was an Arab and whose mother was French. In time, it would come out that Theda was really Theodosia Goodman, a nice girl from Cincinnati, Ohio, and that her movie name was an anagram for "Arab Death." But, meanwhile, the theaters playing Geraldine Farrar and Jane Cowl were

empty, and the customers were lining up to see Fox's "discovery"
—whose eyes were kohled and whose face was talcumed white.
Why? *A Fool There Was* but a picture it wasn't. A soggy tale
about a housewrecking female who "strips a fool to his foolish
hide" and turns him into a rambling wreck, it did show Theda
in a muslin nightie and a bra spun of spiderwebs. But near nudity
was nothing unusual in those days when Will Hays was still a
postmaster. They were always putting Milton Sills in jockstraps
and covering Annette Kellerman, the swimming star, in the
sheerest of gauze. Tarzan would soon debut in a *Folies Bergères*
loincloth; and the orgy would become as common as the custard pie with the release of *Intolerance*.

And it couldn't be, as someone suggested, the clever title cards
(flashed on the screen instead of spoken dialogue). Sure, "Kiss
me, my fool," was catchy, but Anita Loos had written catchier
ones for D. W. Griffith ever since, at the age of twelve, she
sold him the scenario for *The New York Hat*. They didn't go
to the movies to read!

It might have been the allure of the "vamp"—but even those
man-eating dames had been around a while. Mary Hollander, the
first of the screen vampires, was never allowed to pat a dog or
a child in her pictures, and she was followed by a succession
of other pre-Havelock Ellis nymphomaniacs, including Lucille
Younge and Dorothy Dalton (who later reformed and became
a serial queen).

No, it wasn't the vamp gimmick. That had been around ever
since P. T. Barnum sold red salmon by advertising that it was
guaranteed not to turn pink in the can.

It was something else.

What was it?

Why would they go to see Little Mary and this phony Arab
but stay away from Mrs. Leslie Carter like she was Typhoid
Mary. Mrs. Leslie Carter! You couldn't get them to go in even
if you passed out bagels and lox on the house.

TITLE CARD 1: *A light flashed.*

TITLE CARD 2: *Came the dawn!*

CUT TO: Zukor and Goldwyn looking up sailing schedules.

TITLE CARD 3: "They like them FOREIGN."

Dissolve 1:

The Search for Foreign Faces

In New York harbor, the sea gulls flew around the departing luxury liner, while most of the passengers were strolling the deck furiously, trying to find their sea legs. Not so The Producer. Inside the Bridal Suite (he always booked the Bridal Suite), he was hunched over a portfolio of pictures of beautiful women, poring over them with a microscope as if they were precious gems.

The stars of the great Ufa Studios in Berlin and Svenskfilm in Stockholm paraded before his eyes. He quickly discarded the ones that were too perfectly featured, the simpering ingenues who, like gentle heifers, were made to breed. Those he could find in Hollywood. No, what he was searching for was a *face*, one with some striking irregularity that would fasten itself on the subconscious like a leech—a mouth that was too big; cheekbones that were too prominent; eyelids that drooped; a nose that was *retroussé* or even crooked; a forehead that was too high. A *star!*

It might seem, to a snob, that this first- or second-generation American, of some not quite first-class origin—Goldwyn was a glove seller, Jesse L. Lasky a horn player, Carl Laemmle a haberdasher, Louis B. Mayer a scrap dealer—was hardly prepared for the job. The snob would be wrong, for this man was a professional, shrewd and hard of heart as a professional always is, but with a love of what he was doing. To survive he had to spot the proverbial diamond-in-the-rough, the fat Swedish girl, Greta Gustafsson, long before anyone else saw anything in her; long before the world would worship at her large feet; long before, as Garbo, she became a billion-dollar industry.

If the offbeat face interested him, he knew it would interest the world. And it was really only the face that mattered. If she was too short, they would scale the sets down to her size and surround her with midgets. If she was too tall, they would put the leading man on a box in the close-ups; grade the floors so that, in long shots, she did not stand a half a head taller than the other actors. If she was too fat, they would slim her down. If she was too thin—well, that was never a problem, not with the salaries those girls got.

All he wanted was the face. The rest the technicians would take care of. The studios were filled with engineers who could handle that part of it.

It would have to be a face more striking even than Helen of Troy's. All *she* had to do was launch a thousand ships, but the Hollywood star had to support an industry that, by the middle of the 1920's, was the fourth largest in the nation. Everyone said it was a bubble that would burst, but it turned out to be the one industry that was depression-proof. In the early 1930's, when ruined financiers were jumping off tall buildings in Wall Street, the rest of America was watching movies. Their stomachs were grumbling from hunger, they slipped cardboard into the worn-out soles of their shoes, but they went to the movies. There, in those cavernous auditoriums, they searched for Dietrich amid those von Sternberg smogs or suffered heart palpitations when Garbo slunk on the screen and growled, "Give me a viskey, gin-ger ale on the side, 'n' don't be steen-gy, bay-bee!"

To be accurate about it, not all the faces the moguls found in Europe caught on in Hollywood. For every Greta Garbo there were ten Eva von Bernes, actresses who appeared in one picture and then went back home. Some of the faces they found didn't have the stamina to stand up under a sixteen-hour workday that began at dawn and ended after sunset, with the exhausted star memorizing her lines for tomorrow while she lounged in bed.

A strong, athletic girl like Garbo, even, developed anemia under this kind of schedule—but the detached listlessness that was a symptom of her illness only made her more fascinating. Others, even if they did catch on, became impossible to handle, and, like the talented Luise Rainer, had their contracts torn up in their faces.

And so it was necessary to replenish the supply of Venuses every seven years or so—to keep looking—always to be vigilant. There would be good Venus years and bad and, sometimes, as in 1937, there would even be banner ones.

That was the year that Louis B. Mayer went to London to take care of a minor business matter—minor, that is, by the standards of M-G-M, since it involved an investment of less than a hundred million. One evening he decided to go to the theater and, scanning the austere listings in the London *Times*, chose a play called *Old Music,* thinking it was filled with Viennese waltzes. There wasn't a waltz in it, he realized, as he squirmed in his seat. But, just as he was getting up to go, a redhead with a kind of purplish cast to her ivory complexion walked on the stage, and Louis B. Mayer sat right down again. Her name was Greer Garson. She wasn't foreign, since she was English, but they were talking of another war and it was good to have an Ally around for a rainy afternoon. That rainy afternoon came with *Mrs. Miniver,* which Miss Garson, a deft, light comedienne, thought was pretty silly. But Mr. Mayer pulled out all stops in his powers of persuasion—even stooping so low as to wave the flag of Old Britannia—and Miss Garson came around.

After completing his business in London, Mr. Mayer took a short swing to the continent. In Vienna he saw a striking brunette named Rose Stradner, and signed her up, too. And so, on to Carlsbad, where he rhumbaed with an exquisitely lovely Hungarian, Ilona Hajmassy. The strap of her gown broke while she was dancing in his arms, and a light flickered in Mr. Mayer's brain. He would rename her Ilona Massey and make her a star. He did, in *Rosalie.*

Swinging homeward, he stopped in Paris, where he saw a pair of delectable Parisiennes, and signed them up, too. And, en voyage to the United States, guess who happened to be on the same boat?

Well, as director King Vidor once said to his wife when she asked him where he got that lipstick on his face: "Oh! That's just Hedy Lamarr!"

Chapter 3

Pola Negri; Or, Passion's Pulsating Plaything

The first of the great continental actresses to write a chapter in Hollywood history with blood, sweat, and smelling salts was Pola Negri. With her much publicized and anticipated arrival in Lotus Land in 1922, Hollywood's Age of the Baroque, which had gained momentum with the rise of Rudolph Valentino, went into full swing. Pola queened it from the moment she set foot on Hollywood and Vine. When a famous lady stopped to say how charming she was, Pola replied, "I know I am charming. I consider my work great and I am a great actress."

This was just what Hollywood was waiting for—an egomaniac to upstage every other egomaniac in town—and the reign of Pola Negri began. The reign was, alas, a short one. Although Sam Goldwyn and Charles Chaplin, among others, considered Pola the most talented woman in Hollywood, she never quite caught on with the plain folks who were going to the movies at the rate of a hundred million a week. They found her strange meat, too highly seasoned with exotic herbs. They were riveted for a while—she ranked fifth in *Photoplay's* popularity poll of 1924, ahead of her arch rival, Gloria Swanson—but soon the public became disenchanted with the sultry star.

It could have been they sensed that, unlike Dietrich and Garbo, who were playacting all the time, Pola really meant it. There was nothing synthetic about Pola—she was the real thing, a sophisticated, world-weary intellectual and a consummate artist. At a time when ladies blushed if sex was mentioned, Pola talked about it openly and freely, as if it were just another everyday function, like brushing one's teeth. She swore proficiently in seven languages although the English words that had more than four letters proved a stumbling block when sound came in. She even wrote a book, in French, of course—*La Vie et la Rêve au Cinéma*. It never occurred to her that it should be translated into English: "If you don't know French, dar-linkg, you wouldn't like it!"

She made no compromises. When Metro-Goldwyn-Mayer kicked out Mauritz Stiller, the Swedish director who had discovered Garbo and brought her to America, Pola took him under her wing. She saw to it that he directed her next picture, *Hotel Imperial*, one of the few real classics of the Hollywood silent era. For the first reel, the screen was almost entirely *black* —not gray, as in von Sternberg—but *black*. Pola fought to keep it this way at the front office: "If Stiller he want it, thizz izz the way it muzzt be." When things did not go her way, she summoned her chauffeur and left the set—staying home for three or four days until they did it her way. On the set, where even the stars were just plain "Gloria" or "Mary," she insisted on being called *Madame* Negri or *Countess* Dombski, as the mood struck her. After all, who was that little Pickford woman, anyway?

Hollywood, which liked being kicked on its posterior (Ben Hecht once said that every time you kicked they gave you a raise) just loved Pola. There was never a dull moment with her around. She acquired a panther, and took it for walks on a leash. She acquired Charles Chaplin, and took him for walks on a leash. She acquired Rudolph Valentino—but that's getting ahead of the story.

In addition to Little Mary, her consort Douglas Fairbanks, Charles Chaplin, and Gloria Swanson, Hollywood was filled with other spectacular stars and personalities during Pola's reign—the two "Don Johns," Barrymore and Gilbert; Mae Murray of the bee-stung lips; the ebullient Marion Davies; Tom Mix; Erich von Stroheim, who despite his airs of a Prussian officer was just poor boy Erich Stromme, someone said; Colleen Moore; and, last but not least, Warner Brothers' gilt-edged moneymaker, Rin-Tin-Tin.

They inhabited the Hollywood of the pink mansion and the baby blue Rolls-Royce; of the swan-shaped marble bathtub and the throne-shaped gold *chaise percée;* of black silk sheets and silver satin pajamas; of all-white drawing rooms and scarlet red boudoirs; of evening frolics at Falcon's Lair and weekends at William Randolph Hearst's San Simeon,

Just as the Robber Barons, at the turn of the century, bought their way into the Almanach de Gotha via marriageable daughters and million-dollar settlements, so now did the female film stars court the titled bachelors of Europe. Pola already had a title when she arrived, as she let everyone know, but she was outdone when Mae Murray became the Princess Mdivani. So Pola went Mae one better—she divorced the Count Dombski and married another Mdivani, Serge, and became an ex-countess and a princess at the same time. Meanwhile, Gloria Swanson wasn't going to sit back and let everyone else grab the brass ring—she took off for Europe, and came back with a Marquis, a Hollywood first. He was, as everyone who knows his Hollywood alphabet can tell you, the Marquis de la Falaise de la Coudray and he would later marry Constance Bennett, when Gloria divorced him.

Although Henry James viewed American heiresses as innocents who were taken in by wily Europeans, it is unlikely that self-made millionairesses like Gloria and Pola and Mae were babes in the woods. If you had the money, you could afford the best, and these charming, well-mannered, exquisitely groomed bluebloods were delightful playmates and elegant backdrops to the gowns the goddesses acquired on Paris shopping sprees. It was nice to have a prince around the house.

Pola had Serge, and Gloria had "Hank" (as everyone who was anyone called the Marquis), but Adolph Zukor had a headache. An intimate studio like Paramount seemed too small to contain two such major stars. Although they both later denied that there was rivalry between them, Zukor had to separate them by a continent to keep them happy. Gloria was sent to make films "on location"—to Paris, where she starred in *Madame Sans-Gêne*, and to New York, where she ruled the roost at Paramount's Astoria, Long Island, studios. In this way was harmony maintained in the studio family.

Pola thought it only just that Gloria was the one who was sent "on location," even if *Madame Sans-Gêne* made more money than her own *A Woman of the World*, in which she portrayed a tattooed Italian countess. "Mon-yee, mon-yee, mon-yee, what was mon-yee?" It was something for the peasants, dar-linkh! She got along quite nicely on her salary of three thousand, five hundred dollars a week (later doubled).

This extraordinary lady, one of the great Hollywood originals, had a picaresque life style, almost from infancy. She was born Barbara Apolonia Chalupez as the sun sank on the year 1894 in war-torn Poland. Her father, a gypsy violinist, was soon deported to Siberia, but the lovely dark-eyed child attracted a protector, the Countess Planten, who educated her privately and sent her to the Imperial Ballet School in St. Petersburg. A weak heart prevented her from becoming the new Pavlova and Isadora, in one single, dynamic package, but Apolonia was never one to be downed by adversity.

Shortening her name to Pola, and acquiring the name Negri after an Italian poetess she much admired, she began a career in the theater and took on another rich protector, Victor Hulewicz. Pola would always find a Victor Hulewicz, no matter where she went: There was something vulnerable about her, a kind of personal courage that exposed her to danger, and, besides, she was really very beautiful. It was her tragedy as a film star that her beauty was in her skin tone, in her personal iridescence, rather than in bone structure. There was no von Sternberg around to light up her face so that it took on contour. But even Lita Grey Chaplin, who had every reason to despise her, has said that she was the most beautiful woman in the world, with an astonishing personal elegance that diminished every other female in the room. With Pola around, you might as well go home, which is what Lita did when she met her at a party arranged by Ernst Lubitsch.

It was inevitable that such a beauty would be attracted to the camera, and Pola made her debut in a film she scripted herself, based on her own life. It was inevitable, too, that Max Reinhardt, Europe's greatest theatrical impresario, would see it and lure her to Berlin. And, it was inevitable, finally, that Hollywood would immediately begin bargaining for the services of this shooting star, who favored gowns of gold lamé, with little bodice, and who swathed her gypsy-black hair in a turban, from which an ostrich plume cascaded, attached by a single, perfect diamond.

In *Carmen* and *DuBarry*, made by Ernst Lubitsch at the Ufa Studios in Berlin, she was an immediate sensation. Hungry Berliners lined up around the block to see her films at the huge Ufa-Palast am Zoo, Germany's major movie theater. And when the films were released in the United States, the same thing happened all over again. She had that intangible star quality; she was the first great movie Venus.

Pola was in no hurry to go to Hollywood. There was a rich creative ferment about post-World War I Berlin, reflected in the clean, angular excitement of the new Bauhaus architecture and in the rich musical experimentation of Schönberg's twelve-tone scale. Its upper-middle-class Bohemianism was encouraged by the government, which wanted to convert Berlin into another Paris—a tourist attraction that would eradicate the scars of war. The Ufa Studios were financed with government funds, on the sound principle that films of high merit would not only help the nation's image but create a new industry as well. The film industry did that for a time, but Germany did not foresee that Hollywood would rob it of its richest talents. Pola Negri was the first to go.

Held by her Ufa and Reinhardt contracts, Pola was enjoying the show. No matter where you turned at the Ufa Studios, you were sure to bump into a genius—it might be a director like Ernst Lubitsch, G. W. Pabst, Fritz Lang, F. W. Murnau, or Alexander Korda; an actor like Emil Jannings, Conrad Veidt, William Dieterle, or Willi Forst; an actress like Elisabeth Bergner, Greta Garbo (an import from Sweden), or a plumpish daughter of a Prussian officer, Marlene Dietrich, just then getting established. This was the most brilliant collection of cinema talent ever assembled under one roof; and the films they made, up to

1925, represented one of the two or three great bodies of work in the movie medium. They included *The Cabinet of Dr. Caligari, The Golem, Waxworks, Destiny, The Last Laugh, Metropolis, Variety,* and *Siegfried,* as well as the Negri-Lubitsch moneymakers.

We can see, then, why Pola's arrival in Hollywood was a news event. Her *Carmen,* released in America as *Gypsy Blood,* and *DuBarry,* pepped up with the title *Passion,* surrounded her with an aura of prestige that Little Mary never had. Vachel Lindsay was succeeded by a whole new group of critics that would, in time, include Allene Talmey, Robert Benchley, and Robert E. Sherwood. Every major newspaper now had a movie reviewer, of varying levels of competence. A sharp ex-newshen by the name of Louella O. Parsons was covering the film beat for the *New York Telegraph* at $110 a week, when a favorable review of a Marion Davies picture, *When Knighthood Was in Flower,* caught the eye of William Randolph Hearst. He hired her away for his *American* and *Journal* at $250 a week, and she soon became the nation's first syndicated Hollywood gossip columnist. To supplement and encourage this intensive movie coverage, Paramount took full-page ads in the major dailies, as well as in the *Saturday Evening Post.* It was the threshold of the era of movies as Big Business, and Pola Negri—POLA NEGRI!!!—surrounded with continental glamour and decked out in an aura of art, symbolized its arrival. Overnight, Hollywood, that freckle-faced little kid from the wrong side of the railroad tracks, had become a ravishing debutante.

The only real contender for the crown of Venus that Pola faced in Hollywood was Nazimova, the Russian-born mistress of Stanislavski, who had come to New York with the Moscow Art Players and remained on Broadway, where she became a star. She was no beauty, but she had blue-black hair, large dark eyes that cried *Oh, Tschitschornia,* and a body that she could double up like a snake. Her first film, was a Hun-atrocity epic, *War Brides,* in which she was billed as "The Great Nazimova." It was a 1916 success, but her subsequent films, for Metro, were failures. One of them, *Salome,* was a fascinating interpretation of Oscar Wilde's play, inspired by Aubrey Beardsley's erotic drawings. To be true to the spirit of the original, she reportedly insisted that every actor be homosexual—which demand, admittedly, presented no great problem. But though the intentions of Wilde remained pure, the film confused the audiences at the neighborhood Bijou, who assumed that the author had been put in Reading Gaol for eating babies. There wasn't a baby in it.

Another foreign-born enchantress then appearing in silent films was Dagmar Godowsky, a green-eyed sophisticate whose father was the famous pianist-composer, Leopold. Hollywood was enchanted by her, but she was disenchanted by it—"all those empty heads and ermine tails"—and fled to New York, where she took to wearing two live white mice around her neck instead of a fur piece. For years, no really first-class cocktail party was complete unless Dagmar, now grown fat but still green-eyed and serpent-tongued, stopped in "and put on a show," as the ladies commented cattily. But what a show! While beauties stood twiddling their thumbs, Dagmar was the center of interest, with every male in the house gathered at her feet, listening to her tales of Grover's Corners (Hollywood), Nita (Naldi), Sessue (Hayakawa), and Garbo ("All she ever really wanted from life was a plate of okra").

Dagmar's abdication left the field wide open for Pola, with only intermittent harassment from Gloria. But when Gloria insisted on her own studio car, Pola asked for two. And if Zukor arranged for a gala cocktail party in New York so the press could meet Gloria and "Hank," Pola would ask for a larger one so that she could introduce "Serge." In that prohibitionist era, she insisted that a small bar be set up in her dressing room, complete with authentic champagne, chartreuse, and cognac ("I don't care how you get it, dar-linkh; get it"). She also thought it her right to be surrounded with freshly cut flowers, and she let it be known that she liked caviar.

No one had played the role of The Star with such brio. And she had truly Shavian flashes of wit—as, for example, when she was dining with Chaplin, and the butler rushed in to inform the host that a Mexican girl had broken into the house and was sleeping in his bed. Chaplin was for calling the police to have her removed; but Pola thought that was just silly. "Bring her to *me;* I want to talk with her," she commanded. The girl was brought in, and she refused Pola's offer of a glass of champagne in favor of a glass of milk. But Pola chatted with her in her deep guttural voice, completely calm and nonchalant, as if this were a scene in *You Never Can Tell.* She carried it off as if she were Mrs. Patrick Campbell, and housebreakers were an everyday occurrence in her life.

Hollywood did not know what to do with her, after the first flurry of excitement had abated. She was pulling in the carriage trade, but was establishing no real audience rapport, nor was she building a consistent cinematic image. She was not, like Garbo, "the lost lady," or, like Dietrich, "the woman of mystery." Gazing at her movie stills, it becomes apparent that she never looks the same in any two photos. There were times when she was the continental sophisticate; and then again she was the torrid vamp; and then again she was the scullery maid. Her coiffures fluctuated wildly from a frizzy hairdo to short brilliantined bangs. She was exceedingly photogenic in some shots but looked quite banged up and hollow-eyed in others. No single image came through.

This may be because Pola was a real actress, with a method approach to her individual roles. The same thing can be said about Marlon Brando. He never looks the same in any two films, either, and this has curtailed a career that began brilliantly. The ones who went on and on were instantly recognizable personalities—Gary Cooper, Joan Crawford, Katharine Hepburn, Spencer Tracy (a particularly insincere actor, for he always let the audience in on the fact that he was *playing the part*), James Cagney. Not until Luise Rainer would there be another Venus like Pola—a Stanislavskian actress.

Among the films she made in Hollywood, two are remembered today—a delightful Lubitsch comedy, *Forbidden Paradise,* in which she lampooned Catherine the Great of Russia (it was later remade as a Bankhead talkie, *A Royal Scandal*) and, of course, *Hotel Imperial,* a real movie milestone.

Hotel Imperial (1926) illustrates the remarkable strides Hollywood had made in the twelve years since *The Squaw Man.* Directed by Stiller, and supervised by another Ufa import, Erich

Pommer, it was the first movie to be filmed on a composite set—
that is, an entire hotel, room for room, was constructed on the
Paramount lot, with rails above the ceiling on which a mounted
camera could move. As Pola and the rest of the cast went from
one room to another (there were eighteen in all), the camera
could follow them without interrupting the action. This allowed
for a natural kind of continuity, a smooth, unbroken scene-to-
scene flow, which Lubitsch would use in a Dietrich film, *Angel,*
a decade later.

Hotel Imperial was very much in the headlines, for it was
during the filming of this complex and expensive production
that word came through that Valentino was dead. Pola's name
had been linked with that of Rodolfo Alfonzo Raffaelo Pierre
Filibert Guglielmi di Valentina d'Antonguolla (Rudy, for short),
but Pola was Pola, and it seemed unlikely that such a supreme
egotist would be attracted to one almost as imposing.

But when word came through on the set that Rudy had died,
Pola's grief appeared very real. She halted production by disap-
pearing to her Hotel Ambassador bungalow, where she called a
press conference and announced that she and Rudy had planned
to be married. "I have lost," she said, "the one real love of my
life." The army, moved by her histrionics, volunteered to fly
her to New York for the funeral in an airmail plane.

Pola wouldn't hear of it—the funeral would be held up until
she had time to acquire a wardrobe of widow's weeds and could
get there by the more reliable means of rail. There was a press
conference when she left Los Angeles, at which it was announced
that she had ordered a floral offering of four thousand red roses,
six feet wide and eleven feet long, with "Pola" spelled out in
white roses in the center. The cost was reported to have been
$2,000.

Pola held another press conference in Chicago, when her
private railway car was attached to the Twentieth Century
Limited. There was to be still a fourth meeting with the press
when she got to New York, but in Grand Central Station Pola
screamed, fainted, was revived, screamed, and fainted again. That
postponed conference took place instead in the antechamber of

the Campbell Funeral Home, after Pola had again collapsed, this time before Rudy's bier.

She was in the first car that followed the coffin to St. Malachy's Church, for the funeral service, with Mary Pickford trailing behind in the third car. She stayed only a few minutes, and then went back to her hotel and called another conference.

The ensuing events always starred Pola, to the exclusion of Rudy, in the nation's headlines. A crew of publicity men, assigned to her by Adolph Zukor when she left Hollywood, was supplemented with another crew from the New York office. They kept things spinning, and luck was with them all the way. When the nation finally tired of reading about Pola's fainting spells, the doctor who had attended her in New York was exposed as a fraud. Pola was en route to Hollywood when that story broke, and, at San Bernardino, when Marion Davies boarded the train, she collapsed again. At the funeral, she cried openly and passionately, her sobs ringing through the aisles of the church. After the funeral, the newsreel cameras followed her back to her bungalow as, with veil lifted from her face, she entered her house of mourning. Shortly thereafter she filed a suit against the estate of Valentino for $15,000. This amount, she declared, represented a loan she had made him a year earlier. Her claim was substantiated.

Hotel Imperial reestablished Pola as a ranking box-office star after a two-year decline. She quickly followed up that success with *Barbed Wire,* with Clive Brook as her leading man, and *The Secret Hour,* in which Jean Hersholt appeared. That was in 1927, the year in which Al Jolson's voice was first heard in the nation's theaters, saying "Come on, Ma, listen to this!"—an event that changed the course of movie history.

The coming of Vitaphone, just as her career went into high gear, was one of the many cruel jokes life played on this fascinating actress. She flopped in an early talkie, *A Woman Commands,* despite her melodious crooning of the hit song, *Paradise.* She ran into serious tax problems. She was constantly being sued for nonpayment of hotel bills and personal loans.

But the cruelest joke of all was Marlene Dietrich. Dietrich had what Negri never had—cheekbones.

Pola Negri's Hollywood reign is nonetheless the most vivid chapter in Hollywood's social history. Never again would that purple era, which rivaled in lavishness the courts of the corrupt Louises, see the light of day. It was filled with cheating beauties, panderers, liars, fakes, renegades, blackmailers, remittance men, confidence men, thieves, professional fornicators, and despots—but it also had Pola.

Some nonsophisticates think that the era never ended. There is the story of a New York banker who was a guest at a very proper Hollywood dinner party in the late 1940's. He sat through it politely, pausing now and then to remove his rimless spectacles and wipe them carefully.

Finally, he couldn't bear the tension any longer.

He turned to the beautiful young lady on his left, the daughter of one of Hollywood's highest-paid writers, and into her startled ear he whispered: "*P-s-s-st!* When does the orgy begin?"

Chapter 4

Vilma Banky, Queen of the Pleasure Domes

Manhattan's first one-cent picture show opened on the Great White Way on April 14, 1894, in the usual empty, bare-walled store. No rented chairs were required, for the patrons had to stand to see the movies—through a slot cut in the top of a large box. When a penny was dropped into a slot and a crank was ground, audiences saw pictures move before their eyes. These boxes were called Edison Kinetoscopes, and their star attraction was an ice age Venus, Fatima, who did a well-bred belly dance. They lined up to see Fatima, while *Admiral Dewey at Manila Bay* and *Edward VII at the Age of Six* were poorly patronized.

Which just goes to prove something.

This penny arcade was a far cry from the city's great tri-umvirate of movie pleasure domes—the Capitol, the Paramount, and the Roxy—which went up in the 1920's and became Church, State, and Fatherland to the new movie-mad generation. They are all torn down now, but the memory of their lavish interiors, decorated in pseudo-Moorish, quasi-Italian Baroque, or would-be French Renaissance, will not die. As architecture, they may have been synthetic, vulgar, and grotesque, but they had an unmis-takable grand style. "Mother, does God live here?" a little girl in a popular cartoon asked, as she entered one of these great film cathedrals.

She was part of a generation that would grow up thinking that

Chartres and Notre Dame looked like the Grand Foyer of the Roxy. This 6,200-seat theater was the last of the triumvirate to go up (on March 11, 1927) and the first to be torn down (in the summer of 1960). It was also the costliest—its Spanish Renaissance interiors skyrocketing the final figure to $10 million. It had dressing rooms large enough to hold 300 singers and dancers, and a pit scaled for a 110-piece orchestra (led by Erno Rapée, with an electric light at the tip of his baton). It had 108 ushers—well-favored young men, who were drilled with the ferocity of West Point cadets, and whose sky-blue pants were immortalized by Cole Porter in *You're the Top*. It was swathed in rosy velvet, leafed in brilliant gold, and crowned with dazzling crystal. Its likable entrepreneur, Roxy (S. L. Rothafel), often stood in the lobby to greet the customers, who paid fifty cents to get in.

What its twenty thousand patrons a day saw for their money was a "Class A" feature (such as Gloria Swanson in *The Loves of Sunya*) and, on the stage, a Broadway musical revue in miniature, with a visiting Hollywood star. This was the era of the "personal appearance," when even such major stars as the Marx Brothers and Bette Davis appeared live to promote a forthcoming film, and some of them found their way to the Roxy, appearing four times daily except on Saturday, when there were five shows.

But, while everything glittered out front, all was not sweetness and light backstage. Ted Lund, a dancer who was sometimes given featured "spots" in the stage shows, recently recalled that backstage the Roxy was "a factory," with what amounted to a twelve-hour workday. Since the bill changed every two or three weeks, the performers rehearsed the next show while appearing in the current one. Temperament among the "in person" stars was commonplace—Grace Moore demanded a separate elevator and a red carpet, extending from her dressing room to the elevator to the stage. Carmen Amaya's dance troupe cluttered the dressing rooms with empty wine bottles. A mischievous Danny Kaye was forever upsetting the blocked-out dance routines. Bored and frustrated, the chorus kids would camp it up by covering their teeth with rhinestones or dyeing their hair in shades that ranged from anisette to vin rosé. The studio couches, where they were allowed to rest between shows, were crawling with vermin. And, oh yes—their salaries were $35 a week.

But the Roxy seemed a glamorous place to those kids from Cleveland and Oklahoma City and Podunk—somehow they sensed they were participating in theater history—as were, to a lesser extent, the Capitol and Paramount. The latter theater, seating four thousand, had a lobby of Italian marble and a series of fancy nooks and crannies that included the Elizabethan Room, The Chinoiserie, the Venetian Room, the Hunting Room, the College Room, and Peacock Alley. In this spiffy setting the Pola Negri movies were shown.

The 5,300-seat Capitol was the first of the "big three" to go up (in 1919) and the last to go (in 1968). Its entrepreneur was Edward J. ("Major") Bowes, whose name is also associated with radio's Amateur Hour, a depression favorite in which crooning cowboys, tap-dancers, moppets who imitated Garbo, and sopranos who tried to sing like Jeanette MacDonald were gauged for popularity by audience applause. The Major's taste in theaters was completely professional, however. To design the Capitol he tapped Thomas W. Lamb, the most talented of the pleasure dome architects, who chose a restrained Adam and Empire décor for the interiors. Those famous white marble stairs in the lobby (scrubbed every night by a team of ladies from Baltimore) were set aglow by three rock crystal chandeliers originally designed by Stanford White for Sherry's.

New York was not alone in theatrical splendor. In Chicago Barney Balaban realized his dream of "presentation houses" with the Riviera (where, during the showing of *Humoresque,* a live violinist played on stage); the 4,000-seat Tivoli, which featured bands like Fred Waring's Pennsylvanians; and the Chicago, where the Sunday Symphonic Hour starred Tito Schipa or Gladys Swarthout, and which usually had a shortened opera (*La Gioconda, Faust, Madame Butterfly, Carmen*) or an operetta (*The Student Prince, Rose Marie, Naughty Marietta*) on the bill along with a movie feature. A very young Vincente Minnelli designed these productions.

In Hollywood, Sidney Patrick Grauman, who once had prospected for gold in the Yukon, built his fabulous Egyptian in 1922 among the bean fields. Its enormous court, 150 feet long and 45 feet wide, featured such celebrity imprints as John Barrymore's profile and Jimmy Durante's nose. The Fifth Avenue Theater in Seattle had an enormous ceiling dragon reaching down to a white globe ("The Pearl of Attainment"). The décor of Loew's State, in Syracuse, was Hindu; the Fox in San Francisco, French Baroque; the Fox in Detroit, Byzantine; the Kimo in Albuquerque, Navajo. Other great showplaces of the 1920's included the Loew's Penn and Warner Brothers' Stanley in Pittsburgh; Loew's Paradise in The Bronx; the Strand, the Rialto, and the Rivoli in Manhattan; the King in Brooklyn; and Loew's in Jersey City. As is pretty evident, Marcus Loew and William Fox were engaged in open warfare to see who would outdo the other in ornateness, with the odds favoring Loew.

Although the architecture was of the wedding-cake school, the theaters themselves were structurally sound beneath the façade of high Busby Berkeley camp. The lobbies were spacious (the Roxy had room for 2,500 waiting patrons, who curled up in serpentine lines supervised with Marine-sergeant precision by those fabulous ushers). The floors of the auditoriums were well graded, so that audiences did not have to crane their necks or swing their heads as if it were a tennis match. And the temperature was controlled (these were the first public buildings to introduce air conditioning). They attracted new audiences to the movies—well-off ladies with maids at home and time on their hands in the afternoon. And, how could they better spend their time than to motor downtown in their Auburns and take in the newest Vilma Banky? These matinée ladies came back in the evening, and brought their husbands—squirming, tired Babbitts —with them. Babbitt took one look at Banky, and thought she was pretty hot stuff, yessiree! But she was also such a nice refined lady, they came back the next evening with their children, Babs and Bob, in tow. It might teach Babs good deportment to watch Vilma Banky; and she would give Bob an ideal to strive for, so he'd keep himself pure until he met the right girl. Vilma Banky became the darling of the two-car family, the sweetheart of suburbia, the dream girl of the Boosters' Club Ball. Even today she is something of a wonder.

There are blondes, and then there are blondes, and then there is Banky—the distillation of the startling beauty very occasionally found among Hungarians. This comeliness may be due to the wild mixture of national strains in their Magyar background. On the other hand, it may simply be one of those gifts the gods bestow now and then. It should not be probed too deeply; it may just break.

Perhaps Samuel Goldwyn felt this way, too. The press releases in 1925 merely stated that he had discovered Vilma Banky, his "Hungarian Rhapsody," in her native Budapest. One can almost see the peppery Mr. Sam passing a sidewalk café and stopping dead in his tracks as his eyes fell on Vilma Banky demurely sipping an ice-cream soda and totally unaware of her charm. (Of course, they don't serve ice-cream sodas in sidewalk cafés in Budapest, as they do at Schwab's drugstore in Hollywood, but this is a movie, isn't it?)

A little Pinkerton work will send those press releases flying into the wastepaper basket. Miss Banky did indeed once live in Budapest, where her charms had been much admired by a millionaire baron, but he went off to war and she went off to Paris. There, she changed her original name of Vilma Konesics to Vilma Loncit and went into films. Years later, when as Vilma Banky she was Valentino's leading lady, her baron pursued her to Hollywood with a marriage offer—first socking Valentino in the jaw for eyeing his old girl with such unrestrained lechery in their love scenes. But the baron went back to Budapest empty-handed. Vilma Konesics was Vilma Banky the film star now—no longer just his Golden Girl but the entire world's. (One thinks of him, in later years, as a prototype of a character who often appeared in the silent screen—a handsome aristocrat, stout and jolly, except when the wind howls outside the door, singing the words *Vilma . . . Vilma . . . Vilma.* A wine glass falls from his hand and shatters into fragments, to the accompanying rumble from the mighty Wurlitzer. Amidst the slivers of crystal the radiant visage of his Vilma appears while the mighty Wurlitzer again breaks into the act with *Just a Song at Twilight.* Fade Out.)

If you have ever been fortunate enough to meet one of those Hungarian Rhapsodies, you are struck by the practicality that lies beneath the magical brush strokes that tinted their cheeks just that shade of pale pink and colored their hair that precise tone of ripe wheat. Miss Banky ran true to form. She married one of her leading men—not Valentino; she was too smart for that. No, she chose instead debonair Rod La Rocque, born of Chicago bourgeoisie, who wooed her by learning to say "I love you" in Hungarian, no mean feat since Hungarian is, as Edmund Wilson has told us, the most chaotic of languages. But Rod managed it, and Vilma was swept off her feet; she married him, and stayed married. The practical nature behind her exotic golden glow came out again when sound reared its terrifying head in the Hollywood silent screen colony. She made one or two talkies, to see what they were like, and then very quietly and intelligently retired. In the late 1920's she was a star of the caliber of Garbo, but she didn't make a production about retiring—she just retired, leaving behind a very pleasant memory.

In *Sunset Boulevard*, Billy Wilder's 1950 evocation of the silent era, she is remembered with a line of dialogue having an oddly Fitzgeraldian ring: "Vilma Banky and Rod La Rocque must have swum in that pool a thousand midnights ago." When Banky heard it, she howled. She had become an expert golfer, but had never learned to swim. She and Rod were living in a modest stucco house in Beverly Hills. They had saved their money, and were spared the humiliation of scrounging for an existence by appearing in minor roles, the fate of many an old-time star.

New York's Museum of Modern Art still shows *The Winning of Barbara Worth*, in which, like most of her films, she was reverently photographed by George Barnes, and which is also noted in cinema annals as the film in which Gary Cooper made his debut. She gives a special, ethereal quality to the traditional Western heroine, and it is the best of her pictures. Also of interest as scatological documents are her two films with Valentino, *The Eagle* and *The Son of the Sheik*, which were presented to the public with tremulous advertising campaigns, which ran along the lines of:

SEE
—The auction of beautiful girls to the lords of Arabian harems
—The barbaric gambling fete in the glittering casino of Biskra
—Matchless scenes of gorgeous color, and wild free love. The year's supreme thrill—

But, alas, no one bothers to show those lovely love stories in which she co-starred with Ronald Colman—those hymns to romantic love which always brought out the best in such fondly remembered organists as Jesse Crawford. *The Dark Angel . . . The Night of Love . . . The Magic Flame . . . Two Lovers:* four-handkerchief pictures, one and all, in which love . . . love . . . love was ennobled and refined, with all traces of animality removed, and enshrined on a snowy white altar above which stood a castrated cupid. Many a virgin went to her wedding couch thinking *it* was like this, and woke up in the morning a wiser and sadder woman.

Love . . . love . . . love . . . and, always with a Banky picture, came a very special stage presentation: a harp ensemble, a poetry reading, a violin recital. The overture to the program was from *Romeo and Juliet* or *Tristan and Isolde;* and the finale was a pink-and-silver ballet, with music by Tchaikovsky and choreography by Petipas. A special attendant dispensed smelling salts in the Ladies Lounge, along with copies of Elizabeth Barrett Browning's *How do I love thee? Let me count the ways. . . .*

Love . . . love . . . love . . . ah, Vilma . . . Vilma . . . Vilma! You were love!

Miss Banky, like all the continental enchantresses, left behind her some legacies—first, a cool aloofness that was perpetuated some years later by Grace Kelly, although in a much thinner vein. While Vilma had a throbbing sensuality behind an icy reserve, Grace was that nice Irish Catholic girl from Philadelphia even when she was being kissed by Clark Gable or Cary Grant.

Second, there was the legacy of the Colman-Banky "love team," which was perpetuated by Garbo and Gilbert, Gaynor and Farrell, Bergman and Grant, Hepburn and Tracy. To watch two film stars kiss in picture after picture was a perfectly respectable form of voyeurism, by the lights of our society, and no one got hurt—unless it was Colman and Banky, who, in the effort to provide variations on the theme, struck semi-supine postures that must have left them with housemaid's knee.

Third, Miss Banky provided lively copy to the crew of newshens then situated in Hollywood, and helped formulate the "star interview," now a standard adjunct to movie fame. In such interviews, the star gives beauty hints, recipes, pointers on how to attract a man, opinions on world events, and racy comments on her leading men. Miss Banky may have overdone that a bit; Valentino's marriage to Natacha Rambova began to disintegrate after Vilma Told All.

And, fourth, Miss Banky set standards for the Hollywood Wedding, during her nuptials to Mr. La Rocque, which have since become classic. The props included false hams and turkeys, made of cardboard, on the sideboard; an all-star cast of ushers (Rod's included Sam Goldwyn and Cecil B. DeMille) and ladies-in-waiting; and screaming, fainting fans on the sidelines. The casualties included the broken dentures of a sneaky reporter who bit into a pâpier-maché turkey leg to see if it was real, and an ambulance load of lovesick maidens, who were treated for scratches and bruises.

Families like the Babbitts suffered bruises that were more internal, after Miss Banky left the screen. Mr. Babbitt, to whom Vilma came to mean palmy nights and rapturous dawns, kept going to his real estate office every day, but it wasn't the same any more. Mrs. Babbitt missed the recipes. Babs, with Vilma no longer around to show her how to keep cool in a crisis, would sit in the middle of the floor and scream. And as for poor Bob: When Vilma was no longer around to keep him chaste, he took to necking with little girls.

Yes, it all happened thousands of midnights ago, in pleasure domes that looked like kingdoms-by-the-sea or castles-in-the-air, in an innocent America that had yet to drift, smilingly, into paranoia.

Dissolve 2:

The Silent Pictures

Movies were: bigger than ever—Jesse L. Lasky experimented with an enlarged screen, a forerunner of Vistavision, for his road-show attraction, *The Covered Wagon.*

Movies were: better-directed than ever—from Sweden came Victor Seastom; from Germany they brought in Alexander Korda to "style" stars like Billie Dove and Dorothy Mackaill; from the heart of America came one of those rare, fine men who *was* what America was supposed to be all about, Robert Flaherty; from nowhere came Erich von Stroheim, who was finally given pictures to do—in one of them, he ordered wardrobe to issue silk underwear, embroidered with a Graustarkian crest, for all the male extras. (It would, said Von, make them *feel* like Prussian officers.)

Movies were: better written than ever—they were paying real money to acquire properties like Ibáñez's *The Four Horsemen of the Apocalypse;* they were filming classics like *The Scarlet Letter;* they were developing scenario writers like Carl Mayer, Ben Glazer, June Mathis (who along the way discovered Valentino), Anita Loos, and Jeanie MacPherson.

Movies were: better photographed than ever—in addition to George Barnes, cinematographers of note were Griffith's renowned Billy Bitzer (*Way down East*), Bert Glennon (*Hotel Imperial*), Tony Gaudio (*The Temptress*), Lee Garmes (*The Private Life of Helen of Troy*), Gregg Toland (*This Is Heaven*), and Charles Rosher (*Sunrise*).

Movies even started to have messages: *Broken Blossoms, Bluebird*, and *The Miracle Man*. And they were better cast than ever: Paramount imported Elinor Glyn, a lady from London who had daydreamed *Three Weeks* and *It*, and gave her a free hand in casting. She took to Hollywood as a goldfish takes to a bowl—Hollywood being something of a daydream itself—but her eye was good. She discarded one vapid ingenue after another for *It*, until she encountered a tough, profane, flame-haired, black-eyed miss from Brooklyn, Clara Bow. This urchin, decreed the society lady from London, had *It*. Clara, a little uncomfortable about it all, was lifted from a small role in an Eddie Cantor picture, *Kid Boots*, and given the star treatment right alongside Pola and Gloria.

Other silent picture stars were: piquant Colleen Moore, who cut off her curls and became the definitive galoshed Jazz Age Flapper; Lillian Gish, now with Metro, and still suffering; Constance Binney, who played debutantes; Norma and Constance Talmadge, the good/bad sisters; Corinne Griffith, whose beauty only Vilma Banky surpassed; Louise Brooks, gutsy, high-styled, with the ping of crystal; Norma Shearer, The Lady; Joan Crawford, The Would-Be Lady; Dolores Costello, for whom John Barrymore left home, and he really couldn't have done much better; Sue Carol, a Manhattan cocktail; Alice White, a sloe gin fizz; Janet Gaynor, fresh-churned butter; Bebe Daniels, Juicy Fruit chewing gum; Loretta Young, an orange gumdrop; Marion Davies, a truly enchanting soubrette, for whom William Randolph Hearst left home; Mae Marsh, one of the great expressive actresses of the silent screen, as yet not properly canonized; Laura LaPlante, the dimpled doll next door who surprises everyone, except the next-to-the-richest man in town, by marrying the richest man in town; Mabel Normand, Tragedy's Darling; Esther Ralston, Sunshine and Wiener schnitzel; Mary Astor, a hick-town Brünnhilde; Mae Murray, the girl you remember the morning after; and Constance Bennett, *really something*, a kitten with platinum claws—a Diored Cleopatra, barging down the Housatonic—the ultimate martini, with a poisoned onion.

The males of this era were nowhere nearly so distinctive—except for Rudolph Valentino, who could wear the costume of either a sheik or of Louis XIV's court and make it look like a second skin—a born clotheshorse, that one, unrivaled until the advent of Marlene Dietrich. But they were a personable lot: Thomas Meighan, Milton Sills, Wallace Reid, Ramon Novarro, Richard Barthelmess, Ronald Colman, Clive Brook, Richard Arlen, George O'Brien, Adolphe Menjou, Neil Hamilton, John Boles, and Johnny Mack Brown.

Fortunately, none of these walking Arrow collar ads really had to act. About all that was required was good looks, clear eyes, slim hips, and the ability to follow the director's instructions: "O.K. Joe, kiss Norma . . . with some feeling now; what do you think she is, your mother? . . . O.K., O.K., that's enough . . . walk over to the fireplace . . . look into the fire . . . with *soul* . . . let's do it once again now . . . with real *soul* . . . O.K. . . . turn to her slowly . . . you're showing too much cuffs on your shirt . . . pull them up . . . what's the hell with wardrobe anyway giving you a shirt with long cuffs. . . . O.K., let's do it again now . . . turn slowly . . . face her . . . say, 'I can't live without you,' and remember our audiences read lips . . . O.K. . . . walk toward her . . . agitated like . . . throw yourself at her feet . . . those pants are too tight in the ass; Bennie, take a note, *fire* wardrobe . . . no, let's get on with it now . . . we're three days behind schedule as it is, thanks to Norma's *toothache* . . . you heard me, Norma . . . O.K. look into her eyes . . . say, 'Norma! Norma! Forgive me!' . . . what did I tell you about those jerks in Podunk reading lips . . . think I want the General Federation of Women's Clubs after me? . . . say it again, 'Norma! Norma! Forgive me!' . . . O.K. . . . take her hand . . . gently now, what do you think she is? A sailor? . . . O.K. . . . say, 'Norma, I love you' . . . what did I tell you about reading lips . . . O.K. . . . O.K. . . . cut . . . cut . . . cut!"

The successful stars were associated with particular studios. The Big Five—Mary Pickford, William S. Hart, Douglas Fairbanks, D. W. Griffith, and Charles Chaplin—had a studio of their own, United Artists. It took ten lawyers, headed by William Gibbs McAdoo, to draw up their contracts.

Metro had John Gilbert, Mae Murray, Lon Chaney, Joan

Crawford, and Marion Davies; First National had Colleen Moore, Billie Dove, the Talmadge girls, Corinne Griffith, and Richard Barthelmess; Fox had Madge Bellamy, Tom Mix, Janet Gaynor, and Charles Farrell; Warner Brothers had John Barrymore and Rin-Tin-Tin; Goldwyn had Eddie Cantor, Vilma Banky, and Ronald Colman; Universal had Laura LaPlante, Reginald Denny, Mary Philbin, and Norman Kerry; and star-studded Paramount had Pola and Gloria and Clara, as well as Tom Meighan, Esther Ralston, Bebe Daniels, Emil Jannings, and W. C. Fields.

Salaries were higher than ever. John Gilbert stood at the top, with $10,000 a week; Mae Murray got $7,500 a week; a director, Clarence Brown, was taking in a weekly $5,000; and even a title-writer, George Marion, Jr., was pulling in $2,500 a week.

Grosses were greater than ever. The Roxy celebrated its first year with gross receipts of $5,500,000. It obviously wasn't just the pictures that were pulling them in, since the Roxy had to share the best ones; it was the *thee-ay-ter*. The trend in pleasure domes continued to grow, until almost every village in the U.S.A. had a miniature Valhalla which was the focal point around which the town revolved. In the bigger cities, neighborhood theaters became just as elaborate as the downtown palaces—in New York, for example, a rococo, star-studded, gilded cavern went up in the residential area of East 72nd Street; the Sheridan, as elaborate as an opera house, gave grandeur to quaint little Greenwich Village; and the baroque Orpheum swept up almost an entire city block in the "Little Germany" area of the East 80's. These triumphs were engineered by Marcus Loew, who had gained a noticeable ascendancy over William Fox in penultimate pleasure domes.

And, finally, movies were: better than ever. Among the classics of 1923 were: *The Hunchback of Notre Dame, Robin Hood, The Green Goddess, Scaramouche, Safety Last, Rosita* (Lubitsch's first U.S. picture, in which he encountered the dynamic presence of Little Mary for the first and last time), and *Little Old New York*.

The year 1924 saw *The Thief of Bagdad, Monsieur Beaucaire, Beau Brummel, The Marriage Circle,* and DeMille's *The Ten*

Commandments, which celebrated his first decade in Hollywood.

In 1925 came *The Gold Rush* (which stands close to the top of *any* list of the greatest movies), *The Unholy Three*, *The Merry Widow*, *The Big Parade*, *The Phantom of the Opera*, and *The Freshman*.

By 1926 there were *Ben-Hur* (a $6 million spectacle that never recouped its cost), *Beau Geste*, *What Price Glory?*, *The Sea Beast*, and *La Boheme*.

The last great year of the silent film was 1927, with *Seventh Heaven*, Keaton's *The General*, *The Cat and the Canary*, and Murnau's lyric poem, *Sunrise*.

But such masterpieces were as long as a year in production, and could hardly fill the ravenous clamor for movies . . . movies . . . and more movies that sprang from the nation's twenty thousand movie emporiums.

To help fill this demand, almost by accident a truly native American art form emerged—namely, The Western. These were easy to make, since they were filmed outdoors; inexpensive, since the cast consisted largely of horses; and uncomplicated, since the plot lines were as rigid and systematized as Greek drama.

The first great Western star was Max Aronson of Little Rock, Arkansas, better known as Broncho Billy Anderson. Other silent screen cowboys were, alphabetically: Richard Dix, who portrayed the more psychologically motivated Western hero; William S. Hart, an artist and a neo-realist, who attempted to portray accurately the West as he remembered it from his childhood in such films as *Hell's Hinges*; ole' uncomplicated buttermilk sky Ken Maynard; leathery Tom Mix, the most popular of Western stars, whose wonder horse Tony displayed an almost Wagnerian sense of superendurance; and Fred Thomson, a really excellent equestrian, whose skill on horseback was wonderful to watch.

En masse, these gentlemen shaped a genre that is pure American; as native to the United States as the kabuki is to Japan or the Comédie-Français is to France. Some frames in these silent epics convey the rich Americana of Matthew Brady photographs; even the poorest of them will have a redeeming shot of a stampede or a horse bridging a river. It is not surprising to hear them referred to as horse operas; for they have the pace of opera, slow, unhurried, rising to climaxes and then settling down again.

Theaters in rural America also welcomed another form of silent drama, the twelve-part serial. Like the Westerns, these were simple in story lines and easy to make; instead of horses, the principal actors were stunt men, an improvement over thespians as far as temperament, although they sometimes proved equally hard to keep sober. The first great serial stars were women—Pearl White, Ruth Roland, and even Billie Burke. But later the serials took on a science-fiction or jungle-adventure format (*Tarzan* was one of the most popular of serials). These week-to-week adventures were bread-and-butter to small-town exhibitors, particularly on Saturday afternoon when the movies were filled with lethal hordes of children, out to rape, murder, and pillage. The serials distracted the mob for a while, at least.

This, then, was the silent screen. What was it exactly? An art? An industry? A passing fad, like the six-day bicycle race?

No one knew. No one, except a few analysts like Vachel Lindsay and Gilbert Seldes and Robert E. Sherwood (who conducted a department called "The Silent Drama" on the old, pre-Luceian *Life*) really cared. It was something that was happening.

But one thing was sure—everyone was going to the Hollywood-made movies, even in Europe where the great studios of Ufa and Cinecitta were, after a brilliant beginning, going downhill. Ninety percent of all films shown in Europe were made in Hollywood; and this was true in South America, Asia, Africa, and Australia. The American film industry was the greatest single monopoly ever known in the modern world.

Like all monopolies it would slowly crumble but, meanwhile, everyone wanted to visit this wonder. The kings and queens of Europe, after shaking hands in New York with Jimmy Walker and sipping tea with Mrs. Coolidge in Washington, hotfooted it to Hollywood, where they met the real American royal families —the DeMilles, the Fairbanks, the Chaplins, the Valentinos, the Lloyds. To lunch with Marion Davies in her Metro-Goldwyn-Mayer bungalow, where bottles of Heinz's catsup were plunked unceremoniously in the middle of the table, came Winston Churchill and George Bernard Shaw. Churchill's coming passed unrecorded; but Davies and Shaw had been thrown together as if by predestination. If it wasn't for D-d-d-addy, said Marion, she'd have left home. Oh, those d-d-d-arling whiskers. Shaw returned to England and wrote *The Simpleton of the Unexpected Isles.*

By this time, Hollywood had acquired a czar of its own— the ex-Indiana lawyer, ex-Republican national chairman, ex-Postmaster General, Will H. Hays. "The Little White Father of the Cinema" had to fend off the General Federation of Women's Clubs with one hand and tone down the bathtub sequences in DeMille's spectaculars with the other. It was no easy job, and, not surprisingly, he pulled some heady boners—such as excising the udders of an animated cow in a Walt Disney cartoon.

By not taking his job overly seriously, he managed to rule on the side of the angels for more than three decades, although one can detect a faint note of exasperation and despair in his often repeated pronouncement: "No story ever written for the screen is as dramatic as the screen itself."

But, then, could he have been thinking of Greta Garbo?

ParkPlace
—ENTERTAINMENT—

BALLY'S   *Paris*   *Hilton*   CAESARS   GRAND CASINOS   *Flamingo*

Chapter 5

The Divine One

"Greta! Greta Lorjissa Gustafsson!"

It was the voice of Mrs. Gustafsson calling after her tall, long-legged daughter as she ran out of the apartment after supper.

Greta was, for all her strange ways, a nice child.

She sullenly retraced her steps, her broad shoulders sagging, as she reentered the dingy apartment in the working-class section of Sweden.

"Where, may I ask, are you headed?" asked Mrs. Gustafsson.

Her daughter's lashes were long and silken, and a tear, somehow, had got caught in one of them. It sparkled like a jewel in the shabbiness of that single room, where four people lived and slept.

"To the theater, mama."

"But we are in mourning. You know your father's only a few months gone."

"Yes, mama."

"Why don't you stay home this evening, with your sisters, and do some mending then, my child?"

"I can't, mama."

"But why can't you, then?"

"I *must* go—to the theater. They will let me in free backstage. I'll help them with the props."

The plain, honest face of Mrs. Gustafsson looked deeply into her daughter's.

"You are the one most like your father," she said. She moved her hand to brush away the tear in Greta's eyelash, but she quickly dropped her hand. "Go then, Greta," she said finally.

They clung to one another for a moment, the muscular, squat cleaning woman and her gazellelike daughter. There was an understanding between them that would never change in the coming years, although they would be half a world apart. Greta often visualized her mother in the audience as she played roles like *Camille* and *Anna Karenina*. This is what gave her art its simplicity and its universality.

As her daughter ran out the door, Mrs. Gustafsson was for a second so overcome by her grace that she was forced to lean her weight against the door. How could such loveliness have sprung from her sturdy body? But she quickly recovered herself and went back to her chores. When Greta became famous, Mrs. Gustafsson never cashed one of the checks that her daughter sent her. She always made her own way.

Greta Lorjissa Gustafsson had even then at fourteen chosen a theater name for herself: Garbo, meaning "beautiful form" in Italian. By day she worked at odd jobs—she lathered men's faces in a barber shop, she sold fruit at a stall, she clerked in a shop—meanwhile, forming strong attachments to her girlfriends while she dreamed of acting in the theater. She rarely thought of boys; she always said she would never marry. She never did.

Carl Brisson, the Swedish matinée idol, was the first professional to see something in her. She was too tall, too gawky, but Greta had a face that sent out radiations, he said. The great ones always had this gift of gently embracing their audience with love. It was that sliver of projection that separated the actors of genius from those of talent. It was that inward response that illuminated, transfixed an object, until it became divine.

The metamorphosis from peasant to cinema divinity began when she was promoted to a hat model in the Stockholm shop where she worked. A producer, making an advertising film on the store, saw her. Yes, she would do. Other small roles in minor movies followed. In one of them she was a bathing beauty; in another, she flung a custard pie.

But Greta, a child of the streets and wise in the ways of the world, knew that nothing would come of this unless she really learned to act. She yearned to appear in plays like *Anna Christie*, which she saw again and again at the Stockholm State Theater. Now that was a role to play—she grew up among girls like this, girls who had come to Stockholm from farms and soon gave up trying to find jobs in the big city. She had, from childhood, watched them fight with rich homosexuals for the attention of a sailor. She knew what life was all about. She knew, too, that she could not possibly convey it until she had acquired technique. Tremulously, she applied as a trainee at the Stockholm State Theater. The other candidates were the daughters of bankers, the sons of politicians, the children of the Stockholm well-to-do. They made her feel that her clothes did not quite fit, that her shoes were too shabby, that her body was loathsome and ugly, that her voice was too deep and guttural. She wanted to run away and hide from them, to go back into the arms of her mother, to marry a boy of her class. But she endured the humiliation of the tests—why should she, who had already proved herself as an actress, be tested along with these rich, self-assured children? That combination of hauteur and shyness that would prevail through her entire career already came to light.

The directors of the Stockholm State Theater were not aware, at first, of the beauty of her face. They saw a tall, angular girl who might make a good character actress. Let's see—Gustafsson from the Southside slums. She came well recommended and she was ambitious enough. Well, let's give the girl a try.

All the way home, Greta was jubilant. And terrified. What would she wear to her classes? How could she possibly compete with all those rich girls? And what would those elegant young men in her class, like Nils Asther, think of her? A girl from the Southside. And how would mama manage now that she could no longer bring home a salary? But, oh, what heaven! She had been accepted by the Stockholm State Theater. Her future was secure. After she played *Anna Christie* and had grown too old to act any more, they would give her a pension.

The directors of the Stockholm repertory began to see something in the girl. Offstage she was nothing very much, but when they gave her a bit role to play she managed to transform it into something quite magical. What an amusing name she had chosen for herself. Garbo. How like a girl from Soder. But she had something. That Jewess, Sarah Bernhardt, was once an unpolished girl like this. A nobody who could, on the stage, be grander than the grandest lady. How is it that things happen this way? No one knew. No one would ever know. But they happened, and it was what made the theater fascinating.

Mauritz Stiller, the film director, telephoned them one day. He was looking for a young girl, pliable, who could take direction easily. Who had a face that would look foreign on camera. She would play the Italian-born Countess Dohna in his version of Selma Lagerloff's *The Story of Gosta Berling*. Whom could they suggest?

Garbo thought him quite insolent. He arrived late, and said very little. Yes, yes, a good face, he finally admitted, but you are too fat. Even so, some signal of recognition passed between them. She had seen men like Stiller slumming on the Southside. Garbo and Stiller understood one another. They were cut of the same cloth.

To Stiller, the challenge of converting this child of the Stockholm slums into a cinema countess was irresistible. He was a born impresario, and here was raw material he could mold. The face, properly made up, would be magnificent. He would "Greek" that hideous body. The daughter of a cleaning woman and a sanitation worker. How amusing! He stroked his lap dog lovingly.

Unforeseen problems came up. She was so nervous on camera that a twitch eliminated all possibilities of close-ups. But the star of the picture was Lars Hanson, in any case. Meanwhile, he would train her to walk, to sit, to stare into space, to use her hands, to hide those feet. He would photograph her against the beauty of the Swedish landscape so that she would blend into it and become part of it. He would fuse her into the film with the brush strokes of a Rembrandt.

When the picture was, at last, done, Stiller took his new protégée, who had made herself indispensable, with him to Berlin to market it. They were enchanted with her, the Germans, as he knew they would be. Already she had the hauteur of the international star. Already she was the great new Swedish discovery.

They bought *Gosta Berling* and talked of financing a new film, which would star Garbo. But the deal was never completely consummated. Stiller returned to Sweden, leaving Garbo behind to do *The Joyless Street* for G. W. Pabst.

The film, a neo-realistic study of postwar Berlin prostitution, frightened Garbo; Berlin frightened her; Pabst frightened her. The twitch reappeared—and Pabst began to tear his hair, until a clever cameraman discovered that, by shooting at double the normal speed in the close-up scenes, it was eradicated. A studio extra in *The Joyless Street* was Marlene Dietrich, a few years older than Miss Garbo, and already married and carrying a child. The attention the raw Swedish actress was getting didn't disturb her particularly; Dietrich had adjusted to the fact that she was not photogenic and that consequently she'd never get anywhere in movies.

Meanwhile, Louis B. Mayer, in Europe on one of his peripatetic scouting trips, had seen *Gosta Berling*. It was, he decided, a good example of the Swedish psychological tragedy, and Stiller might make a good director for Gish. He offered Stiller a contract. What! said Stiller, hadn't he noticed Garbo? Who, asked Mayer, was Garbo? The actress who played Countess Dohna. Yes, he'd noticed her, said Mayer. That big girl. But they already had Lillian Gish, who was far prettier. Well, said Stiller, Mayer would have to sign up Garbo if he wanted Stiller in Hollywood; they traveled as a team. Mayer reluctantly agreed, telling Garbo that Americans did not like girls with fat legs. "*Ja, ja,*" said Greta Gustafsson nodding eagerly. She did not understand a word he said.

Hollywood to Garbo was a shock. Even the working-class section of Stockholm where she grew up had handsome old buildings and festive ancient theaters, centuries old, which gave the place a sense of history. Here everything seemed an open field, dotted with what looked like farmers' huts and palm trees which (her Swedish sense of housekeeping told her) badly needed dusting. The tiny Hollywood women had enormous heads and breasts that made them look like plump pigeons, and the men walked with an odd tilt, like roosters. A funny kind of barnyard to which she had come. She wanted to go home.

Hollywood found Garbo just as bewildering. The leading men of that period—Ricardo Cortez and Ramon Novarro—were slight of build; Garbo not only towered over them but outweighed them. The studio decided she was the athletic type; they put her in bathing suits, on the tennis court, in rowing machines, behind the wheel of sports cars. Once they photographed her modeling trick garters. When she wasn't posing for publicity stills, she was put to work greeting visiting exhibitors. In her one and only suit, a cheap black-and-white check, she was presented as the new Swedish discovery. "*Ja . . . ja . . . ,*" said Garbo, as she enthusiastically grasped their limp hands in her enormous paw.

Then, one day they found there just wasn't anyone around to put into the role of the Spanish girl in *The Torrent*, which starred Ricardo Cortez. What about the big Swede? someone said. Her, for Christ's sake, why she'd make Ricardo look like the groom on a wedding cake. But they pulled out a test made by Stiller, which showed them how to photograph her. Well, maybe; and, anyway, even if it flopped in America they'd go for it in Europe. *The Joyless Street* was a hit over there.

Garbo, to their amazement, said no, she didn't want to do it. She had come over with Stiller, and would make pictures only with Stiller. The director assigned to *The Torrent* was Monta Bell.

Hollywood was intrigued: a girl who said No! The studio was filled with minor little contract actresses who would lie down on a couch for a chance to appear in a Ricardo Cortez picture. And here was this big Swedish liability telling them No! Now, they decided, they just had to have her. Louis B. Mayer got down on his knees and pleaded with her, his style somewhat hampered since he first had to address his comments to a translator who transposed his words into Swedish for Garbo. Irving Thalberg smiled his tight, little juvenile smile and tried to charm her. Garbo still said No!

While production was held up, they decided to try a new tactic—convince Stiller, soft-soap him somehow, that Garbo should do it. It worked.

The rushes came in. Louis B. Mayer sat up straight in his seat. Irving Thalberg played it cool, as he always did, but his eyes narrowed conspicuously. He drummed his fingers; and decided to open the picture at the Capitol.

The critics started tossing their hats into the air when they saw her, but New York critics will always buy a new face. They waited for *Variety*, the tough, cynical, don't-kid-me-Buster of Show Biz, to come in. *Sime*'s words were wired to Culver City: "The discovery of the year!"

Quickly they starred her in another picture, *The Temptress*, this time complying with her request for Stiller as her director. But Stiller's slow European way of engineering a film—it can be compared with the product of an English bootmaker's meticulous craftsmanship and loving concern, as contrasted with an American machine-tooled pair of shoes—had the powers-that-be at Metro frothing at the mouth. The picture was pulled from Stiller, and farmed out to one of Metro's yeomen, Fred Niblo, to get it to the Capitol on time. He got it there—with scenes that didn't match the ones before and a happy ending tacked onto a tragic story—but her growing army of fans was too overcome by the Garbo mystique to notice. Her co-star this time around was Antonio Moreno, one of a dozen Latin lovers rushed into service after the death of Valentino. That none of them had Rudy's charisma was a foregone conclusion, but Antonio was one of the nicer ones.

Thalberg and Mayer and Harry Rapf—nicknamed "M-G-M's Unholy Three" by disgruntled stars—now knew they had a gold mine on their hands. She was not only standing them up at the Capitol, she was sitting them down in Paris, Berlin, Rome, Sydney, Cairo, Port Said, Walla Walla, Bombay, Shanghai, and London. In London, as a matter of fact, she was sitting them down three deep, piled on top of one another like acrobats. And she was doing this in a half-assed picture, in which her coiffure and costumes changed in a split second (depending on whether a scene of Stiller's or a scene of Niblo's was used), and in which the continuity was wobblier than a stepladder with one leg sawed off.

They had come—Mohammedans, Catholics, Buddhists, Jews, Presbyterians, and Holy Rollers—to see *That Face!* They had come—Australians, Indians, Italians, Hungarians, and Chinese—to Worship at the Shrine. They had come, and Garbo knew it.

The Torrent and *The Temptress* were not made as Class A films, but were more in the nature of substantial programmers, ground out to meet the laws of supply and demand. Now Mayer was prepared to pull out a few stops with the next one—*Flesh and the Devil*. They weren't going to spend $6 million on it, but they would give her a leading man who was a big star, John Gilbert, and one of their best directors, Clarence Brown. They would also assign Billy Daniels, who had found a way to photograph *That Face!* that could hardly be improved, and throw in Lars Hanson, a fellow Swede, so she wouldn't feel so alone and lost on the set. (Hanson, who had starred in *Gosta Berling*, was now demoted to third in the cast, a not unusual pattern with a strong life force like Garbo.) Mayer could hardly wait to tell his new star the good news, but he had trouble finding her. She had quietly gone on strike.

Her salary of $750 a week, said the cool Swede, was hardly commensurate with that of Gilbert. She wasn't asking for $10,000, but $5,000 a week seemed only fair.

Mayer tried cajolery first. He sent her large plates of corned beef and cabbage, her favorite American food, and promised to have the palm trees dusted. This was all very nice, said the Swede, sending the empty dishes back, and she thanked him. As for the palm trees, they should have been dusted a long time ago. As for coming back to work at her old salary, No.

It was time to get tough, Mayer decided. Did she know she was in the United States on a work permit, and he could have her deported if she refused to work? Garbo, who had gotten reports on the world grosses of her first two pictures, didn't bother to reply at all. She had grown up in the slums of Stockholm, and she knew there was one way, and one way only, to handle the taunts of bullies—ignore them. If ignored, the wind will go out of their sails until they find another vulnerable object to taunt—and then they will expand again. Meanwhile, preparations on *Flesh and the Devil* had stopped. Every star at M-G-M was considered for it, but each time they had decided on someone else a new report would come in saying that *The Temptress* had broken all records in Manitoba or North Dakota. Negri was losing money for Paramount, and here they were with a hot Cold Swede on their hands . . . well, offer her $2,500.

Flesh and the Devil differs from the usual pleasure-dome pablum in that it is based on a good story—Hermann Sudermann's novel, *The Undying Past*. In the scenario, some of the flavor gets lost but enough chicken paprikash and champagne remain to give the characters—two Austrian officers in love with the same married woman—a bit of zing. It was handsomely directed in the Ufa manner by Clarence Brown. Above all, it was lovingly photographed by Billy Daniels, who converted scenes that could be clichés, such as a dueling episode, into silhouetted cameos. It would be interesting merely as an example of Hollywood Mandarin Art (to apply Cyril Connelly's literary allusion to film) were it not for the fact that at some point in the picture Gilbert, reportedly having a love affair with Dorothy Parker between marriages, fell madly in love with Garbo. That the love was not reciprocated is suggested by some eyewitness reports at the time—which indicate that Garbo remained cool and amused, while Gilbert fawned on her with moonstruck eyes. When he presented her with a robe of his to keep as a memento of his love, thrifty Greta rushed over to wardrobe with it and asked them to cut it down to her size. Perhaps she knew Gilbert would fall out of love as quickly as he fell into it; in any case this balmy kind of American love must have struck her hard European pragmatism as quite ridiculous. She refused to marry him.

But his passion, and her interested indifference, created love scenes of startling intimacy that sent Mrs. Babbitt and her ilk speeding to the downtown pleasure domes in their Auburns, in numbers that had not been recorded before. The Babbitts' Auburn was joined by the Scott-Smythes' Pierce Arrow and the Jones's Model-T Ford to create traffic jams of lovesick ladies that tied up transit for blocks. A love like this crossed all income levels, as Mrs. Scott-Smythe grabbed the arm of Mrs. Jones, seated next to her, when Gilbert kissed Garbo. "There, there, dear," said cloth-coated Mrs. Jones to chinchillaed Mrs. Scott-Smythe, "it's only a moving picture." Short of breath, and barely able to walk, Mrs. Scott-Smythe found her chauffeur and asked to be taken directly to Dr. Rosenkrantz, who diagnosed "no more photoplays!"

But that's like telling an alcoholic, "no more whisky," and all three of these ladies were right back at Loew's the following afternoon. *Flesh and the Devil* was held over a second week; a third; a fourth; a fifth; a sixth. When Mrs. Babbitt put on a beaded negligée that looked like Garbo's, the exasperated Mr. Babbitt was heard to say, "For Christ's sake, Agnes. What's come over you anyhow—change of life?"

There were three more—Garbo-Gilbert pictures, that is— *Love*, a silent version of *Anna Karenina*, with a happy ending tacked on; *The Divine Woman*, which was intended as a biography of Sarah Bernhardt but ended up closer to the life of Eva Tanguay; and, inevitably, *A Woman of Affairs*, in which Garbo played Michael Arlen's Iris March. American womanhood has never been the same since.

Garbo was now the top-ranking foreign star in Hollywood. Louis B. Mayer was ecstatic. Loew's stockholders were waving miniature Swedish flags. Robert E. Sherwood joined John Gilbert among the hordes of the infatuated. He wrote in *Life*: "Anyone who says that Garbo isn't the most ravishing, alluring, enthralling, etc., etc., has me to fight."

Whatever happened to Dorothy Parker? Chances are she went home and wrote one of those rueful little love lyrics.

Chapter 6

The Late Flowering of Marlene

At the age of two she was a tiny Dresden doll, with hair the color of marigolds and eyes of periwinkle blue. She was "correct"—the little body well formed, the features neatly buttoned on her tiny face, the skin properly tinted: a little paragon of Prussian supremacy.

It had taken years of careful breeding to create so perfect a child, so scrumptious a sample of middle-class aristocracy. Unsuitable suitors had been banished, cold and love-starved, into countless bitter nights, trembling with delirium; maidens who did not have the dowries or the beauty or the fortitude were cast aside ruthlessly by pugnacious *grandmères*, so that the Wolfgangs and the Erichs would have a wife at their side that they could proudly present to the Empress. Maria Magdalene, for that was the child's name, did not just happen into this world: She sprang from good seed, seed that had been carefully fertilized, seed that had been polished until it sparkled like gold.

To understand this middle-class aristocracy one must grow up in it, day after stultifying day, year after stodgy year, decade after unbending decade, generation after impassive generation, lifetime after pernicious lifetime. It is an aristocracy of heavily curtained windows and securely locked doors and carefully nurtured money. Often four generations live in one household: grandparents, parents, children, and grandchildren. It lets in little sun and air. It is final.

Thus sprang Maria Magdalene Dietrich, for Dietrich was the child's last name. Her mother was born Wilhelmina Felsing, the daughter of a prosperous merchant; her father was Louis Erich Otto Dietrich of the Royal Prussian Police. At the age of two her hair was neatly combed, parted, and beribboned; her spotless white dress had insets of handmade lace; her sash was neatly folded; her feet were shod in white high-buttoned shoes. Everything was in order—until one looked at the eyes. They were dreamy, and it was not the dreaminess of a child who grew up listening to *Gretchen am Spinrade*. No. It was the dreaminess of a poet, of a revolutionary even. Those eyes were not "correct."

Frau Dietrich, soon to be widowed and then to remarry (her second husband was Edouard von Losch, Regiment of the Grenadiers), seems to have done very little about the visionary fire that lurked in Maria Magdalene's eyes. Usually such fire is fought with fire, until the child is either made or broken. But the problems of being a young widow may have distracted her. She even encouraged Maria Magdalene's first artistic expression, which was music, and arranged for her to study at the Hochschule für Musik.

The Dresden doll had by then grown up into an enchanting fräulein, the very flower of Germany. All was as it should be, except for that love of music. But, that was a most ladylike predilection, after all. She would soon make her debut as a violinist, and Frau von Losch, although a bit alarmed, was also proud. Research has not as yet unearthed what that debut recital consisted of, but we can be sure it included Schubert and Brahms. Schubert and Brahms, the soul of Germany, to be interpreted by one of the fairest flowers of Germany. *Sehr Schön.*

And then, on the eve of the debut of Fräulein von Losch, tragedy struck. Her wrist snapped. The Dresden-doll wrist was not made to pull a bow across a violin. No. Frau von Losch gave a quiet sigh of relief. Well, that was the end of that.

But it wasn't. Maria Magdalene stood in the waxed and polished front parlor and stunned them all by announcing that she wanted to become an actress! It was like a slap in the face. Nor would she listen to reason. For every point that was made, she had a counter-point. She was cool, calm, collected—

and obviously demented. For, finally, she announced that, despite their objections, she fully intended to pursue a career in the theater—and she would change her name to Marlene Dietrich to save them the embarrassment.

Her first call was to Max Reinhardt, the great German impresario who had discovered Pola Negri and who attracted every society girl in Europe with theatrical aspirations.

Reinhardt looked at the fair officer's daughter, and did not see too much. She was pretty, yes, but a common type in Germany. She did not engulf you with her presence, as did Negri. She was not exotic. But, if she came back in the fall, he might take her on as a student. Quietly, he hoped she would just go home and marry some nice German boy.

Marlene Dietrich didn't go home. She, Maria Magdalene von Losch, became a—chorus girl! She toured Germany with a slightly ratty troupe of dancers, keeping her eyes and ears open, learning everything there was to learn. No neophyte was ever more ready, willing, and able. None was more fascinated by the tough slang of the theater. Quietly, calmly, coolly, she *watched*—and if you have ever seen Dietrich at an opening night on Broadway, you will have noticed how she *watches*. She *watches* with the sublime indifference of a cat.

She presented herself to Reinhardt at the appointed time. He sighed, and took her on. She played a bit here, a second lead there. And then, like a moth drawn to a flame, she headed toward the studios of Ufa. It was now that her career would really begin.

In the next seven years, she appeared in nine films—none of them distinguished (except for *The Joyless Street*, in which she was an extra). Sometimes she was the leading lady; sometimes her roles were little more than bits. Nonetheless, she came in contact with many of the major figures then working at Ufa—with Emil Jannings, William Dieterle, Willi Forst, director Maurice Tourneur, Karl Freund, Alexander Korda, Paul Leni. Every year she was "discovered" and then quietly dropped. Reinhardt was right. She didn't project. She didn't grab you by the throat, like Negri, or sneak up on you like Garbo. She had no consistent style or screen personality. She was competent, yes, but really unexciting.

The great German actress of this period was Elisabeth Bergner. Bergner was a mere wisp of a thing, nowhere nearly so attractive as Marlene, but no matter what she did—if she lifted an eyebrow or crooked a little finger—she was Elisabeth Bergner. And Bergner knew how to act. She could take a line, "Where are you going?" and break your heart with it. She could pick up a lover's coat, and by holding it in just that precise way for a short second, she expressed the depth of her emotion. Her costumes were superb—she knew when to be dowdy and when to dazzle you with her Berlin elegance. You could not take your eyes off her—you went back to see her a second, a third, a fourth, a fifth time in the same play or movie. And each time you went, you found something new, a nuance that you had missed before, a revelation of character that she had shaded so carefully it was not immediately apparent. Berlin sat at her feet, as soon would audiences in London and New York.

How could Marlene compete with exhibitionistic displays like these? With her Prussian officer's mind, she knew that she just didn't have it in her. For a few years she even retired from the screen completely—to marry Rudolph Sieber, a production assistant at Ufa. On their daughter Maria she lavished the love that she once put into her career.

And yet she could not give up acting entirely. She was now close to thirty and a nobody. But she would not give up. When roles in films became harder to find, she appeared in musical revues, in comedies, in anything. She filled up her time by reading omnivorously—Hamsun, Lagerloff, Mann, Goethe, and, above everyone, the poet Rilke, who captured her sunlight-and-shadow moods.

It was in this frame of mind, and at this point in her career, that von Sternberg saw her for the first time.

He happened to be in Berlin to direct Emil Jannings in *The Blue Angel*. The papers were full of it; and the gossip backstage had it that he had rejected producer Erich Pommer's choice for the role of Lola Frobisch, the café girl who seduces the professor, along with every other important actress in Germany. But it did not seem to Dietrich a particularly promising part and, in any case, it was unlikely that this famous American director would consider her for it.

Then one evening he came quite by accident to see the stage comedy *Zwei Kravatten* (Two Cravats), in which she played a bit part. The other members of the company, wanting to make an impression on von Sternberg, played at the double. Marlene thought them ridiculous, and glared at them insolently.

That insolence was the very quality that von Sternberg had in mind for Lola Frobisch. No one else in hungry, battered, starving, between-the-wars Berlin had it. The city was filled with eager glad handers, who would do anything for a few of the inflated German marks. This girl did not have to; or was too proud to. It was, he suspected, a little of both. He was fascinated, and the next day he sent for her.

She arrived in one of those moods of deep melancholia from which she suffered. When she talked of herself, it was to speak negatively. She made no attempt to be attractive or "cute." She stared at him sullenly. Now his curiosity was piqued even more. She was the antithesis of the glib actress, who recited her credits as if by rote. Each bit of information had to be coaxed out of her. When she uttered it, she gave it a sardonic twist of phrase, talking down about herself. She was, he decided, the most sophisticated woman he had ever met. He knew, then, that the part was hers.

But she did not know, nor did Jannings, nor did Pommer. All three of them fought the idea, with a savage fury. Jannings said she would ruin the picture. Pommer said she was too much of a risk. Dietrich said she did not photograph well; and even if von Sternberg could, as he said, manage it, she had not been impressed in the past by the way he directed women. She was really not too terribly interested.

But von Sternberg overruled the lot of them. He coaxed her into signing the contract, and shooting began. At some early point in the picture, Jannings knew that the picture was Dietrich's. He was the first to know; von Sternberg was the next to know;

and Dietrich never knew, until it was all over. Meanwhile, Svengali Joe had wired Paramount that he thought he had an important discovery on his hands. Trusting his judgment, they prepared a contract—and thus it was that Marlene Dietrich, a new "sex symbol of the century," was brought to Hollywood.

It had taken the Dresden doll a long, long time to become a star—but, when she finally came out, she would reveal a legendary luminosity for decade after decade.

Dissolve 3:

The Talkies Come Marching In

"Hollywood is a sewer with service from the Ritz-Carlton," Wilson Mizener once said. To Evelyn Waugh, it was a land where everyone was "deep in thrall to the Dragon King." Clifford Odets thought the sun had baked everyone's brains right out. "A celluloid Babylon," said Don Blanding. "Not so much a business as it is a racket," said Harry Cohn. "Hollywood is the land of Mother Goose platitudes and primitive valentines," said Ben Hecht. "I never drink anything stronger than gin before breakfast," said W. C. Fields. To Fred Allen, the place was so unreal he always expected the prop men to come and remove the palm trees at five o'clock. "A Necropolis," said Sterling Hayden. "A dream factory," said Hortense Powdermaker. "Bloody, bawdy villain! Remorseless, treacherous, lecherous, kindless villain!" said John Barrymore.

And now it was learning to talk, at a cost estimated to be $500 million, a modest figure when one considers the havoc wrought by the coming of sound. In those halcyon days, a number of silent pictures that were already in the can were pulled out and entirely reshot: This happened with Howard Hughes's multimillion-dollar epic, *Hell's Angels*, which originally starred Anna Q. Nillson, who "couldn't talk." (She was replaced by a sexy blonde from a St. Louis finishing school, Jean Harlow, who could.) In other instances, the entire crew was recalled to film a one- or two-reel "all-talking" sequence, which was tacked onto the end of an otherwise silent picture. (When the sound finally came on, it seemed as if the figures on the screen were disinterred and given the voices of babbling idiots.) The director, traditionally at the helm of a picture, now moved over for the "sound technician," a ruthless overlord "from the East," who told *him* what to do. Big studio stars rushed out to have their voices trained, only to discover, as did Vilma Banky and Pola Negri, that no amount of study could eradicate the guttural sounds that issued from their lips; or, as did Norma and Constance Talmadge, that a Brooklyn accent was a Brooklyn accent was a Brooklyn accent; or, as did Janet Gaynor, that pear-shaped tones did not fit her screen personality and to please to put it back the way it was.

Producers huddled in dark corners, wringing their hands with despair. Could Ronald Colman "talk"? Could Clara Bow "talk"? Could Lillian Gish "talk"? "What about Gary Cooper's mumble?" "What about Marion Davies's stutter?" "What about Kay *Fwan*-cis?"

The giant silent star system, which had taken a decade or longer to build up, was wrecked. One by one they rode into the valley of Vitaphone or the meadow of Movietone, and never emerged, the great super-stars: Little Mary (a born fighter, who went down kicking); Gloria, the Marquise; Tom Mix, with his gallant horse, Tony; Clara Bow, with her glorious shimmy; Jack Gilbert; Doug; Colleen; Dick Barthelmess; Bill Haines; the orchidaceous Corinne Griffith; the beautiful Billie Dove.

A gallant few came through. Joan Crawford "could talk." Norma Shearer "talked." The grand old vaudevillians—Marie Dressler, W. C. Fields, Will Rogers, Wallace Beery—"talked."

Others talked, but it didn't sound American—John Barrymore was eased out of his Warner Brothers contract; Tallulah Bankhead made six talkies, all of them flops; Ina Claire, with her Broadway stage diction, came over too brittle. Major stars from Broadway and London were rushed to the Coast—Leslie Howard, George Arliss, Jeanne Eagels, Ruth Chatterton, Helen Hayes, Alfred Lunt and Lynn Fontanne. Although their pictures did well in the big cities, they did not catch on in the hinterlands. Strictly Broadway favorites—Harry Richman, Sophie Tucker,

Belle Baker, Fannie Brice, Bobby Clark, Rudy Vallee, George Jessel, Marilyn Miller—turned out to have limited cinema appeal. So did opera stars Lawrence Tibbett and Grace Moore and John McCormick. So, incredibly, did Kate Smith, whose *Hello, Everybody* was pulled out of the Paramount, after only a few days.

A group of talented younger performers from Broadway—whose technique was not "frozen" and who could adapt themselves to the new talkie medium—fared best. They included Spencer Tracy, Paul Muni, Claudette Colbert, Bette Davis, Fredric March, Miriam Hopkins, Irene Dunne, Humphrey Bogart, James Cagney, Joan Blondell—and they would become the backbone of Hollywood in the 1930's and 1940's. But it didn't happen easily—Davis was said by Carl Laemmle to have the sex appeal of Slim Summerville and Bogart not even to have that. They were let out of their contracts and they scrounged around for parts, until slowly, very slowly, they made their way to the top. These Broadway performers, intelligent and attractive rather than sexy and beautiful, were supplemented with young players discovered on the West Coast—Clark Gable (developed for the screen by Lionel Barrymore and signed by M-G-M over protests from Thalberg), Myrna Loy, Carole Lombard. Gradually, other young Broadway personalities would make their way to Hollywood—Katharine Hepburn, Margaret Sullavan, Henry Fonda—and a whole new star structure would be erected over the bones of Negri and Banky and Swanson and Pickford and Fairbanks and Davies.

It was cruel and senseless and expensive, and it could only have happened in Hollywood, the last frontier of American free enterprise—a throwback to the Robber Baron era of the post-Civil War. After it was wired for sound, Hollywood would mend its ways and operate as a cartel in which industry procedures were established and maintained. It, too, would become a Detroit or a Pittsburgh or an Akron, an industry town supervised by a handful of moguls and financed by the great investment houses. The late 1920's were the blithe soft-shoe dance that preceded a more decorous waltz.

The old soft-shoe was set in motion by the Brothers Warner,

who, while Paramount and Metro and Universal and First National had gradually evolved individualized star systems, and while Fox was combining the lowbrow (Tom Mix) and the highbrow (F. W. Murnau) into a successful package, were left far behind in the races.

About all WB had was a dog, a silent Shakespearean actor, and the licensing rights to a primitive sound system, Vitaphone, in which sound was recorded on discs and projected, separate from the film, through a system of amplifiers that cost $20,000 for a theater to install. Warners' sound-on-disc was viewed by most film people as inferior to a system evolved by General Electric, in which the sound was photographed directly on the film strip, and another, perfected by RCA, in which the sound track was kept separate from the film but run concurrently. To complicate matters, William Fox had secured the rights to a rival European sound-on-film system, which he called Fox-Movietone, and there were any number of independent sound processes, such as Powers Cinephone, available on the market.

Warners introduced their Vitaphone with fair success in 1926 at the Mark Strand on Broadway, during the engagement of Barrymore's *Don Juan*. There was no spoken dialogue on the disc, only a musical accompaniment, but the film was preceded by a series of talking and singing shorts which gave audiences some idea of what sound movies would be like. *Don Juan* was viewed by the industry as something of a novelty, nothing to be taken very seriously, and production of silent pictures continued at the normal pace.

Terror struck when some singing sequences (including "Mammy," sung by Al Jolson) were introduced into Warners' major feature of the year, *The Jazz Singer*. This was an adaptation of a hit Broadway play that starred George Jessel, who was originally slated to duplicate his role on the screen. When Warners decided to film it as a "part-talkie," however, Jessel demanded more money, and Warners gave the role to Jolson. It made Jolson the first big talkie star, and accomplished what *Don Juan* failed to do—it created a sensation. Audiences lined up for blocks to see and hear *The Jazz Singer*, as they did the first all-talkie, a low-budget melodrama, *The Lights of New York*, that grossed a million.

If, at this point, the industry hadn't panicked, a gradual transition to talking pictures could have been worked out over the next decade. Silent pictures, as a result of the foreign invasion, had achieved new levels of artistry by 1927. There was every indication that the medium would evolve further and that even greater masterpieces would join a blue-ribbon list that already included *The Gold Rush, Hotel Imperial, Ben-Hur, The Big Parade, Flesh and the Devil,* and *Sunrise.* But panic the industry did. Fox broke into the soft-shoe act with its Movie-tone News (George Bernard Shaw, inevitably, was one of its prime attractions) and the first "100% talking picture produced outdoors," *In Old Arizona.* Paramount, utilizing the RCA sound system, came on strong with *Wings,* the first aviation epic with sound. The slumbering lion, Metro-Goldwyn-Mayer, awoke with a roar and rushed "the first 100% all-talking, all-singing, all-dancing picture," *Broadway Melody,* into the market. Carl Laemmle, at Universal, filmed plays like *Broadway,* musicals like *Show Boat,* and brought in Paul Whiteman to do *King of Jazz.* (The latter film, incidentally, deserves a special niche in the Hall of Fame for two reasons: It introduced Bing Crosby to the screen and it was one of the first movie musicals made in color. Since only two colors—red and green—were used in those days, Gershwin's *Rhapsody in Blue* sequence presented a special problem. Director John Murray Anderson solved it by tinting it peacock green.)

Now everyone got into the act, even Little Mary, who ruthlessly changed her screen image to a vamp and made her first talkie, *Coquette.* She and Doug then made *The Taming of the Shrew,* also deserving a place in the Hall of Fame, if only for its credits, which listed "additional dialogue by William Shakespeare." Janet Gaynor and Charles Farrell, who had emoted silently in *Seventh Heaven,* now sang in *Sunny-Side Up* ("If I Had a Talking Picture of You-Hoo, You-Hoo"). Maurice Chevalier, a star of the Casino de Paris, was brought to Hollywood by show-wise Paramount, and, when he chirped lilting

"Louise" in *Innocents of Paris,* silent pictures received their kiss of death.

It was, recalled Cecil Beaton recently, a time when Hollywood was alive. In those pre-labor-union days, stars stayed at the studio till well past midnight as the overwhelming production problems were nailed down. The big problem in the first talkies was mobility —since the cameras (together with cameramen) were sealed in soundproof vaults to prevent any foreign noises sneaking onto the sound track. The studios themselves were padded in horse-hair and the stars were dressed in cottons (silks and satins came on like Gangbusters). It was not unusual to do a scene thirty or forty times before it came through.

These technical problems, plus the additional ones of evolving a more subdued acting technique for talkies, inspired young, pliable professionals like Bette Davis to new heights. They were fascinated by the possibilities of the new medium, while the older stars despaired. Thalberg, whose contributions to silent films were negligible, also came into his own. He knew the value of good writers—and brought in Scott Fitzgerald, Charles Mac-Arthur, Vicki Baum, P. G. Wodehouse, Frederick Lonsdale, and Dorothy Parker. He developed directors like George Cukor and Rouben Mamoulian, who got their first training on Broadway. To escape the flatness of the immobilized cameras, he rehearsed his casts for three weeks, as in a play, so that the polished acting could compensate for the lack of action. He placed new emphasis on costuming (Adrian) and set designs (Cedric Gibbons, who developed a high gloss that will forever be associated with M-G-M movies of the 30's). He shot and reshot (the studio became known as "retake valley"), until the final product was as sleek and purring as a Rolls-Royce. Jesse Lasky, at Paramount, was just as finicky, and just as tasteful, although he lacked Thalberg's personal magnetism. And Samuel Goldwyn continued to buy the best of everything—the best writer, the best director, the best star—and blended them in his mixmaster into palatable, salable concoctions.

As a result of this ensemble feeling, new to Hollywood, the early talkies were often superb and, as viewed four decades later on television, always interesting even when they were bad. William Haines's *Just a Gigolo* is a Lonsdale comedy à la Thalberg that brings back the days when Lucky Strikes were sold in tins, men parted their hair down the center and then flattened it with Brilliantine, and young ladies went to tea dances in flowing peach organdy gowns, carrying gold-chained Coty compacts. It is a perfect artifact. So, in their way, are *The Virginian*, from Paramount, with Gary Cooper, the classic cowboy hero, and Mary Brian, the classic 1929 ingenue; and *Night Nurse*, with a heroic Barbara Stanwyck and a villainous Clark Gable (in those days before they pinned his ears back). These films crackle with a vitality that has disappeared from Hollywood.

In addition to such Smithsonian relics, a handful of the early talkies rank with the finest films made anywhere, anytime. If there has been a more effective, pictorially stunning anti-war film than Lewis Milestone's *All Quiet on the Western Front*, it's been kept a secret; and King Vidor's *Hallelujah!* has never been surpassed as a filmed folk epic. *Dracula* and *Frankenstein* are true classics of the macabre, very skillfully made; and *Little Caesar*, *Public Enemy*, and *Scarface* are three bulletproof survivors of the gangster era. *Trader Horn* is the adventure film at its peak; and *Steamboat Willie* (recorded on Powers Cinephone) is a fine piece of animation, from Walt Disney. The early Marx Brothers comedies from Paramount, *Duck Soup*, *Cocoanuts*, and *Animal Crackers*, live, as do the Chevalier-Lubitsch musicals, *The Love Parade, One Hour with You,* and *The Smiling Lieutenant*, the wittiest film musicals ever made and among the most tuneful. For high Thalberg-30's camp there is nothing like *Grand Hotel, Dinner at Eight,* and *Rasputin and the Empress*, the latter with three—count 'em, three—Barrymores, which still line them up around the block when they are shown in art theaters.

By the time *Grand Hotel* was released, in 1932, all the nation's theaters were wired for sound. The Vitaphone disc was obsolete, and the Western Electric and RCA systems were the accepted ones. The silent film had disappeared from the landscape, mourned by only two of its pioneers. "A good silent film had a universal appeal . . . now it was all lost," said Chaplin. "We have taken beauty and traded it in for a rusty voice," said D. W. Griffith.

The era of the photoplay had gone the way of the horse and buggy, long winter underwear, and the hand-churned ice-cream freezer which sat on the porch.

And, life went on.

Chapter 7

Garbo Talks!

They still like to tell Garbo stories in those pink Canyon villas, over cocktails on Sunday afternoons, as they gather around handsome fireplaces that have never been lit. Garbo has been gone for many years now, and there has never been anyone to take her place, so the legend keeps growing.

She was unique in Hollywood, for no one could ever pin anything on her—in a town that liked to pin things down; in a town that tolerated the duplicities of Hedda and Louella, and trembled at their thrones. But, as Mae West said, Greta was a lady: She never borrowed money; she paid her bills on time; she never got drunk; she did once run off to Ravello with Leopold Stokowski, but that elopement had a Kareninan flavor of romanticism about it—Ravello! What could be more nineteenth century!

In her prime, she demanded and got a good salary, but she was never on one of those "ten highest incomes" lists, published in the 1930's, to the vicarious delight of a nation that subsisted on corn pone and baked beans. In 1938, when Claudette Colbert earned $426,944 and Irene Dunne $105,222, Garbo's salary was given as $270,000. Through careful savings and wise investments, she was said to have departed with a $3-million fortune when she left Hollywood, but that, too, is hearsay.

One story that is more fact than fantasy concerns Garbo's encounter with the now anonymous and forgotten M-G-M press agent who thought up the brilliant slogan, *Garbo Talks!* He was introduced to her one day as the one and only begetter of this advertising gem. Garbo acknowledged the introduction, a rare thing with her, by looking at him straight in the eye and saying, "Aren't you ashamed!"

But, as Garbo knew, he had no reason to be. The slogan was carried around the world as a news item, and whipped up interest in *Anna Christie*, the film to which it was attached, so that it broke existing records in many theaters, including the Fox Criterion, one of the more lavish Los Angeles pleasure domes. This was at the height of the depression, in 1930, when the sky was falling down.

Anna Christie opened in a year of lush M-G-M duds—including Cecil B. DeMille's *Dynamite*, in which he attempted the sublime and achieved the substandard; *A Lady's Morals*, a biography of Jenny Lind, with Grace Moore, that never reached high-C; *Let Us Be Gay* with Norma Shearer, one of those films that make us think *twice* about Thalberg; *A Lady to Love*, which had Vilma Banky tripping up over consonants in a screen version of Sidney Howard's *They Knew What They Wanted*, thus allowing Edward G. Robinson, as the Italian winegrower, to run off with the picture; *Way for a Sailor*, in which John Gilbert fell flat on the deck, thus allowing Wallace Beery to run off with *that* dodo; and Lon Chaney's *The Unholy Three*, one of those jinx pictures which was followed, sadly, by the death of the "man with a thousand faces."

It was a black year at Culver City, and perhaps that's why they gave Garbo her head and let her do *Anna Christie* instead of a studio-toasted marshmallow. She went about it professionally —choosing Clarence Brown, the American Murnau, as her director; Billy Daniels as her photographer; and Charles Bickford as her leading man. Bickford was a particularly happy choice— a manly actor who projected a pug-nosed sex appeal that made him exactly right for the role of Matt. Garbo had spotted him on the *Dynamite* set, shortly after he arrived from New York and before he took on Thalberg, Mayer, and Rapf in a colossal barroom brawl that hijacked him to Monogram. She liked him; but fled, when she saw him walk toward her to say hello. He ran after her, catching her by the ears, and told her she ran like a rabbit. She invited him in to her dressing room for tea. Production on *Dynamite* stopped that day; some say on orders from Mr. Mayer himself, who was informed by studio spies in five minutes as to what had taken place.

As Garbo knew, Bickford's gruff voice made her own basso profundo a little easier to take; as did the growl of Marie Dressler, who was cast as Marthy. Furthermore, Frances Marion, the scenarist, went over the dialogue with a fine-tooth comb— carefully snipping any of O'Neill's dialogue that Garbo would trip over. A policy was established: Keep Garbo's dialogue spare, and keep it down to words of one or two syllables. Let the other actors talk; let Garbo *emote*. Thus, an approximation of silent-film technique was maintained in all the Garbo talkies, with the exception of the disastrous *Two-Faced Woman*, a talky talkie.

As the rushes on *Anna Christie* came in, Mayer and company didn't know what to make of it. In all her silent films, Garbo had played a woman of mystery, elegantly gowned and coiffured, surrounded with smooth-faced leading men. Here she was, playing a waterfront whore, with that Irish brawler Bickford opposite her. It might be art, but it was too goddam risky. Better have them run off a German-language version, so they could sell it in Berlin, Germany, if it flopped in Berlin, New Hampshire. The German version was made in two weeks, with Garbo repeating her original role, after the English-language version was finished. Thus, another important milestone was reached with *Anna Christie*—it was entirely reshot for the foreign market, a particularly lucrative market that would soon bring Charles Boyer and other continental performers to Hollywood. This industry within an industry was rarely publicized, for obvious reasons: In Europe they thought they were seeing the original *Anna Christie*, when what they were really seeing was a foreign-language remake.

Anna Christie was released in the United States in February, a slow time for a movie, since the better product was generally saved to coincide with the holidays. As was Garbo's first silent film, *The Temptress*, it was thought of as a programmer, with the studio's major promotional effort going into some now-

forgotten Shearer drawing-room comedies. The *Garbo Talks!*
slogan had caught on, and was being bandied about by comedians
on the radio, but would the picture? Hollywood Boulevard was
ankle deep in the bones of silent film stars who had crashed
with the talkies.

Mr. Mayer need not have worried. Mrs. Babbitt, who had
traded in her Auburn from the Vilma Banky days for a Chrysler
77, was queued up at the box office on opening morning, along
with hundreds of other ladies in Empress Eugénie hats, which
they made themselves, using dyed turkey tail feathers, or bought
for a dollar in bargain basements. Many of these ladies recognized one another on sight, as do opera buffs or prize-fight fans.
Mrs. Babbitt nodded to two familiar faces—Mrs. Scott-Smythe,
who had traded in her Pierce Arrow for a beige Cadillac which
had a matching beige chauffeur, and Mrs. Jones, still driving her
Model-T Ford. The rich and the poor are always with us, and
have always been Garbo fans. Millionairesses and paupers alike
stood clutching their quarters—the admission price before noon
—suffering heart palpitations at the thought of hearing Garbo
talk.

They were put through a particularly cruel ordeal before
they would have their curiosity satisfied. In those days, they
really tried to give you your money's worth at the pleasure
domes. The early 30's were the heyday of the "unit shows,"
which traveled from city to city, changing theaters each week
until they had as many as forty bookings. Each "unit" was built
around a theme—"In a Persian Garden," "The Melting Pot,"
"Pompadour's Fan," or "The Story of Jazz," and it featured
dancers, singers, jugglers, dog acts, and midgets, along with
the Beethoven *Sonata* or Ravel's *Bolero*. They were lavish, and
sometimes even artistic, and they kept scores of vaudevillians
and chorus girls alive. If the "unit" was one of Fanchon and
Marco's, you were generally in for a special treat: There was
always a ballet of sorts; always a chorus of "Sunkist Beauties,"
most of whom hailed from Bloomington, Indiana, but who might
include a promising newcomer like Doris Day; and, especially,
an exotic, spectacular finale which recalled the great days of

the Roman empire, the glory that was Greece, the T'ang dynasty, or the Egypt of Cleopatra.

Ordinarily, the ladies loved "the stage show," since it was generously sprinkled with handsome males in swimming trunks or tights, along with dogs and chorus girls. But, during the run of *Anna Christie*, they sighed with relief when the final feather and spangle disappeared behind the lavishly tinseled *art nouveau* curtain. They were Garbo lovers, first, last, and always. Now, at last, they would hear her talk.

But, no. The stage show was followed by an organ recital, playing Grieg's *Peer Gynt Suite* as a tribute to Garbo—Grieg was Norwegian, of course, but what the hell!—and after a mild rustle of impatience the ladies sat back and listened with the air of being in church that always came over them in the pleasure domes.

As the theater lights darkened, they applauded politely and concealed a need to go to the ladies' room. The familiar M-G-M lion appeared on the screen, roaring ferociously as he had ever since *Broadway Melody*, and they leaned forward in their seats only to discover—that it was a Charlie Chase comedy! This time the ladies made no attempt to conceal their displeasure; they booed and made a beeline to the ladies' room, trampling a number of the West Point cadets who were moonlighting as ushers in the process. They returned in time to see the M-G-M lion roaring at them from the screen once more. They leaned forward again—only to discover it was one of the Fitzpatrick travel talks!

Mr. Fitzpatrick sank into the sunset to stony silence, and then the M-G-M lion roared yet again, and *at last!* the Garbo picture came on.

The ladies loved *Anna Christie*. Who, indeed, could not? Sound editor Douglas Shearer (Norma's brother) bathed the sound track in vibrantly mooing ship's signals; cameraman Billy Daniels drenched the celluloid with fog; Marie Dressler hammed it up as she'd been doing since she was an ingenue with Weber and Fields at the turn of the century; Bickford came on sincere, sinister, and sexy. Even without Garbo it would have been a good picture. Garbo, of course, elevated it to the stature of a nearly great one. When the matinée ladies heard her say, "Give me a viskey . . . 'n' don't be steen-gy," there was, for a second, stunned silence, followed by a howl of nervous laughter, followed by volumes of thunderous applause that echoed through the movie cathedral like claps of thunder.

THE GODDESS TALKED! GARBO TALKED!

It was not a soft and pretty voice. It sprang from her throat like a caged jungle cat, leaping to get out, violent, angry. It sent shivers down the spine. It sent the ladies rushing again to the ladies' room, knocking down a fresh replacement of West Point cadets. It was—well, it was—it was *very heaven!*

The ladies didn't leave the theater after they sat through *Anna Christie* once. They stayed a second time. A third. Lines of impatient ticket holders formed around the block. Police were summoned to keep them under control.

Here, finally, was a great star in a good story. It was nothing like anything they had seen or heard before. It didn't insult their intelligence. Its people were recognizable people. Its sets were recognizable places. Every small role was perfectly delineated. It ticked like a good Swiss clock.

Meanwhile, back at Culver City, they were dusting off their little Swedish flags. They were also dusting off some stale marsh-mallows they had on the shelf, and they rushed Garbo into them—*Romance*, a war-horse of a play, in which they cast their Swedish discovery as an Italian opera singer; *Inspiration*, in which they teamed her with Robert Montgomery, a nice enough man, but it was like combining vodka with crème de menthe; and *Susan Lennox*, one of the unwed-mother epics so dear to the hearts of Hollywood moguls in the early 30's, in which they paired her with Clark Gable. Gable, who had built up a lucrative career by socking M-G-M's expensive galaxy of lady stars—Norma Shearer, Jean Harlow, Myrna Loy, and Joan Crawford—was a bit more subdued than usual in this one. "If I'd socked her," he said of Garbo, "she would have socked me right back."

Her first decent role, after *Anna Christie*, was in that all-star bit of moonshine and roses, *Grand Hotel*, in which she spun out the role of a fading ballerina with the skill of Pavlova dancing *The Dying Swan*. Most of her scenes were played with John Barrymore, the greatest actor of his day, and they are miraculous. He put her at her ease immediately by kissing her hand when they were introduced, and saying, "My wife and I think you are the loveliest woman in the world." It was precisely the way to handle this shy, insecure artist, and they became fast friends. After one particularly grueling scene, she surprised everyone by kissing him. "You have no idea," she told him, "what it means to me to play opposite so perfect an artist." Barrymore, she later said, had the divine madness of every great artist. She understood him, as he understood her.

Grand Hotel, which broke a box-office record in San Francisco a few years ago, more than three decades after it was first released, also starred Joan Crawford (to whom Garbo rarely spoke, although they had adjoining dressing rooms) as well as Wallace Beery and Lionel Barrymore. They were all steady, reliable performers, but it is Garbo's picture. She was secure before the microphone by this time, and she was playing opposite a very great professional. Scott Fitzgerald and Charles MacArthur are said to have howled with derision when they saw the picture, and they had every right to—it's a light bit of Viennese pastry, nicely baked by Vicki Baum, and not really very important. Compared to the usual toasted Hollywood marshmallow, though, it's a rare treat—a Thalberg special, oozing with real whipped cream. It is so very well done, as a matter of fact, that Hollywood, which remakes its classics with inferior casts, has let this one alone. (Or almost—*Weekend at the Waldorf*, an ersatz derivative, was a stale, store-bought cookie.)

It was followed by two other interesting films, neither of them particularly good, but dear to cinema addicts: *Mata Hari*, in which Garbo does a modified hootchy-kootchy and pulls it off (this entire film is a throwback to the heyday of Negri), and *As You Desire Me*, in which she wears a platinum wig, fends off Erich von Stroheim, and meets the Pirandello dialogue head on. Stilted though it is, this movie never fails to draw entire regiments of very attractive and very long-haired young men and women, carrying Eisenstein's *The Film Sense* in one arm and a collapsible sleeping bag in the other. It is *their* picture.

But a true cinema classic was to come along in *Queen Christina*. It was Marie Dressler, of all people, who first suggested that Garbo play the eccentric seventeenth-century regent, who liked to read Descartes and dress in men's clothes. When the movie was added to her schedule, a few years later, in her innocence she did some real research in an attempt to recreate the true Christina. She voyaged to Sweden to bone up on how Christina looked and dressed, and talked with historians to get to the root of her personality. Back in Hollywood, she came face to face with Louis B. Mayer. So Christina had a hooked nose; so what? They weren't making movies for a few Swedish history teachers. They had to fill the Capitol. And what the audiences at the Capitol wanted was a love story. Now, be a good girl, Greta, and don't make with that hooked nose.

We'll send you over some corned beef and cabbage and you can keep the plate. Greta, I'm talking to you like a father, Greta; please, Greta; your own nose is good enough.

Greta liked Mayer; Mayer liked Greta. He once told Robert Morley, the British actor, that the cinema had given one great artist to the world: "Greta Garbo, unless you count that damn mouse." She didn't make with the hooked nose.

Nonetheless, a character *does* emerge in *Queen Christina*. This is in spite of Rouben Mamoulian, the talented Russian-born director who had come into fame through his staging of Gershwin's *Porgy and Bess* for the Theatre Guild. His first movies were for Paramount: *Applause*, a realistic evocation of Minsky burlesque that starred Helen Morgan; *City Streets*, a garish gangster melodrama with Gary Cooper and Sylvia Sidney; *Doctor Jekyll and Mr. Hyde*, the great 1932 version with Fredric March and Miriam Hopkins, orchestrated with music by Bach and employing camera effects that have never been surpassed; and *Love Me Tonight*, in which he toyed with the Lubitsch touch, starring Chevalier.

Mamoulian was as fascinated by Christina as was Garbo, but it was her love life that intrigued him. *Queen Christina* is the most erotic film ever made, but the eroticism has been fined

down, gauzed, Greeked. There is that morning-after scene where
Garbo moves about the bedroom, touching objects that have
come to have a new meaning for her through her love, touching them tenderly, gently, as if they were toys that would
break. There is that scene of Garbo eating grapes—she lies back
and lets the grapes touch her lips, caressing them with her
mouth. There is, finally, that scene of Garbo bringing the body
of her dead lover to Spain—she stands at the prow of the ship,
her face expressionless, garbed in men's clothes.

Still and all, despite Mamoulian's sly and evil grace, Christina
comes through. She is a person. Mayer and Mamoulian couldn't
stop her. The whole M-G-M machinery couldn't stop her.
Christina lives.

The portrait is all the more remarkable when one considers
that Greta Garbo was a young woman in her late twenties at
this time. Three more masterpieces were yet to come—*Anna
Karenina*, *Camille*, and *Ninotchka*. Then, in her mid-thirties,
the divine one would retire from the screen and the legend
would begin. It keeps growing year after year—like all legends
an intricate tapestry woven of fiction and truth, of dazzling white
unicorns and soft lavender skies.

Chapter 8

The Marlene Fad and Goldwyn's Folly

Anna Christie, which proved there was money in them thar foreign stars, was a pivotal picture, not only for Metro-Goldwyn-Mayer but for all the other studios as well. Paramount rushed *Morocco*, the first American-made Dietrich, into production, and, after its huge success, wildly promised their exhibitors "two Dietrichs a year." Samuel Goldwyn was next to "take the bull by the teeth." He had been making a fortune with the early Eddie Cantor talkies, in which Ruth Etting, Charlotte Greenwood, and Ethel Merman were the leading ladies, but while Cantor, like the United States mint, was nice to have around the house, he hardly surrounded Goldwyn with the aura of art. "Man cannot live by cake alone," said Sam, as he dreamed of a talking Venus he could call his own.

It was at this point that Anjuscha Stenski Sujakevitch came into his life. She was a Ukranian beauty who had appeared in Pudovkin's *Storm over Asia* and other Russian silent films, and then had hoofed it to Ufa, where she made three German talkies. The last of these was *The Brothers Karamazov*, in which as Gruschenka she managed to capture the essence of soul and bile which is the root of Dostoevsky. "A true earth goddess," said the European critics, and "goddess" was the word that Goldwyn wanted to hear. He decided to "strike while the lead was hot," and bring her to Hollywood. After all, if Metro had captured Sweden, and Paramount held Germany, he had the right to a chunk of Russia. Thus, Anna Sten was on her way.

Meanwhile at R-K-O (Radio-Keith-Orpheum), one of the more crazy-quilt studios in Hollywood, things looked pretty bleak. A balding Broadway hoofer and a slangy little Broadway showgirl had yet to strike electrical sparks, and, as Astaire and Rogers, sweep the studio into solvency. The current management, which succeeded the blue-chip team of Joseph P. Kennedy and David Sarnoff, was at wits' end trying to evolve a formula that would work. Warners had gangsters, Mayer had Garbo, Zukor had Dietrich, Cohn had Capra, even Monogram had Frankie Darro—but all they had were several hundred strategically located pleasure domes, originally the Keith-Albee-Orpheum chain, headed into bankruptcy.

Someone mentioned that Pola Negri was still kicking around, madder than a wet hen at being abandoned for Dietrich. "Dietrich!" proclaimed Madame Negri. "Why Reinhardt wouldn't even let her polish his boots!"

R-K-O took a dim view of the Madame, but, hell, they had tried everything else—why not? They put her under contract at $3,500 a week, her salary in the old Paramount days, and found a creaky bit of Graustark, *A Woman Commands*, for her to do. If the customers wouldn't buy Ann Harding in Philip Barry's *Animal Kingdom*, maybe they'd buy Pola singing "Paradise." Hope sprang eternal in the depression heart.

Fox, too, had fallen into thin days. They had Janet Gaynor, but that dimpled darling had them jumping through hoops with an ironclad contract that gave her story approval. Their matinée idol, Charles Farrell, had retired from the "squawkies" to open the Racquet Club in Palm Springs, which he inaugurated with a splash by dressing in white tie, top hat, and tails and diving into the swimming pool. Charlie was happy with his exclusive club, which had a glass-walled bar, one facing the tennis courts and the other the swimming pool, and he had no intention of exchanging the social whirl for the cameras. The new Fox regime, which had replaced the founder William Fox, then latched on to Lilian Harvey, an international star who had appeared in a successful European-made musical, *Congress Dances*, and entered her into the Garbo-Dietrich sweepstakes.

Neither Sten nor Negri nor Harvey proved to have starpower. They interested a few cinema connoisseurs, but cinema connoisseurs didn't fill those cavernous movie palaces—the Mrs. Babbitts and Mrs. Joneses and Mrs. Scott-Smythes did. Once you got these ladies by the throat—as Garbo and Dietrich had, as Joan Crawford and Bette Davis were about to—you were in. Even Warner Brothers, who had made a splash with their gangster melodramas, knew that this was not enough: They developed Ruth Chatterton and Kay Francis, as well as Bette Davis, into matinée stars who brought the ladies in, come rain or come shine.

Negri's talkie comeback was a particularly dramatic flop. The storminess of her nature—she was often seen at Falcon's Lair, after Valentino's death, screaming, ranting, raging, and tearing at her lustrous black hair—had taken its toll of her looks. Although she was svelte and handsomely gowned in *A Woman Commands,* the critics thumbed her down and, disconsolately, she headed back to her home in Versailles. But Pola's career was to end with a bang rather than a whimper. Hitler's henchmen were looking for a star to rebuild the Ufa studios and, having been turned down by Marlene Dietrich, offered the spot to Pola. This marriage of brimstone and fire was doomed from the beginning, and rumors came through that the Polish beauty was being interned in a concentration camp. Friends, who understood her tempestuous nature, intervened to get her out of Germany, but this was the end of Pola Negri as a star.

Lilian Harvey, on the other hand, faded out quietly. A swivel-hipped, pixie-faced, madonna-eyed soubrette, she spoofed the "continental enchantress" vogue with dry, delicious humor. In one of her films, she is seen befurred and befeathered à la Dietrich, as she regally descends a glistening white von Sternberg staircase, her expression one of extreme hauteur. As she nears the bottom of the lush staircase, grand enough for Catherine the Great of Russia, she trips over her sequined train and falls flat on her *popo.* Her gamine charm, despite an extensive Fox build-up, just never caught on in a nation that worshiped its Venuses and didn't see anything funny in them. She was a bit of Moët et Chandon in Nehi territory; a stylish Pulcinella in a wax museum; a genuine chocolate soufflé in a land that liked brownies.

The stars were just not right for the delectable Miss Harvey; for the entire consumer apparatus of cosmetics and fashion, an industry that annually runs into the high billions, was by then geared to the *femme fatale*. To dramatize the changing face of American pulchritude, *Vanity Fair*, the irreverent and never-replaced magazine for mavericks, ran a picture series titled "Then Came Garbo." Joan Crawford, Tallulah Bankhead, and Katharine Hepburn, among other stars, were shown before and after they remade themselves in the image of The Divine One. The change was startling: Frizzy hair was slicked back into plastered-close-to-the-skull coiffures; eyebrows were removed entirely and replaced with thin penciled lines; lips were widened and broadened through applications of paint that did away with the bee-stung look popular a decade earlier; shoulders were, by some miracle of the dressmaker's art, widened; torsos, which had been fore-shortened in the era of short skirts, were lengthened into flowing Grecian lines; hips, which once formed two luscious melons that hung below the small of the back, were now slimmed down until they looked like Tom Mix's; and, as a final triumph of art over nature, feet, once petite and prettily buckled, became elongated and severely classical.

Floppy felt hats and low-heeled walking oxfords were introduced by the millinery and footwear trade; and the Garbo jumper, from which floated bits of organdy or satin, jumped at you everywhere. *Queen Christina* brought back the starched Buster Brown collar, and no American beauty in her right mind was seen without a pair of dark glasses. A million or so Garbos, aloof, headed for some obscure destination or rendezvous, paraded the oak-lined Main Streets of America, to the bewilderment of Pete and Sam and Joe, who never even heard of Herbert Marshall, and, in quiet, dark, male despair, took up skeet shooting, billiards, and bowling. The seeds of a new wave of homosexuality thus were sown.

But the Garbo Fad was as nothing compared to the Marlene Fad. To lengthen her rather tiny hands, Dietrich grew her nails until they extended two inches beyond her fingers, and painted them blood-red so that they would *really* stand out. All over

America, on remote farmsteads where there were cows to milk, or in little cottages where there were diapers to be washed, "long nails" became the vogue and a new billion-dollar industry —fingernail lacquer—was born. Dietrich dressed in pants; and Pete and Sam and Joe, looking for that pair of slacks they bought last week, let out blood-curdling roars when they suddenly realized that Betty Lou and Mary Jane and Sara Sue were wearing them. Dietrich made a thing of crossing her legs, so that her slender ankles almost kicked passers-by on the nose, and, after long hours before the dressing-table mirror, Betty Lou and Mary Jane and Sara Sue mastered that most delicate art—or thought they had, until Pete and Sam and Joe were rushed off to the county hospital with facial lacerations.

More was to come, including the see-through bodice, but, meanwhile, this throwback to the courtesan era of Ninon de Lenclos had the American female so enraptured that she took to naming her daughters after her. No longer were there little Betty Lous and little Mary Janes and little Sara Sues; now there were Marlenes (often mispronounced Mar-leen instead of Mar-*lay*-na). These miniature Marlenes also took to painting their nails, and another billion-dollar industry, children's cosmetics, was born. When they got to high school, they rushed to take courses in French, so that they, too, could sing *Quand l'Amour Meurt*, as did Dietrich in *Morocco*. Soon, the low, sultry, sexy whisper would blanket the American continent, as once did the voice of the turtle.

As the century that Marlene ushered in progressed, she consolidated her gains by publishing *Marlene Dietrich's ABC*, which replaced *Lady Godey's Book* as a guide for young women. From its pages one could glean such pearls of wisdom as:

"LOVE: Before you love/learn to run through snow/leaving no footprints"; *or*
"GIRDLE: An unattractive object"; *or*
"MILK: I have my doubts about milk being necessary for the growing body."

As the nice girl, who kept her apron on until five o'clock,

gradually began to disappear from the native landscape, there were some prudes who claimed that Marlene Dietrich was Germany's secret weapon, undermining us from within—a Mata Hari, tempting us with chicken soup; a vamp who smelled of bread; a grandma, disseminating the doctrines of Nietzsche and Freud. She is nothing of the sort—Marlene Dietrich is only a grand stylist, a witty woman, a masterful promoter, a fair actress, and the most exotic female the twentieth century has yet turned up. And, it appears, no one will come along to top that.

While the Marlene Fad engulfed the nation, Sam Goldwyn back in Hollywood was busily at work molding his own goddess, Anna Sten. It proved to be more of a job than he bargained for. Miss Sten had an undeniable appeal, but it was of a more common dandelion variety. She was a sturdy, intelligent, amiable woman, without a shred of mystery and allure about her. If he had let her alone, and gradually introduced her to the American public in small roles, she might have caught on and even become a major star. But so engulfing was the Garbo-Dietrich tidal wave, that Goldwyn tried to reshape her along more lilylike lines.

This monumental task required the services of six special tutors, who trailed the pleasant Miss Sten from morning to night. There were (1) an English coach; (2) a dancing instructor; (3) a singing teacher; (4) a speech therapist; (5) a masseuse; and (6) a dietician, for she was addicted to Ukranian-sized meals.

After a year of this, Goldwyn was ready to take the plunge and put her in a picture. Again, he goofed. Emile Zola's *Nana* is one of the most realistic and unvarnished portraits of a prostitute in all literature; a lass with a heart of dross instead of gold. Sten, a trained actress, might have done her convincingly, but Goldwyn tidied up the story, bathing it in Edwardian sentiments and costumes, and at the end has her sacrificing herself for the war effort instead of dying of smallpox. At one point, Nana even sings a ballad by Rodgers and Hart—"That's Love."

Even the intrepid Mr. Goldwyn may have sensed that something was amiss as he journeyed to New York for the February 1, 1934, opening of *Nana* at the Radio City Music Hall. For months the newspapers had been filled with huge ads featuring retouched photos of Miss Sten in provocative poses, with provocative adjectives to describe her charms. This advertising campaign, one of the cleverest in Hollywood history, was supplemented with a strong publicity effort, directed by Lynn Farnol, which kept her name in the news almost daily. Since Miss Sten, unlike Pola Negri, was a quiet and reserved lady, this took some doing. Finally, the Russian Orthodox Church came to Goldwyn's rescue—on the eve of her film's debut, at the Music Hall, special services were held all over the nation, wishing the Ukranian-born star success. On the dawn of the premiere, huge crowds had already formed outside the theater to be among the first to get in to see Anna Sten. Many of them had come directly from the special masses.

This was high-style hoopla, carefully engineered, neatly executed, with that special finesse of the truly professional Broadway tom-tom beater. Would Sten live up to it? No one knew for sure on opening day, when all records were broken, including those of *King Kong*. But the next day, when the reviews came out, the receipts tapered off and the dream of cracking *Kong*'s record—it took in $89,941 in four depression-scarred days of March, 1933—vanished in thin air.

The more discerning reviewers, including Richard Watts, Jr., then writing for the *New York Herald Tribune*, saw a "vigorous peasant type" in Miss Sten, lost in the lavish period costumes and the banal treatment of Zola. Other reviewers were not even that kind—Miss Sten was a disappointment, they said, and the picture was lousy. Garbo was still queen, and Dietrich had nothing to worry about.

Goldwyn was already on the train back to Hollywood. If his discovery was a peasant type, why not cast her as a peasant? And what more popular peasant was there in literature than Katuscha in *Resurrection?* He summoned Maxwell Anderson and Preston Sturges, an odd couple, to work on the screenplay of the Tolstoi classic; got Mamoulian to direct it; and browbeat Fredric March into taking the role of the officer who seduces the girl. Freddie had smelled out the fact that the critics would again be hostile, and he was right; *Resurrection*, hopefully retitled *We Live Again*, had the boys and girls in the screening rooms gleefully pulling off its shimmering Mamoulianesque wings and exposing the shriveled body that lay beneath.

This would send a lesser man back to Eddie Cantor. Not so Samuel Goldwyn, goddamit!

The third time out, he bought an original story of Polish-American tobacco farmers, *The Wedding Night*, which had a juicy role for Sten as a farmer's daughter. He surrounded her with a fine cast: Gary Cooper, as a spiritually bankrupt author "trying to find himself" by going back to the land (a recurrent character in the fictions of the 1930's); Helen Vinson as his wife; Ralph Bellamy as Anna's Polish fiancé. Then he made a brilliant choice, in King Vidor, as director. Vidor, who had been an assistant to both Griffith and Ince, and whose silent films included *The Big Parade*, *La Boheme*, and *The Crowd* as well as the talkies *Hallelujah!*, *Street Scene*, and *Our Daily Bread*, was just right for it. If anyone could contrast the European folkways of immigrant farmers with weary New York intellectuals, and make cinematic poetry out of the stew, it was this fine American-born director, whose work ranked with the best Europeans.

So far, so good. But though Goldwyn was discerning in choosing the right people, he all too often didn't know how to handle them. Vidor made a real attempt to get to the root of the problem—as he saw it, Sten was essentially a silent-picture actress, steeped in Russian cinematic technique. Her pantomime flowed freely, but her words had no relation to her emoting, the dialogue often following as an afterthought. He urged that the script be pared down, as were those of Dietrich and Garbo, to get her over this initial hurdle. Furthermore, he asked that words with the "th" sound, so deadly to Middle Europeans, be deleted wherever possible. Here, Goldwyn turned his back stubbornly. Having spent all that money on writers, he wasn't about to throw out a word that cost $300. *The Wedding Night* was budgeted at $2 million, and each word stayed in. Money didn't blow off bushes.

Vidor pleaded—an altogether wrong approach with Goldwyn. Never *plead* with Goldwyn, said the sages; it only makes him more bullheaded. In the key love scene, Sten was scripted to say, "*Earth* returns," which, of course, emerged as "*Earse* returns." Goldwyn would not change it. But, after the preview, he was seen to rush up to Vidor and was heard to say: "You'll have to reshoot that big love scene. That girl can't say *Earse!*"

Vidor's efforts did at last produce a good picture. *The Wedding Night* has scenes of pure cinema, including a ribald wedding party as it is celebrated in many Polish-American communities. The picture is adult in its handling of the farmers; they are neither sentimentalized nor made villains of. The characters are motivated to do the things they do; their actions are consistent and logical. It is one of the better pictures of the 1930's.

But, by this time, all interest in Sten had vanished. It was, you could say, gone with the *Earse*. Years later one would catch glimpses of her in minor films—by then she was slim, trim, and had her "th" under control. Just about right for Goldwyn's *Nana*, and she would have been a sensation in it.

Fade-Out 1:

John Gilbert

On the Metro-Goldwyn-Mayer lot—forty acres of neatly clipped lawns, dotted with executive offices, shops, laboratories, and glass-enclosed sound stages—he was the Prince Charming in residence, his dressing room a small Renaissance Palace. He had earned it. No other leading man in Hollywood was so flexible a performer—he could play a doughboy in *The Big Parade* or Prince Danilo in *The Merry Widow* with equal ease. He drank and wenched a bit too much, but it didn't seem to affect the warm, human image he cast on the screen. Total strangers wrote him by the thousands every week, and he was rewarded with a new studio contract which gave him $250,000 a picture, a record high for that time.

He was one of those rare male stars whom both women and men liked—there would not be another one until Clark Gable—and he seemed "in" for a run, even with talkies around the corner. To Garbo he was *Ja-kee;* to everyone else, from Thalberg to the studio carpenter, he was Jack. In addition to his palace on the lot, he had a private palace on the hill, where all he had to do to touch the stars was stretch his arm.

His easy, flippant way of talking occasionally got him into difficulties. When he joked with Mayer, telling him that he had every reason to believe that his mother was a whore, the studio boss became so enraged he tried to strangle him. When, at a game of charades, he suggested to William Randolph Hearst that he be the pill in the pillbox, Hearst left the room, slamming the door.

Suddenly, the word went out—"*Get* Gilbert." Put him in lousy pictures; tell the sound lab boys to take no trouble with his voice; break him up with Garbo. Let the word get around that he was *out*.

Gilbert never knew what hit him. He just thought he was no damned good in the talkies. Anyway, there was nothing they could do about it; he was under contract, and he would drink it out. Ben Hecht and Charles MacArthur, like Angels of Death, sometimes moved in and helped him do it. So did lively Marie Prevost, another silent screen star on the skids. So did every other rummy in Hollywood.

Word got around that he had become suicidal. He would walk for hours in the blinding rain; swim too far out in the angry ocean; turn himself in to the police and ask to be arrested.

Garbo, who had seen one lover, Stiller, slowly die, tried to help him. When Laurence Olivier was signed to play opposite her in *Queen Christina*, she refused to ignite in their scenes together. By playing it cool, she shanghaied the British star, and the producer was forced to comply with her demands and give her Gilbert.

But John Gilbert just didn't seem to have it any more. The particular iridescence that was his—that glow that once lit up his screen image—had faded. Suddenly, the screen's most beautiful leading man had become just another guy with a moustache. *Queen Christina* was, he knew, his swan song. They were talking of building him into a character actor, and letting him play drunken bums. This was the way Barrymore would end his days in Hollywood, but it wasn't the way for Gilbert. The drinking sessions grew fiercer; he and Marie Prevost made bets as to which of them would first die drunk.

It is often a minor incident that will push a suicidal man over the edge. Just one little thing, and he finally knows he has had it. With Gilbert it happened when a wig he wore to cover a bald spot slipped off his head at an important Hollywood party. It tangled in his heels, and he couldn't lose it. Everyone laughed.

It was perfectly all right to laugh at a failure. A few years ago they wouldn't have dared. They would have pretended not to notice.

Anyway, the next morning he was dead. They said "of a heart attack."

Part II

Just Plain Folks in Hollywood

Chapter 9

Venus Straddles the Hays Code

"Is it not time," editorialized William Randolph Hearst in the 30's, "that Congress did something about Mae West?"

Miss West, a satirist of the Venus vogue, had by then taken off Garbo's grape-eating scene in *Queen Christina* with a single, devastating line of dialogue—"Beulah, peel me a grape!" Her classic film, *She Done Him Wrong*, had also saved Paramount (which had $400,000 to its name when the movie was released) from bankruptcy by garnering $2 million in its first three months. Goodness had nothing to do with it, as both Miss West and Mr. Zukor knew; and, yet, the tide was turning against the sex-goddess. The biggest moneymaking star of the decade (who enriched 20th Century-Fox by $20 million) was that sprightly, fife-voiced moppet, Shirley Temple, whose curls covered her head like limp egg rolls. She was followed in popularity by a displaced faun, Mickey Rooney, and the tragic, teen-age Judy Garland, whose voice roared from the sound track like Niagara. By 1937, another child actress, Jane Withers, ranked Number 6 at the box-office polls—yards ahead of Dietrich and Garbo; and, standing on the horizon, was a pie-faced coloratura, Deanna Durbin, whose trills and bobbysocks would "save" Universal, which had fallen into lean times.

To keep up with the small fry, the grownups shed their glamour and began to pose in layouts for *Picture Play* or *Silver Screen* that showed them watering the lawn or washing dishes at the kitchen sink. Such pictured domestic bliss was sometimes marred by the telltale silhouette of a dry martini, peeping from beyond a wet glass of milk, or an unmistakable glassiness of eye. As one press agent of that embattled era recently stated, "We had to put them to bed for a week, if the layout was in color. Color couldn't be retouched, like black-and-white, and told sad stories."

Hardly appropriate settings for such "at home with" photo layouts were the grand mansions of the 1920's—like John Barrymore's on Tower Road, equipped with a Spanish garden, three swimming pools and an aviary (heated for tropical birds). Such symbols of conspicuous consumption were gradually scuttled for more modest ranch-style dwellings in San Fernando Valley or colonial-styled "cottages," often decorated by William Haines, in Brentwood. In such "and-baby-makes-three" settings, Joan Crawford forsook the Charleston to sponsor a milk fund for underprivileged children; Claudette Colbert married a doctor; Melvyn Douglas's wife ran for Congress; and Carole Lombard designed furniture (including a dining-room table that could be converted into a dice board with a flip of a wrist). Even Tarzan felt the impact of middle-class mores: His once meager loincloth grew looser, and longer, and wider, until, eventually, it hung forlornly around his manly knees, looking more like a dirndl than a jungle chastity belt.

Hollywood, that baroque old courtesan, aped well-heeled suburbia with such finesse that soon it was marrying into society. Constance Bennett crashed the billionaire barrier by wedding a peanut prince; and soon a Norwegian enchantress-on-skates, Sonja Henie, wed a Topping; Douglas Fairbanks, Jr., a Hartford; and Randolph Scott a Du Pont. The radio king, Atwater Kent, moved to Hollywood and amused himself by entertaining cinema favorites in his lavish court; and both Howard Hughes and John Hay Whitney were involved in making movies. Frequent seasonal visitors to the Gold Coast included the Vanderbilts, the Kennedys, the Posts, and the Guests—as well as two marriageable millionairesses, Doris Duke and Barbara Hutton (who would, eventually, add Cary Grant to her collection). John Cabot Lodge, a very proper Bostonian, even *acted* in the movies—sporting a pre-East Village shoulder-length bob, he was Marlene's chatelain in *The Scarlet Empress*—and the marriage between Hollywood and society would be made official by the entry of three certified debutantes—Cobina Wright, Jr., Gene Tierney, and Diana Barrymore (an Oelrichs, on her mother's side)—into stardom.

The traditions of old-style baroque shenanigans were upheld by a handful of names—most notably, still Lolita-prone Charles Chaplin; Mary Astor, diary-prone; and accident-prone Jean Harlow, the brilliant comédienne who became tragedy's new darling. With Negri in retirement, lavish fur wraps went out of style, but Myrna Loy made news by protecting a peach tree with one of her mink coats; Paulette Goddard trimmed a Christmas tree with ermine tails; and Kay Francis urged ladies not to throw away their old ermine jackets: They made divine bath mats.

The Production Code was evolved in 1930, but no one paid it much mind until 1934, when the National Legion of Decency came into power and the Purity Seal was uncorked. Will Hays, paid $100,000 a year (at that time a figure larger than the salary of most corporation presidents) to look the other way, now had to look twice when Mae West gyrated her hips and invited 'em to—*um-m-m-m*—come up 'n' see her sometime. This invitation was, as time has proved, innocent barnyard fun, presented with undeniable style and theatrical expertise by the showwise Hour Glass, but it came over dirty in the Bible Belt. To appease the upholders of the nation's Blue Laws, Hays forced La West to tone herself down, and even ordered her to change the title of one of her films from *It Ain't No Sin* to the innocuous *Belle of the Nineties*. This created havoc in Paramount's publicity department, where fifty parrots had been trained to say *It Ain't No Sin* prior to embarking on a nationwide tour of the pleasure domes. So dastardly a deed, which a musicologist said may have deterred the birth of a new art form, helped give Mr. Hays the sobriquet of "Mr. Scissors."

Just what havoc was wrought on the already established art form of the cinema by the Production Code, no one will ever know. The perspective of history reveals that some form of censorship has always existed to plague the artist, ever since the spoiled darling first began to draw pictures on the walls of his family cave, while his mother was out hunting a dinosaur to keep him supplied with fresh blood. In the year 2000, censorship will still be driving the artist to silence, suicide, or psychosis: We can be as sure of that as death and taxes.

The Hays Code,* as it came to be known, created an Eden in which there were no "lustful" or "open-mouth kissing"; no sex perversion "or any inference of it"; no brothels; no obscenity in "words, gesture, reference, song, joke or by suggestion"; no double beds; no nudity "in fact or in silhouette." A middle-class child, who spent as much time in the movies as he did at home in the 1930's, was thus astonished to learn that kissing *could* be lustful and open-mouthed; that perversion was as American as cherry pie; that every hamlet had its brothel; that obscenity was in common usage in the locker room and in many living rooms; that his mother and father slept in a double bed instead of twin beds, like William Powell and Myrna Loy; and, most astonishing of all, that when he took off his clothes he was nude.

It seemed for a time that these strictures would put Venus out of business; and they might very well have, were it not for the lucrative international market, where sex was in to stay. These were the harvest years of Hollywood's global reign, and Louis B. Mayer's office was now the shrine where prominent pilgrims came. They found "L. B.," as he liked to be called, in a white-and-silver office, a kind of benevolent halo surrounding his white-and-silver head, his body firmly encased in a white-and-silver suit, which emitted further radiations of its own. God was in his heav'n and all was right with the world, as, full of Old Liederkranz grace and Boston brown bread moxie, L. B. pointed out an enormous map where M-G-M's branch offices crisscrossed the five continents. Visiting heads of state did not exactly bow, as they departed the throne room, but, said an observer, they sort of half-curtsied.

For, the 30's, British producer Roy Boulting has said, "were the halcyon days of Hollywood supremacy—with its stars glistening, its techniques unrivaled, its abilities to neutralize competition by buying up talent wherever and whenever it appeared, and its films dominating the screens of the world. These were the days of Empire."

---

* For the Production Code in its entirety, see Appendix B.

As a salute to the Empire, *Variety* expanded its movie coverage and moved it to the front of the paper. Back in *The Great Train Robbery* days, Sime had ordained, "The picture show is essentially a poor man's amusement." Although *The Birth of a Nation*, a two-dollar "hard ticket" when it opened at New York's Liberty Theater in 1915, and Garbo, in the 1920's, gave it respectability, it remained the poor country cousin of Legit and Vaude until sound came in. Now, in the 30's, Sime issued a new dictum: "The Hollywood Story is the Number One story today." As this new chapter was writ in the Show Biz Bible, headlines switched from

SHUBERT'S NEW POLICY

to

STIX NIX HIX PIX,

pausing along the way to note

WALL ST. LAYS AN EGG.

But how could the Empire make pictures that would please the bluenoses at home and the sophisticates abroad? Fig leaves were an unknown ornament in Europe, where children splashed happily in fountains that were decorated with statuary of nude lush maidens and naked husky males. The doves of Sorrento did not croon *It Ain't No Sin*, but the medium was the message.

This problem would be resolved, a few decades later, by financing European-made films and producing "family trade" pictures at home. By that time, the theater structure would have changed radically—many of the ornate pleasure domes would have come down; more of the small, intimate art theaters would have gone up. But, in the 30's, they were still faced with those block-deep Arabesque vaults, filled with Wurlitzer organs, pickled mummies, electric stars, and six thousand seats. And they still had Dietrich and Garbo under expensive contracts.

The solution was to reengineer the Hollywood product so that it would fit the demands of the Hays Code and could also be marketed in Wicked Paree. This would take the most highly skilled writers in the world, and one of the happy by-products of the Code was that Hollywood went out and searched for them. Every major novelist was lured to Hollywood during this period—not only Fitzgerald and Faulkner, but Aldous Huxley, Christopher Isherwood, and Evelyn Waugh. The playwrights in residence included S. N. Behrman, Sidney Kingsley, Robert E. Sherwood, Lillian Hellman, and Clifford Odets. Noel Coward flitted in and out of town, as did Somerset Maugham and Ernest Hemingway.

Working with professional scenarists, such as "And George Oppenheimer" (so named by Dorothy Parker), they pulled off the job—with the Garbo pictures, at least. Dietrich, one of whose pictures was scripted by none other than John Dos Passos, was a more pesky problem. She was less of an actress than Garbo, for one thing, and, for another, in the haste to put her over before American audiences her publicity got raunchy.

Her lurid press campaign began with her 1930 success, *Morocco*, in which Marlene, to tantalize Gary Cooper, kisses a woman on the mouth. A light flashed in the collective minds of the Paramount publicity department when they saw this scene— for they had been tearing out their hair at the way the new German import was interviewing. All she could talk about was her daughter Maria and her husband Rudolph, whom she had left behind in Berlin, and this *hausfrau* image was hardly consistent with the high-class strumpets she was portraying on the screen. In this, her von Sternberg period, she was a lady spy (*Dishonored*), Shanghai Lily (*Shanghai Express*), a transvestite entertainer (*Blonde Venus*), a Pola Negri siren (*Song of Songs*), Catherine the Great (*Scarlet Empress*), and a Spanish lady of uncertain morals (*The Devil Is a Woman*).

Mystery is what sold a star in the early 30's, and the press boys found that by giving the very feminine Marlene a decidedly mannish look, they broke all the wire services around the world and cast a most welcome shadow of a doubt on her propriety. This shadow is what made the cash registers ring—as well as carefully planted stories linking her romantically not only with von Sternberg but with Maurice Chevalier (he was most willing to be linked with Marlene, Maurice says in his autobiography),

Erich Maria Remarque, and Ernest Hemingway (he, too, was willing, but the stars were never right).

The circumspect Hays Code put an end to Dietrich's lesbian-and-loose image. Now, she was photographed at the races in frilly chiffon gowns, seated between her daughter and her husband. True, von Sternberg sometimes lurked satanically in the background, but he was on his way out—to be replaced by the newly named head of production at Paramount, Ernst Lubitsch, who would grapple with the problem of what to do with Marlene Dietrich in the "Just Plain Folks" era.

His solution was, as might be expected, sly, wicked, and witty. In one of the unrecognized masterpieces of this period, *Angel*, he created a drawing-room comedy that ticked as neatly as one of Wilde's and was as stimulating as one of Shaw's. In this film, Lubitsch probes the question, "What is woman?" and his answer, delivered with a characteristic shrug of the shoulder, is "Who the hell knows?"

Angel unfolds like a rose—from the opening shot, which has the camera panning the exterior of a Paris townhouse until the audience slowly becomes aware, via the comings and goings, that it is a *maison de joie*. Inside, a lovely lady (Marlene, of course) is engineered into a liaison by the madame (Laura Hope Crews). It turns out that her amour for the night (Melvyn Douglas) is an old friend of her husband (Herbert Marshall), who gets wind of the affair by accident. Nonetheless, he returns to her, in a scene that takes place back at the *maison de joie*. When his call-girl wife glides toward him, as in a dream, the husband no longer cares what she was, is, or will be. All he knows is that she has come back to him and that he needs her.

By handling infidelity as if it were myth, Lubitsch manages to straddle neatly the Hays Code and performs a bit of cuckoldry of his own. It is a classic example of how the artist can find a way to thumb his nose at the censor and put across his message for posterity. At the height of the most puritanical era in films, Lubitsch made his naughtiest film.

Chapter 10

The Viennese Teardrop

She carried a leather-bound Latin dictionary with her wherever she went, ostensibly because Latin helped her with her English, but also because she was a girl who liked to get at the root of things.

Her name was Luise Rainer, and, unlike most Venuses, who appealed primarily to the matinée ladies, men fell in love with her on sight. This seemed, at first glance, curious, since she was far from a *femme fatale:* She was slight (five feet three), thin (one hundred and one pounds), not interested in clothes (she liked to wear sweaters and slacks, and varied this costume with an occasional $5.95 print), and her huge, luminous eyes had a perpetually lost and forlorn look. Yet, Luise knew that the more red corpuscles a man has, the harder he'll fall for a waif.

In reality, she was far from a waif. Although she had grown up in the aftermath of World War I, when most of Europe was paying the piper for its game of tin soldiers by subsisting on beef lung and black bread, her father was a substantial merchant (of solid fertilizer, as she told nosy interviewers). The Rainers (they pronounced the name Rye-ner) were bourgeois of an intellectual bent, inclined toward medicine or publishing. There was no need to put on airs, not in public anyway. Such families are apt to be ingrown and intensely devoted to one another. When Luise was starring on Broadway in *A Kiss for Cinderella,* her father fell ill and wouldn't allow anyone but her to nurse

him. This she did happily, rushing from her matinées to his bedside, as would any other well-brought-up *jeune fille.*

In the tough carny world of Hollywood, Luise was quite different—more like a foreign exchange student at Vassar than a
star. She was also the most interesting actress (as opposed to personality) since Negri, but she crashed Hollywood by a fluke.

The fluke was a strike against M-G-M by one of its more popular contract actresses, Myrna Loy. Miss Loy, who had grown up
along with Hollywood, graduating from bathing beauty to Ori-
ental siren to the other woman to the perfect wife, was tired of
it all. She walked out of a projected remake of a continental
comedy success, *Maskerade,* and sailed for Paris, where everyone
fell in love with her freckles. While French cosmeticians tried to
simulate "Loy Freckles" on olive complexions, "L. B." was pacing
his white-and-silver floor. He had the rights to this wonderful
picture; he had William Powell signed as leading man; he had
one of those sparkling M-G-M supporting casts, this one including Mady Christians; but where was Myrna Loy?

William Powell without Myrna Loy, in the 30's, was like
bagels without lox, eggs without ham, spaghetti without meat-
balls, chop suey without suey, *coq* without *vin.* Im*poss*ible! You
might as well have a bowl of corn flakes.

"Why not try 'the Viennese teardrop'?" said one of those
shiny-suited men who periodically popped into his white-and-
silver office and then popped right out again.

The buzzers buzzed. Secretaries flew. Junior executives jumped.
Senior executives scurried. Writers hid the brandy in the toilet.

"The Viennese teardrop! Of course, she'd be perfect!"

She would have been, too, if Constance Collier had taught her
basic English words such as "up" and "down" instead of trans-
lating *Measure for Measure* from German into English with her.
Oh, well, turn a liability into an asset. Have her say "settling up"
when she means "settling down" (as she did in a trailer for
her first picture) and they might go for it. Only ask her, please,
to leave her Latin dictionary at home and get herself a Webster's.

Of course, Luise ignored this request. If she had complied, she
wouldn't have been a star—and a star she was, all one hundred

and one pounds of her. Furthermore, while everyone else connected with the production, retitled *Escapade* in its American reincarnation, studied the original film each morning before reporting to the set, she refused to join them. She would do it *her way*, and not as it was done by Paula Wessely.

Her way was a distinctive blend of the techniques of Eleonora Duse and Elisabeth Bergner, with a touch there of Stanislavski and a soupçon here of Reinhardt. It was absolutely unique, and it had made her a sensation on the continental stage while she was barely out of her teens. In addition to *Measure for Measure*, she had appeared in the German language versions of *An American Tragedy* (opposite Joseph Schildkraut) and *Men in White* (opposite Conrad Veidt). Her technique, like all good art, seemed effortless, but it was the result of intensive study that began when she was sixteen, when she became a pupil of Luise Dumont, an actress who had played with Duse. This was followed with further training under Reinhardt, who saw her as the logical successor to Bergner—an actress who had moved on to New York, to the joy of the handkerchief buyer at Macy's, for *Escape Me Never* had them bawling the moment she crept on stage and smiled her crooked little elfin smile; and, by the time she spoke her first line of dialogue, something mundane like "Hello," you had already dampened your third handkerchief.

Those were the good old days, when you went to the theater to *cry*. *Escapade* was a comedy, but Luise managed to wring a tear or two out of 1935 audiences, who otherwise found it a wooden remake of *Maskerade*, leaden where it should be light, frumpy where it should be fragile. Rainer's hunch—that anything that was copied rather than reinterpreted would fall as flat as a bride's first wedding cake—proved correct. Like Garbo, she immediately became a critic's darling, garnering an ecstatic set of notices that made the film a success. Luise had mystique, it was discovered, as the acclaim spread to London and on to the continent, where the vogue for Loy freckles was replaced with one for Viennese teardrop eyes. The ladies of the Western world overnight became wistful, and Myrna decided it was time to head on back to Hollywood and make her peace with L. B., before freckles went out altogether.

Luise Rainer, at twenty-two, was a star. In four years' time, at the age of twenty-six, she was, in Hollywood parlance, *through*. A Texas congressman, Martin Dies, precipitated her fall, as did the closing of the foreign market on the eve of World War II. But, above all, it was Luise's own outspokenness that did her in. As Kyle Crichton, who interviewed her for *Collier's*, noted, she was the one girl in Hollywood who would always say exactly what was on her mind. And, in a patriarchy like M-G-M, back in those days of Empire, this was not wise.

Meanwhile, Luise experienced, at first hand, the perils of instant stardom. On a trip to New York, she was surrounded wherever she went by hordes of fans who pressed in on her and demanded autographs, buttons off her coat, feathers off her hat, a snip of her hair. Even the most experienced stars had learned to fear "the mob," for they could turn on you in a second, screaming for blood instead of a souvenir. No one could foretell what would cause them to turn—a gesture of annoyance might do it, a hint of boredom, the suggestion of being late for another appointment. Even Joan Crawford, the most publicly geared star in Hollywood, feared them.

For a shy, intellectual, self-contained personality like Luise, the experience was torture. A special police detail was assigned to keep the fans at a distance, but the mob crashed through, putting terror in her heart. She found she could no longer shop for a $5.95 print or go art-browsing on West 57th Street. She began to frequent those special haunts geared to give a star some privacy, and to avoid the places she liked—places like the Russian Tea Room, which was filled with Viennese refugees like herself. On certain evenings, the Tea Room looked like a setting for *Tovarich*, with the Viennese colony in New York taking it over lock, stock, and barrel, but Luise couldn't join them now; she was Luise Rainer, the Hollywood star. They, too, came to hate her, thinking it was an affectation.

Another problem was that of the interviewers. She was, from the beginning, a favorite with the press, and they begged for an hour, a half-hour, fifteen minutes of her time. They terrified her. Her English was still uncertain; her very nature forbade her to be dishonest. Her interviewers often noted how totally unlike a star she was—her hair windblown, her conversation frank, her manner unguarded. But she generally gave them direct, quotable copy: No, she didn't hold acting in particularly high esteem, she told one reporter. She had, more or less, gotten into it accidentally. Unlike Paul Muni (one of her co-stars), it wasn't her entire life. It was sometimes boring, and Hollywood could be a dull place. Why didn't they make more films like *The Informer*, honest films with worthwhile themes? Hollywood's basic misconception was to think that anything good couldn't make money. *The Good Earth* made money—wads of money, by recession standards, when even a Joan Crawford-Clark Gable *mittel*-Culver City romance would end up with a net profit of fifty dollars. *The Good Earth* took in $3.5 million. In any case, she was planning to give it all up, eventually, and go into medicine.

The boys and girls on *PM*, New York's liberal daily, loved it. *Collier's*, still doing some of their old-time muckraking in the 30's, loved it. And who else but Luise could say, when asked what she thought of New York: "The city is tall and magnificent and frigid like a forest in winter."

Well, Ernest Hemingway, maybe.

Meanwhile, back at God's Golden Acres, they were searching frantically for stories that would suit their new star. They had the literature of Ibsen, of Chekhov, of Zola, of Balzac, of Turgenev to draw from; they had serious contemporary novels, *The Magic Mountain, The Years, Christ in Concrete*, that would make excellent films. But, no, they teamed her up with Powell again in a bit of froth called *The Emperor's Candlesticks*, in an attempt to cash in on the success of *Escapade*. They also rushed her into the role of Anna Held, again with Powell, but this time also with Myrna Loy, in *The Great Ziegfeld*.

Ziegfeld was one of the ponderous musical biographies of that day—others were built around Victor Herbert, George Gershwin, Cole Porter, and even poor Stephen Collins Foster—which managed to totally discard any genuine flavor that might have recreated an era or the man, and settled for a kind of safe Grape Nuts schmaltz. This was more fun than most, but it would have passed into that special graveyard where musical biographies rest were it not for a brief telephone scene—in the hands of a lesser actress, merely a short, transitional scene which telescoped an important plot line, so that the picture could go on—that became one of the high points of the decade's movie experience and brought Luise her first Academy Award.

On the morning that the scene was to go on camera, Luise had taken her dog to the vet. On the way out, she stopped to admire a golden-haired cocker spaniel puppy in a cage, and petted it. The vet told her that the dog would be put to death in an hour.

As the camera ground away on the telephone scene, Luise thought of that lively canine, now dead, and her voice quivered with real tears. The banal dialogue took on the overtones of true tragedy—only Elisabeth Bergner could outperform Luise in this regard—and everyone in the audience had a good cry. This is perhaps the most classic example in the history of film of converting a sow's ear into a silk purse. And a silk purse, for M-G-M, *The Great Ziegfeld* turned out to be. Only Bell Telephone was unhappy about it: For years, people would pick up the telephone, think of Luise, and burst into tears.

But Luise Rainer would be remembered only as a passing Hollywood oddity—as is Lilian Harvey—were it not for *The Good Earth*, her next picture and her most successful one. No one knew how to film the book—it had been bandied about from writer to writer for almost two years—until an actress who had the emotional depth to play O-Lan came along. Luise, Irving Thalberg knew, was that actress—and suddenly the problems of condensing a story that had a thirty-year time span began to clear up.

Talent from all parts of the globe was poured into *The Good Earth*—including Paul Muni, the carefully honed and intense actor who played Wang, the Chinese peasant who abandons O-Lan for a fancy second wife, once his peach trees make him rich; Walter Connolly and Henry Travers, two of the brilliant character actors who enriched the Venus vehicles of this era; Tilly Losch, in a *Caligari*-styled make-up, who burns up the screen with one of her hedonistic dances; Lin Yutang, the Chinese-born

author, one of several technical advisers called in to authenticate
the décor; and Karl Freund, the great Ufa cinematographer of
the 1927 tone poem, *Berlin: The Symphony of a City*, whose
magnificent locust plague scene drove up production costs to
$2,816,000 but made it seem money well spent.

Without a believable O-Lan, though, this might have ended up
as just expensive costume jewelry, as most Hollywood epics
have a way of doing. Rainer, in the role, was the diamond-hard
pivot around which the film revolved, pulling out all stops from
the rich bag of theatrical tricks she had acquired under Reinhardt.
Hers was a Mother Courage, Viennese Teardrop style; but, then,
why not? It elated the handkerchief buyer at Macy's, who had
noted a drop in business after Bergner left town; and she sent
out cables to Ireland and Switzerland for fresh supplies. There
wasn't a handkerchief left in those countries, though; Rainer's
fans had bought them all up. Undaunted, Mrs. Babbitt tore up
an old pillowcase, and spent long afternoons at Loew's crying
her heart out. She never had a more wonderful time at the movies
in her life, she told Mr. Babbitt, her face angelic, her eyes red
and swollen.

"Agnes, are you sure you're not going through change of
life?" repeated Mr. Babbitt, who drew the line at going to see
The Good Earth, although he sure went for that Hedy Lamour,
yessiree!

As for Babs and Bob Babbitt, they were now nearing college
age, and, although a certain overproduced feeling marred their
enjoyment of it, they loved Luise, they adored Karl Freund, and
they began to bone up on director Sidney Franklin, for they
were early *auteurs*. "Of course, only Eisenstein could have really
done the theme justice," said Bob, as he and his handsome sister,
totally recovered after being abandoned by Vilma Banky, sipped
black-and-white sodas at Chapman's drugstore, after seeing *The
Good Earth* a third time.

Babs, who hoped there would be a course in the history of film
at State (there wasn't; that would happen a generation later),
shook her head vigorously between sips.

"No, no!" she said, as she lifted her head from the straw.
"Not Eisenstein—Murnau!"

Mr. Chapman, a good friend of Mr. Babbitt, looked perplexed, as he stood by, wanting to join the conversation.

"What are you goin' to take up at State, Babs? Teachin'?" he finally asked.

"No, I hope to study the history of cinema," said Babs, in her newly acquired Katharine Hepburn drawl.

"*Sine*ma!" said Beau Chapman. "Holy Moses, what will you kids come up with next?"

The Good Earth, which won a second Academy Award for Luise, might have been another milestone picture in the development of Hollywood, pointing the way toward a new maturity, but a mood of ugliness had fallen over the movie capital, as it had over the land.

For, this was the era of Congressman Martin Dies, who was to write the first chapter in the Hollywood history of "loyalty investigations," and who would leave a clearing for further chapters to come. In the late 30's, he was competing with the Los Angeles District Attorney, Burn Fitts, in conducting headline-making "inquiries" directed at prominent members of the film capital.

An orphan of the storm was Luise Rainer, who had married the leftist playwright-turned-scriptwriter, Clifford Odets, after an off-again, on-again courtship which had transformed her from a sweater-and-slacks gal to a glamorous Viennese belle. Odets was brilliant but unsteady, and this marriage, like his others, was doomed, but it had brought Luise into close contact with the sizable Hollywood left, about to go into a state of civil war with the equally sizable right.

Now, her outspoken views on Hollywood—as innocent and naïve as a Vassar girl's—took on an ominous twist. L. B. remembered how Luise had to be dragged bodily to an Academy Awards presentation, her hair still uncombed, to collect an Oscar; also remembered, by other Hollywood powers, was her criticism of "our fine pictures."

Suddenly, Luise Rainer's pictures began to get shabbier. She, who had won two Academy Awards and was one of the few actresses since Garbo with that indefinable golden glow, got what is called in the trade "the Gilbert treatment." They didn't fire her—that would be too honest and direct, not to say obvious. They just slowly pulled the rug out from under her feet.

Various official or semi-official explanations are given for her sudden departure from the screen. One is that she got into a quarrel with Mayer over some traffic tickets. Another, suggested by Bosley Crowther, is that she wouldn't sit on Mayer's lap like other actresses when it came time to discuss a contract. Still another, and perhaps more valid, reason is the approach of America's entry into World War II and the subsequent decline of the foreign market. This would, inevitably, put the emphasis on the *Andy Hardy* type of family picture and the *Panama Hattie* musical. Whatever the reason, before what remained of her contract was torn up in her face, her pictures went from bad to worse.

One, co-scripted by Dore Schary, was called *The Big City*, an unintentionally funny rewrite of the classic Sacco-and-Vanzetti case that had our Luise falsely accused of blowing up a factory. She is about to be deported, but is rescued when a bevy of heavyweight champions (all of them under contract to M-G-M), discover the real perpetrator of the crime just as the boat is ready to leave for her native Slobotka. On her way back home, she has a baby in her husband's (Spencer Tracy) cab. The film was originally to have co-starred Freddie Bartholomew, but along the way he got written out. It still makes a good parlor game to try to figure out exactly how Freddie would have fitted into the original story line.

In an act of true sabotage, another film of the late Rainer period, *Dramatic School*, pairs her with Paulette Goddard—a tough actress to play against in any case, but she drove shy, windswept, fragile Luise up against a wall. Not that it mattered; the picture was so terrible she was better off there. After that Luise was at liberty.

Luise Rainer's career did not stop here, although she was never again the great international star she was in her Metro period. She went to London, where she was enormously popular, and starred in a West End comedy. She toured in summer stock, and made a brief foray on Broadway. She remarried; she did volunteer charitable work. One of her last recorded New York appearances was a free performance of Jean Anouilh's *Antigone* at Cooper Union.

But the memory of those luminous eyes and that lilting voice lingers on, and you remember her, no matter how distantly, with pleasant people you have encountered over the years.

And, every now and then, when you look at a telephone. . . .

Chapter 11

Up and Down the Highways and Byways of Love with Hedy Lamarr

Then love was the pearl of his oyster,
And Venus rose red out of wine.
                    —Algernon Charles Swinburne

Among her six husbands were two of the richest men in the world—a German munitions-maker and a Texas oilman. The other four she acquired as she traveled the highways and byways of love; they included a titled British actor, an Acapulco hotel-owner, a Hollywood screenwriter, and a Los Angeles lawyer. She had known love, in all its manifestations, from the age of fourteen, when she broke an ivory statuette over the delicate part of an indelicate laundryman. She once told Harry Cohn that she had had perhaps a hundred lovers since. According to *Ecstasy and Me*, a memoir written in the tough, back-lot lingo of Hollywood and later repudiated, they included a cowboy who had no idea what a famous lady he made love to under the wide-open western skies; a young Catholic artist, who went to confession after enjoying her delights; and a German nobleman, who almost succeeded in hanging himself in her presence. She was the most beautiful Venus since Banky, and her name was Lamarr —Hedy Lamarr.

This perfect-featured brunette, whose face, particularly in repose, suggested a cool woman-of-the-world sensuality, might have been the prototype of the heroines that Garbo portrayed in her sexy silents. Born Hedwig Eva Marie Kiesler, the only child of a Viennese banker, she was petted and pampered from infancy, as pretty girl-children are inclined to be in the city of wine, women, and song. She grew up secure in the knowledge that she was a beauty, adept at the ability to attract men, and jaded by her easy conquests. She might have been content to play that game of easy flirtation that Viennese beauties of the upper middle class indulge themselves in were it not for a gnawing ambition to become an actress—first fulfilled as a schoolgirl when she got a bit role in a silent film.

For all well-connected beauties—whether you were Rosamund Pinchot of Philadelphia, Lady Diana Cooper of London, or Maria Magdalene von Losch of Weimar—the road led to Max Reinhardt. Reinhardt was the first to note that Hedwig Kiesler had a limited range as an actress but an uncommon ability to project sex through her face. All Hedwig had to do was *stand* there, and every male in the audience began to cartwheel up and down the aisles. Reinhardt left her standing on stage, in ingenue roles that required minimal acting, so that, as a theatergoer of that era recently recalled, long-curled Hedwig was always putting flowers in a vase and saying the German equivalent of "Anyone for tennis?" She was an enrapting vision even then, and, inevitably, caught the eye of Gustav de Machaty, a Czech film producer. He was looking for a leading lady of virginal but overpowering beauty for a film, *Symphonie der Liebe*, which would portray a young girl's sensual awakening. It was scripted without the nude scene, so that the unsuspecting Hedwig Kiesler signed up for it not knowing that it would become the most notorious movie ever made.

De Machaty cut off her curls, took off her clothes, and stuck pins in her behind to get her to simulate sexual passion. As *Ecstasy* the result was shipped to the United States, where it was immediately seized by the Collector of Customs in New York and burned. A second print of this inflammable film was then flown to the Circuit Court of Appeals (one would like to think, by doves), who, after screening it a number of times, eventually allowed it to corrupt the morals of the nation.

It is still a good film—so good that the *nouvelle vague* remakes it a dozen times a year, not even bothering to alter its plot line, that of a sexually frigid young woman who is *awakened* by a handsome blond stud after a swim in the nude. Its rather obvious Freudian symbolism—including, of course, a runaway horse—gives it a museum-piece quality that is rather endearing. And, *the awakening* may very well be Hedy's finest hour as an actress.

In addition to inspiring an entire new motion picture genre—the Lady Chatterley and the Horse genre—*Ecstasy* also has the distinction of being the most "burned" picture ever made. Not only did it bring out the pyromaniac in the Collector of Customs, but it sent her first husband, Fritz Mandl, the millionaire's millionaire, searching the dark corners of the world for prints that he would ignite in his fireplace. "A lady is a woman who knows what jewels go with the right clothes," said Mr. Mandl piously, and not a film actress who cavorted in the nude. But no matter how many prints he bought and burned, new ones kept turning up. *Ecstasy* just wouldn't get lost.

Neither would the actress in the beauteous Hedwig Kiesler Mandl. Although she now owned as many jewels as some of the crowned heads of Europe, she was unhappy in the castle where Fritz kept her under lock and key, releasing her now and then to show her off to high Nazi officials. One evening, during dinner, she excused herself—and, bejeweled from head to toe, fled the Mandl manse by crawling out of a bathroom window. Inevitably, she would wind up in Culver City, under a personal contract to Louis B. Mayer. After all, where else could she go?

It seemed for a time that the usually astute L. B. had pulled a blunder with his new discovery—for this was not the Age of the Baroque, where Hedy could have bathed in champagne and cream in a swan-shaped tub along with the best of them—but the Just Plain Folk era. Hedy in an apron was unthinkable; Hedy behind a lawn mower was unforgivable. They fussed and they fumed—at one point even calling on Josef von Sternberg for Hell-ubh—but they just did not know what to do with this gorgeous lady, whom they had rechristened Hedy Lamarr, in that Anti-Glamour day. It looked like back to the castle for Hedy for a while there, but then Prince Charming, in the guise of Charles Boyer, came along with a glass slipper.

Boyer's first view of Lamarr was from the back. Anyone with a back like that must be beautiful from the front, too, decided Charles with typical Gallic perspicacity. Her front more than lived up to the promise of her back, and, there, in the midst of a Hollywood party, he got right down to the business at hand. How would she like to co-star with him in *Algiers*?

Algiers was an anachronism in those *On the Good Ship Lollipop* days, a steaming love story with dialogue—"Come wiz me to the Cazz-bah"—that sounded like silent movie titles with a foreign accent. Its producer, Walter Wanger, was at wit's end trying to cast it: Negri and Banky were retired; Garbo and Dietrich were not available; Harlow was dead. The kind of slumber-eyed sexuality it required just couldn't be faked; you either had it or, like Irene Dunne and Myrna Loy, you belonged in the other twin bed. It possibly might never have reached the screen if Charles Boyer hadn't caught sight of Hedy Lamarr's back.

Wanger lost no time in getting in touch with L. B. and arranging terms for a loan-out. The terms were steep—Mayer would get Boyer, an established star, for one picture, in exchange for lending Hedy Lamarr, an unknown commodity, to Wanger for *Algiers*.

In addition, Wanger, who had produced *Queen Christina* and had played a part in the Dietrich build-up, would put over the new foreign import—something that M-G-M was no longer able to do.

It was Hollywood hoss-trading at its sharpest, and it would seem that Mayer got the best of the deal. Such was not the case. Without Lamarr there would have been no *Algiers*. And, the picture that Boyer did for Mayer was *Conquest*, one of the big Garbo flops. You flipped the coin, but heads sometimes came out tails and tails became heads. You never knew, in Hollywood.

Wanger's build-up of Lamarr was cautious and careful—he

knew all the tricks of the trade and avoided the pitfalls. If, for example, the star of *Algiers* was invited to appear on radio, he blue-penciled the script and excised any words she might trip over—a policy that von Sternberg had established in the early days of Marlene Dietrich, when her English was shaky. By Hollywood standards, Hedy was not particularly well endowed —her breasts were small, her figure lithe rather than voluptuous. He resolved that by stressing the perfection of her face, in still portraits that are among the most exotic ever made, and releasing them to Hollywood's multitude of news correspondents, three hundred strong and Venus-hungry.

By the time *Algiers* went into release, in the early fall of 1938, everyone knew who Hedy Lamarr was, but everyone, including the new Venus herself, was a trifle skeptical. Goldwyn's folly was still a livid scar with movie exhibitors, and Garbo was down to No. 34 in the popularity polls. Dietrich was labeled box-office poison, and Rainer was already on the skids. The prospects for *Algiers* appeared gloomy.

It opened in the nation's leading pleasure domes, but the exploitation stressed that it was a quality picture. Boyer, in Show Biz parlance, was "carriage trade," and could be counted on to bring in the ladies with blue hair. The picture would also appeal to the then rather small audience for foreign films, who may have remembered it in an earlier incarnation as *Pepe Le Moko*, when the sound track was French and the star was Gabin. Some curiosity seekers might traipse in to see the star of *Ecstasy* (which had been banned in most states) but then, if it was a sunny day, they might be out selling vellum-bound Bibles. No matter how you looked at it, *Algiers* was a risk.

The "soft-sell" build-up paid off. *Algiers* didn't hit the nation's screens like Rin-Tin-Tin; it drew audiences to it gradually. Its box-office receipts followed a pattern: low the first day, better the next, and then building up to a crescendo that held it over for a second week. And, everyone who saw it fell madly in love with Hedy Lamarr.

She was, by her count, twenty-three when *Algiers* was released, but, whatever her age, she was at the peak of her beauty. It was a "rolled hem" and snooty beauty—as unique in its way as the Delft tile tracery of Garbo or the Goyaesque splatter of Dietrich. It brought to mind the perfume that ladies leave behind them in the lobby of the Adlon at eleven o'clock in the morning: pressed from hothouse blooms, nurtured by champagne-drinking hummingbirds, that perfume, and then sifted through tiny diamonds mined in some secret interior of Africa.

Cool, that perfume, but letting you know that the lady was, well, not available exactly . . . but. . . .

Pete and Sam and Joe caught the scent the moment the first close-up of Hedy Lamarr appeared on the screen. They had been dragged, quite unwillingly, by Betty Lou and Mary Jane and Sara Sue to the neighborhood Bijou, "to see Heady Lamour," when they wanted to go to the Palace next door to see Alice Faye. They were still pouting, their legs slung casually on the seats in front of them, when an electric charge passed through them that knocked them to the floor.

Then a combined wolf whistle, shrill, terrible, beautiful, rocked the walls of the Bijou as they have never been rocked before or since. "So *this* was Heady Lamour. Well, well, well. What do you know!" Pete and Sam and Joe then proceeded to fling themselves up and down the aisles of the Bijou in a series of fancy gymnastics that included not only cartwheels but single, double, and triple backspins.

Betty Lou and Mary Jane and Sara Sue weren't even aware that they were gone. Their eyes were riveted to the screen, taking in every tiny detail of the new love-goddess, for they were tired of their pageboy bobs (which they had copied from Margaret Sullavan) and were looking for a new hairdo. And here, before their eyes, was the very hairdo they had been dreaming of—a soft shoulder-length bob that began with a severely classical part at the center of the head, and then cascaded dramatically in gently undulating waves. Betty Lou and Mary Jane and Sara Sue were blondes but they would have their hair dyed black to look like Hedy Lamarr.

And that hairdo would require an entirely new wardrobe—severe, Chanel-like suits and simple cocktail dresses, ornamented with a pair of elegant brooches. Well, Pete and Sam and Joe could just wait one more year before trading in their Buicks.

While the boys were back-flipping and the girls were plotting, Hedy, back in Hollywood, had been propositioned by Wendell Willkie, had had her feet rubbed by Clark Gable, and had taken on her second husband—the writer Gene Markey—whom she soon discarded because he was too cynical. Shortly thereafter, she would meet the British actor, Sir John Loder, who was so overawed by the new Venus that, according to Hedy, he kept his shorts on under his pajama bottoms until they were married.

M-G-M now had a real 180-carat star in their heavens; but the great and grand old showmen—those tough, unpolished movie merchants who always gave you value for your money—were dying out, and a new breed of mogul, tailored in Savile Row and educated at the Wharton School of Finance, was coming in. They put Hedy through a computer, unaware that Venus cannot be computerized, and the results were mostly dismal—*Lady of the Tropics*, with Robert Taylor; *I Take This Woman*, with Spencer Tracy; *Comrade X*, with Clark Gable; *Come Live with Me*, with James Stewart; *Tortilla Flat*, with John Garfield; *White Cargo*, with Walter Pidgeon; *Crossroads*, with William Powell; *Her Highness and the Bellboy*, with Robert Walker. The computer said: Hedy Lamarr will bring so many dollars; and William Powell so many dollars. The computer said *Ninotchka* made so many dollars, so *Comrade X*, another Communist spoof, will make so many dollars. The computer said: James Stewart will bring in the teen-agers and Hedy Lamarr will draw the middle-aged males. The computer said: Hedy's running downhill.

Hedy managed to escape the M-G-M machinery and work with the old-style artisans now and then—notably with King Vidor in the film version of J. P. Marquand's *H. M. Pulham, Esquire*. But back into the computer she went, after this brief and welcome respite, until she found herself strangulating and asked to be let out of her contract to produce her own pictures. She made two fairly decent ones, *The Strange Woman* and *Dishonored Lady*, and then Cecil B. DeMille cast her in *Samson and Delilah*, opposite Victor Mature and a Miltowned lion.

But her true individuality—that delicate perfume that separated the men from the boys—was going, going, going fast. Hedy Lamarr reverted to being Hedwig Kiesler, a flirtatious Viennese beauty, now of middle age, with a lover or a husband around every corner. She had earned $30 million, but now she was often broke. At auctions, they would sell her nylon panties for ten dollars and her custom-made housecoats for forty; then, as things got more desperate, she would put up her old wedding rings (she had a generous supply) for sale, next her outsize bed, and, finally, her leather-bound movie scripts.

One day she woke up to find that the delicate perfume had vanished altogether, that there was no husband around to keep her, that there was nothing in the refrigerator to eat, and that she had nothing left to sell.

It was not an unfamiliar story in Hollywood, where stars lived like kings and queens on their income, never dreaming that it would end. But it was a tragic story, nonetheless, for this Venus arose so magnificently red out of so sparkling a wine. When, later, a Los Angeles department store brought charges against Hedy for shoplifting—at the very time her old films were shown almost daily on television screens—the sympathy of many people went out to her. Spectators applauded in court when she was cleared, for they knew that it was they who made her a Venus—and a Venus can do no wrong. As the 70's descend upon us, she remains an incredibly beautiful woman, one who still makes news cameras pop and men go into triple back-flips— a Venus for all seasons.

Dissolve 4:

The Changing Pleasure Domes

The great motion picture palaces which once graced America were a phenomenon of the 1920's, designed to surround the silent photoplay with the live sound of the organ, the symphony orchestra, the opera, and the musical revue. With the coming of sound films, they were doomed to obsolescence; a Garbo who talked was a compleat entertainment unto herself, and the "stage show," whipped together with spit and polish as it often was, was more of a distraction than a complement. The mute wife had learned to talk, and the paraphernalia which surrounded her muteness seemed more of a nuisance than anything. There was, too, a polarization of taste that developed in America in the later 30's. Condensed versions of *Carmen*, which once pleased all brows, now struck the highbrow as a desecration of a great work of musical art and the lowbrow as so much yowling. If you wanted to hear *Carmen*, all you did was flip your radio dial to a Metropolitan Opera broadcast and you could hear the great Rosa Ponselle do it, in a sensuous voice and with a magnetic style that made the little tab-*Carmen* sound like Kate Smith with adenoids. A growing sophistication was sweeping the country; a higher taste level was developing. Mr. and Mrs. Babbitt sadly reflected they did not know what Babs and Bob were talking about half the time: The generation gap, which three decades later would rip America apart, already had reared its head.

But there would be one glorious throwback to the great

pleasure dome era before it all came to an end; one final manifestation of middlebrow *kitsch*. This was the great and glorious Radio City Music Hall, which opened its doors on Tuesday evening, December 27, 1932, with a program of vaudeville that included Weber and Fields, Ray Bolger, Gertrude Niesen, the Tuskegee Choir, the Rockettes, the Wallendas—and, sure enough, *Carmen* condensed. No movie was shown; that would come later. Meanwhile, everyone could marvel at the giant proscenium arch, sixty feet high, whose semi-circular design was carried out within the entire auditorium. The walls and ceiling were formed by a series of arches, each one larger than the next, until the effect of a sunrise was achieved.

The Music Hall was an engineering marvel—for example, it allotted forty cubic feet of conditioned air per patron per minute. Its gold curtain weighed three tons. It consumed six billion watt hours of electricity a year. Its stage was one hundred and forty-four feet wide. Its screen measured seventy feet by thirty-five feet. Its mirrors were backed by gold deposits (it was, after all, a Rockefeller enterprise).

And, blissfully, it's all still there today—all those watt hours, all that gold, all that air conditioning—*there*, to reassure us as the earth turns, as the seasons change, as we crumble slowly from within.

One reason it's there is that, in designing it, the Music Hall's architects managed to avoid the baroque clichés of the usual pleasure dome and to reflect, instead, the Bauhaus tradition then sweeping Europe—a clean, trim new classicism that withstands the ravages of time with ease. The murals and the sculptures (by such artists as Kuniyoshi, Stuart Davis, and Henry Varnum Poor) are for real and are not Brooklyn-made copies of Egyptian burial urns. Underfoot, the era of early cubism is recollected with tasteful carpeting; and, overhead, the lighting fixtures are Swedish modern.

Everyone went to the Music Hall, everyone loved the Music Hall, but a new trend toward small neighborhood theaters had taken shape as the 1930's developed, a trend that would eventually crush the Roxys and the Paramounts and the Capitols. The new trend was for movie theaters that were small, simple,

and intimate. In New York it could be observed at the Plaza
Theater, once an old Vanderbilt carriage house off Fifth Avenue,
which now became the fashionable place to watch movies. The
social-registered patrons were greeted by vases of freshly cut
flowers, as they entered the lobby, and a checkroom, where
they left their hats and coats. Then they had coffee and cookies
before ascending a flight of pleasantly creaking old stairs to
see *Rasputin and the Empress*. When the lights came on, they
observed that the chain-smoking lady who sat nearby was
Tallulah Bankhead and the fat man who kept putting his arm
on the chair arm that was not rightfully his was Alexander Wooll-
cott. It was a charming little bit of "Old New York."

In the newly developed Sutton Place area, Miss Anne Morgan
and friends could be seen at the Sutton, a bank that crashed
early in the depression and was quickly converted into a movie
emporium, its Greek-revival façade intact. On the West Side of
town one went to another remodeled carriage house, the 55th
Street Playhouse, to watch Noel Coward impersonate the pub-
lisher Horace Liveright in a celebrated film called *The Scoundrel*;
or to the Little Carnegie, then a handsome old relic, complete
with a Ping-Pong room, where you passed the time until the
Dietrich revival came on. Hart Crane and Edna St. Vincent Millay
were among the patrons of the 5th Avenue Playhouse in Greenwich Village, particularly when the picture was Jean Cocteau's
The Blood of a Poet; and on the upper West Side, you might
run into Gloria Swanson, Louis Wolheim, or Norma Talmadge
in the first of the city's twin-decker theaters, the Thalia-Sym-
phony, situated in a Tudoresque apartment development called
Pomander Walk.

The trend toward small neighborhood theaters spread throughout other cities of the country. In Pittsburgh, one went to
the little Regent rather than the large Loew's Penn; in Chicago,
to the Esquire; in Los Angeles, to the Brentwood. Some of
these theaters changed their pictures three times a week, and
alternated the best of the new product with revivals of the good
old ones and the first wave of the great European talkies—*The
Baker's Wife* and *Grand Illusion* from France; *The Private*

Theda Bara

Nazimova

Pola Negri

Vilma Banky

Greta Garbo

Marlene Dietrich

Anna Sten

Luise Rainer

Hedy Lamarr

Ingrid Bergman

Zsa Zsa Gabor

Simone Signoret

Brigitte Bardot

Sophia Loren

Gina Lollobrigida

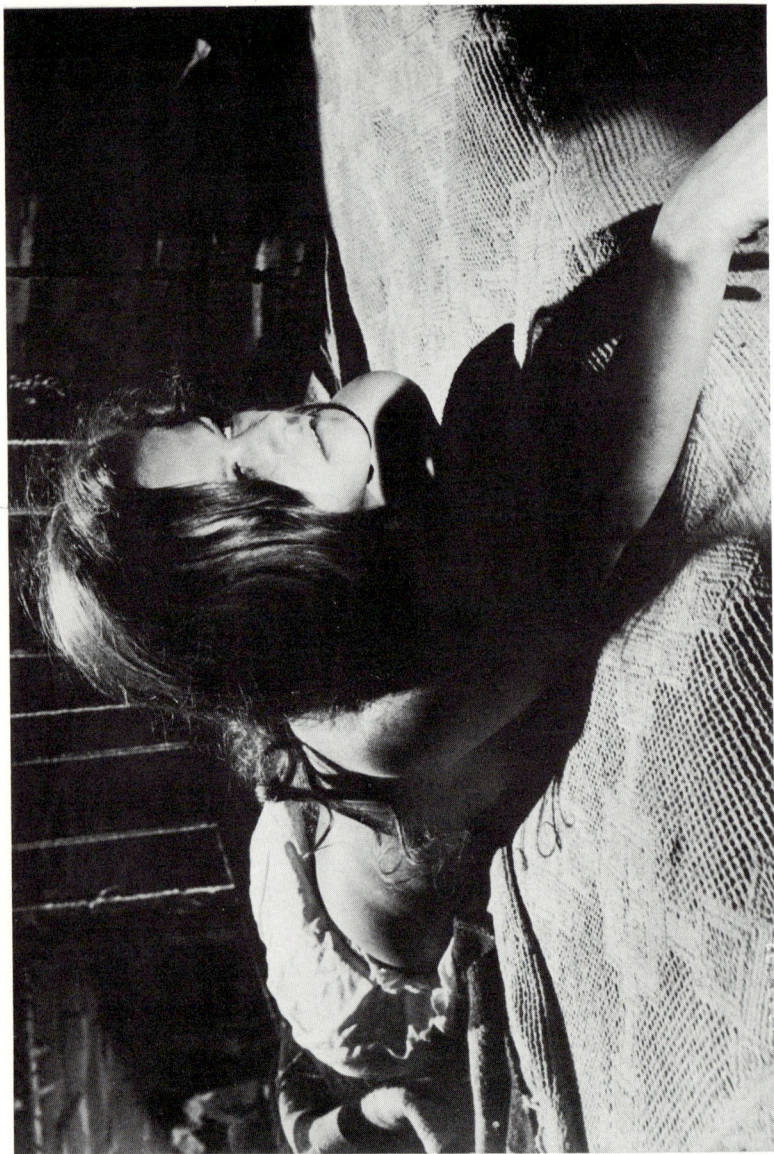

Claudia Cardinale

Life of Henry VIII and *Catherine the Great* from England; *Mädchen in Uniform* from Germany.

Throughout the 30's the grand old pleasure domes, located on prime real estate sites, still flourished—but, until the boom war years in the 40's, it was pretty much a Saturday night trade. The stage shows began to change to fit the customers: Symphonic recitals and condensed operas were out; big name bands and radio comedians were in. This was the era of Kay Kyser and his College of Musical Knowledge, of Guy Lombardo and his Royal Canadians, of Wayne King and his waltz music, of Eddie Duchin and his piano, of Benny Goodman and his swing, of Fred Waring and his Pennsylvanians, and of the great, great Bunny Berigan and his "I Can't Get Started with You." In New York, Tommy Dorsey held court at the Paramount; Xavier Cugat, at the Strand; and Jimmie Lunceford, at Loew's State. The band vocalists, then unknown and unbilled, included Frank Sinatra, Jo Stafford, Doris Day, Ella Fitzgerald, Peggy Lee, Perry Como, Ginny Simms, and Martha Tilton.

The name bands alternated with the name comics—Jack Benny, Eddie Cantor, the Marx Brothers, Joe Penner—who traveled the circuits with "tab shows" which replaced the Fanchon and Marco revues of the early 30's. These shows were noisy, amplified, and brief, to allow a fast audience turnover. They were enormously popular—Benny and Cantor never failed to draw Saturday night audiences every afternoon of the week.

This shift in theater habits during the recession era coincided with the decline of the continental film star. The two brilliant Dietrich comedies made at Paramount under the Lubitsch regime were failures, and, at Metro, Lamarr and Rainer were on-again, off-again draws. Other studios continued to experiment with imported enchantresses with even less success. RKO, for example, brought in a trio of ladies from La Belle France—Lily Pons, Danielle Darrieux, and Michèle Morgan—and starred them in high-budgeted, neatly stitched comedies (*I Dream too Much,*

Rage of Paris, and *Joan of Paris*) that had little box-office appeal. The *chic* of the opera star Lily Pons dazzled the estimated three thousand American ladies who bought their clothes in Paris salons, but the Hollywood Venus school of couture (furs, fishnet, and feathers) was what audiences wanted to see. Another Venus who didn't make it was a striking blonde from Italy, Isa Miranda, hailed at first as the new Dietrich, but after appearing in a remake of Negri's *Hotel Imperial* she withdrew from the fray. Sam Goldwyn, having invaded Russia and lost, tried again with a "Norwegian," Sigrid Gurie, but she turned out to be a fake who grew up in the Flatbush section of Brooklyn.

At 20th Century-Fox, cradle of Shirley Temple, they brought in a great continental star and one of the most refreshing beauties of that era, the really lovely Annabella. She had been discovered by René Clair, who starred her in *Le Million*. She had next gravitated to London and the then prospering Gaumont-British Studios. *Wings of the Morning*, filmed in Ireland in shades of diffused green that certainly must have spurred the tourist trade, brought her to the attention of American audiences and Tyrone Power, who quickly married her. But it was the old story: Fox just didn't know what to do with her. She was put in heavy costume dramas (*Suez*) and, finally, cast as a villainess (*13 Rue Madeleine*). The kittenish Simone Simon fared no better at Fox, but Darryl F. Zanuck pulled out all stops for Sonja Henie, an authentic Norwegian skating star, and cast her in a series of icebound operettas still prevalent on television. There were others, many others, among them Gwili Andre, a Dietrich-ish type from Denmark, Tala Birrell, and Olympe Bradna.

The daft, daffy, and deft comédienne, Carole Lombard, meanwhile, satirized the whole bit by portraying a Brooklyn girl (no doubt inspired by the real-life Miss Gurie) who impersonates a Swedish princess to get a Hollywood contract. In the 1936 film, *The Princess Comes Across*, she runs the gamut from Dietrich to Sten to Garbo ("I lo-o-o-ve Meeck-ee Moo-see!"). It was diabolically clever, and tinged with true bitterness.

After all, Carole seemed to be asking, what's so awful about being an *American*?

Chapter 12

The Great White Goddess of the Cinema

So enormous was the prestige of Greta Garbo in the late 30's that the world's richest and most commercial studio— the super-studio, Metro-Goldwyn-Mayer—did not care whether her pictures made money or not. She was "a good will asset," an ambassadress of Art ("you spelled that with a capital 'A,' honey, when you wrote of Garbo"), and above mere monetary considerations.

During the last eight years of her career, Garbo made six films—highly crafted productions that rarely recouped their cost in local distribution. But, by the time the profits rolled in from Rio and Nome and Brisbane, the red ink turned to black and Garbo's salary of $270,000 per picture was considered well worth the price.

This, the final phase of the Swedish star's career, might be called her "White Period"—as opposed to her "Rose Period," which extended from *Anna Christie* through *Queen Christina*, and her "Blue Period," which ran from *Gosta Berling* through *The Kiss.*

Each period was to make her more and more ethereal, to remove her further and further from the flesh, and to rocket her higher and higher into the heavens, until, finally, she became the undisputed Great White Goddess of the Cinema.

During her White Period, Garbo was very much aware of

her status, and tried to live like a film star, but her Swedish sense of thrift kept getting in the way. She did once rent a standard Beverly Hills mansion, although she shopped around until she found one where the rent was five hundred dollars a month, and then furnished only two of the rooms. She never even bothered to look into the empty rooms upstairs, telling an inquisitive friend, "Why should I go upstairs to look at rooms I don't even need?" She much preferred climbing a tree, and shouting "Nobody home!" when anyone rang her doorbell. A hired couple, paid $125 a month, took care of her material needs, but she carefully supervised the grocery bill, which could run as high as $60 a month if she didn't keep costs down. A second-hand Lincoln town car took her to and from her appointments; she often dismissed it and walked eight miles home rather than keep her chauffeur-butler waiting. As she explained, he had things he could do.

It was to this house that the Great White Goddess one day summoned Aldous Huxley. After he was all but frisked for concealed weapons—Garbo never totally lost the combined feeling of awe and distrust that the lower middle class has toward the writer—the Goddess herself appeared. Somewhat starchily, she told Huxley that she would like him to write a script based on the life of St. Francis of Assisi, just for her. The star was perhaps unaware that Huxley was the author of two of the most wickedly witty novels—*Point Counter Point*, which vivisects the British literati, and *After Many a Summer Dies the Swan*, which invades the private world of William Randolph Hearst—ever written in English. Or, perhaps, she thought that her divinity was so firmly entrenched that this ultrasophisticate would just fall at her feet and tell her he would be honored to serve her with his pen. Huxley gave her the classic British upper-class freeze. But didn't St. Francis, he asked her, have a beard?

He was, rather abruptly, dismissed.

As her films phased in to White from Rose, she made *The Painted Veil*, adapted from one of those patchwork novels that W. Somerset Maugham stitched to pay for a Renoir. It was scripted by Salka Viertel, a writer who, unlike Huxley, became one of Garbo's devout retinue. Herbert Marshall, an experienced hand in the Venus mill, played her husband; George Brent, her lover. The director was Richard Boleslawki, another specialist in Venus vehicles, who directed in the Murnau manner.

In this sweaty opus, Garbo is Katrin Fane, who cuckolds her doctor-husband (*poor* Herbert Marshall, he always got the short end of the stick), but is reunited with him after a cholera epidemic. Such insubstantial plot threads sustained her through the Blue Period, and well into the Rose Period, but now Garbo is more subdued. There is no mouth-to-mouth kissing in *The Painted Veil* and little décolletage. Turbaned à la Negri, she, nonetheless, maintained a cool reserve.

Then came *Anna Karenina*, one of her masterpieces. The production was gilt-edged from head to toe—Clarence Brown, the director; David O. Selznick, the producer; S. N. Behrman, Clemence Dane, and Salka Viertel, the writers; and Billy Daniels behind the camera. The leading man was the competent Fredric March, and Freddie Bartholomew and Basil Rathbone were in the supporting cast.

Surrounded with the best of everything, Garbo glowed from the opening scene—the famous railway station scene, where the smoke from the train clears to reveal *That Face!* It was truly never so beautiful—her new spirituality was becoming to Garbo and seemed to heighten her forehead, narrow her face, and lengthen her eyes. The audience gasped when they saw it, and continued to gasp, as in the picture hats and flowing tea-gowns of czarist Russia she composed one portrait after another, each more striking than the last. If it wasn't acting— and Kenneth Tynan, among others, suspects that it was not—it was at least portraiture of the highest order.

Garbo, when surrounded with people of competence, had a tendency to relax on the set and even to become outgoing. It was when she wasn't sure that she froze and stiffened and kept her distance, as a forest animal will do. On the *Karenina* set, she was smiling and friendly and even flirtatious. Her tone with March and Rathbone was light and bantering but, at the conclusion of the picture, when Rathbone asked her for an autographed picture, she turned her back.

"I never," she said, "gif picture," and she never addressed another word to him. It may be a coincidence, but Basil Rathbone did not become the major star he was equipped and endowed to become.

On the set of *Camille*, Garbo was more guarded. Her Armand was a too-beautiful young man with a limited acting range, Robert Taylor, who was cast in the role for his undeniable box-office appeal. He was obviously frightened to death at the company he was keeping, and even the simple demands of Armand were way over his head. Garbo, true to form, became edgier as Taylor literally grew petrified. It is an amusing *contretemps* in an otherwise almost perfect picture.

Camille had proved itself a hardy cinematic vehicle ever since Bernhardt had first filmed it, back in the Ice Age, with Lou Tellegen as her Armand. Subsequently, it had served Theda Bara in 1917; Nazimova in 1921 (Valentino was the Armand to her vamp); and Norma Talmadge in 1927. It threatens to go on and on—a mod version of the tale, *Camille 2000*, being its latest manifestation.

But it is unlikely that any more definitive version of Dumas's sturdy love story will be made than M-G-M's 1937 version—produced by Irving Thalberg, directed by George Cukor, photographed by Karl Freund and Billy Daniels, with a screenplay by Zoë Atkins, Frances Marion, and James Hilton. The supporting cast, culled from the Who's Who of the London and Broadway theater, included Lionel Barrymore as Papa Duval; Henry Daniell, neatly diabolical as the Baron de Varville; Lenore Ulric, absolutely right as Camille's rival, Olympe; Laura Hope Crews as the whore-turned-duenna, Prudence (one of her many great characterizations for the screen, each as accurate as one of Toulouse-Lautrec's sketches from life); and Rex O'Malley, who gives a homosexual tinge to Gaston.

Utilizing something of the *tableaux vivants* style of *Anna Karenina*, the film takes its time (it is 109 minutes long, which in 1937 was something of an endurance contest) and pauses often to note the Belle Époque décor and costuming. Ulric and Crews and Daniell and O'Malley ham it up to a faretheewell, sometimes even appearing to dig their sharpened claws right into the very lens of the camera. It is possible that on a very good night at the Comédie-Française you could see acting like this—possible, but not very likely, for everyone seemed aware that he was playing to posterity—everyone, that is, except Robert Taylor, who apparently thought he was in the senior play at Fayettesville High School.

And how does Garbo fare among all these elegant bitches, these great virtuosi, this *crème de la crème* of mummery? Like a queen among bees.

"Go ahead; hit your high C!" she mocks. "It's nice, but you don't know how to really play before the camera. Your audience is not up there in the gallery; it is right here in front of your nose. Whisper to it; woo it by lifting your eyebrow, not your voice. It is your lover, not your enemy. Brush it gently with your lips; arouse it." Well, she *is* Marguerite Gautier, and the graduate seminar in Stanislavski can just go right on pretending they are trees.

Camille is an annal in twentieth-century art, akin to the Hunt Armory Exhibition of 1913. In New York, Howard Barnes called it "sheer magic"; in London, the dean of critics, James Agate, said it was "cinema gold"; even in darkest Africa, natives who got restless and bored when shown one of the Tarzan pictures stood stiff as statues for the entire 109 minutes, and then went out and performed a dance in honor of the white goddess of the moon.

Today, hardly a week goes by that it is not screened in some art theater in New York; on the evening it was shown on television in Rome, the movie theaters reported that business was off by 75 percent; in Paris *Camille* days are unofficial holidays. Recently, one lady who has seen *Camille* twenty-one times emerged from a theater into a New York landscape that was thick with the blood of the young and acrid with the smell of tear gas. She placed her left hand on her breast, a ladylike gesture of emotion that she remembered from her genteel, moss-covered manse in Old Atlanta. Then she shrugged her shoulders and said, "Still, a civilization that gave us *Camille* can't be all that bad." And, starry-eyed, she walked home.

After this startling exhibition of witchcraft—the most stupendous since the Maid of Salem's in the seventeenth century—it was inevitable that Garbo would go into decline.

This she did in *Conquest*, her next film, a love story based on Marie Walewska's affair with Napoleon—despite the direction of Clarence Brown; despite the photography of Karl Freund (who made her look very young and vulnerable, instead of mysterious, as did Billy Daniels); despite another gilt-edged cast that included Maria Ouspenskaya and Dame May Whitty; and despite the quite brilliant Napoleon of Charles Boyer.

M-G-M spent $3 million on this rather absent-minded epic; and therein lay its fatal flaw. A Garbo picture had to be built around Garbo. To build one around the Napoleonic Wars and put Garbo in it was to cancel out two great forces of nature. Still, some of the *tableaux* would look at home in the Prado: Garbo standing among the Cossacks who have invaded her home; Garbo pleading for Poland's liberty before a cold-eyed Napoleon; Garbo bringing her son to visit Napoleon after his defeat at Waterloo.

Garbo addicts remember 1939 as the year of *Ninotchka*, and only incidentally as the year that Hitler occupied Czechoslovakia. For in this film, her dry humor, which showed itself in totally unexpected places in her earlier films, was given full rein. Garbo laughed, and somehow the terror of the twentieth century seemed a little easier to take.

Ninotchka has an interesting history. Garbo had wanted to do the film of *Tovarich*, the Jacques Deval comedy that was a hit on the Paris, London, and New York stage and poked delightful fun at the White Russian emigrés. But Claudette Colbert had got hold of the film rights, and an entirely new variation of the same idea—telling the same story from the Soviet Russian point of view—was scripted by Charles Brackett, Billy Wilder, and Walter Reich. Lubitsch was available to direct it—Garbo had admired him ever since *The Love Parade*, which she liked so much that she left a bouquet of flowers at his door —and now, at last, they could do a picture together.

This film, unlike her previous ones, was a commercial success at home and even played the Radio City Music Hall, where it opened on November 9, 1939, with a stage show that included Ravel's *Bolero*. Its genre—political satire—is the most difficult in drama, with Aristophanes and Gogol (in *The Inspector-General*) among the few who have pulled it off. It was an ambitious project, and certainly the most intelligent film in which Garbo ever appeared. The final judgment on it must wait thirty years or so, but we can be sure it's one they'll be watching.

We envy the critics of 2000 A.D. the pleasure that this mischievous film will bring them: the delight of Garbo as a lady commissar; the deft Count Leon d'Algout of Melvyn Douglas; the slightly Alice-in-Wonderlandish Grand Duchess Swana of Ina Claire. Above all, we envy them its Lubitschism.

Then in 1941 came the disastrous *Two-Faced Woman*, in which Garbo was miscast in the kind of lightweight marital farce that Jean Arthur did well. "As shocking as seeing your mother drunk," said *Time*, referring, no doubt, to the grand seduction scene, which took place on a rather moth-eaten couch left over from *Flesh and the Devil* days. Surrounded with such fancy farceurs as Roland Young and Ruth Gordon, Garbo's ironic comedy turns to lead; pitted against Constance Bennett, she looks like a leftover troll; with featherweight dialogue, she becomes a deadweight; asked to rumba, she moves with the grace of a snowplow trampling a field of paper daisies.

It was a sad swan song for The Great White Goddess of the Cinema. She settled her contract with Louis B. Mayer, surprising him with her fairness, packed up her two rooms of furniture, and left town.

Who is Garbo?

For one thing, the most written-about theatrical personality of the century. The Garbo literature—most of it in European languages, and never translated into English—would fill a good-sized library if it were assembled *in toto*. It includes books published in Buenos Aires, in Basle, in Berlin, and in Bremen. Surrealist poets have written studies of Garbo, as have *avant garde* novelists and fashionable critics. Some authors, such as François Mauriac, see her as a cultural phenomenon; others, like Raymond Durgnant in his erudite study, relate her to the growth of film.

She is beautiful to some and ugly to others: Graham Greene thought her merely a gawky woman; to Isabel Quigley, "her very bones were eloquent." Kenneth Tynan was certain she was a female impersonator—really a high-ranking Scandinavian diplomat in disguise—until he met her. Then, he was just as certain she was a girl. Parker Tyler, on the other hand, is not altogether convinced—Garbo, to him, seems to be some kind of mannequin, no doubt wound up each morning by a Dr. Coppelius and turned loose in the housewares department of Bloomingdale's. Alistair Cooke has written of Garbo, as have Cecil Beaton (who finds she grows more beautiful each year) and Simone de Beauvoir and Pare Lorentz (who thought her more slow and stupid with each picture). So have Clare Boothe Luce, who didn't like her, and the hobo-writer Jim Tully, who didn't either. On the other hand, two of the important movie critics of the early 1940's, James Agee and Cecilia Ager, thought her sublime.

There is not a magazine in the world that hasn't "done Garbo": Hardly had she set foot on American soil than Arnold Genthe photographed her for *Vanity Fair*, the most influential magazine of its day, and the publicity mill hasn't stopped grinding since. Her newspaper clippings number in the millions, and still come in from all parts of the world. She appears regularly in the Manhattan gossip columns, doing things she never knew about until she reads of them. The nightclub press agents know they can "break Winchell" if they feed him one usable item about Garbo along with two other nondescript ones that mention their clients, and the very name "Garbo" sets Earl Wilson drooling. Amid the bracken of Broadway, Garbo is a patch of pure white lily of the valley where the tough and the unholy denizens stop to pay homage, and its shopworn courtiers still grow misty-eyed at her very name.

As if this were not enough, hardly any memoir of a Hollywood celebrity is complete without a chapter on Garbo. A notable exception is Charlie Chaplin's *My Autobiography*, which pointedly omits any mention of the Divine One. This is odd, for Chaplin knew everyone of any consequence in Hollywood, and Garbo and Chaplin surely met at San Simeon, if nowhere else. But The Little Tramp clamps a total blackout on The Big Swede—probably another instance of Gimbels not touting Macys.

Colleen Moore, though, paints a charming picture of a shy, elusive woodland creature who was also a highly polished flirt. John Gilbert's favorite name for Garbo was "Svenska flicka," says Colleen, but his proximity did not prevent James Montgomery Flagg from telling the radiant star, "You're my dream girl!" Garbo replied: "All I vant to do is come and live in your studio." Anything might have happened, but Gilbert interrupted this tête-à-tête with flame pouring from his nostrils.

Charles Bickford, too, found Garbo a born flirt, the shyness and aloofness just a blinder to ward off people who bored her. Tallulah Bankhead found her just as much fun "as the next gal" and Mae West thought her a lovely lady. Before they had a falling out over her autograph, Basil Rathbone saw her as a real beauty, with a skin of such exquisite texture that it required no make-up. She was an all-around athlete, he said, and swam like a faun. George Oppenheimer, who had been warned she was forbidding, was delighted to find "her beautiful face smiling, her eyes sparkling . . . she was warm and friendly."

Attractive men always brought out the belle in Garbo, it appears, just as more mature performers always noted her respectful good manners. Although she never bothered to say "good morning" or "good night," noted Lionel Barrymore, "she was very, very nice, and likeable and kind." That she had true simplicity—"the true simplicity of genius"—was a fact also noted by the great character actress, Marie Dressler, who observed that Garbo was a most dedicated actress, who seemed to live for her work and just blended into the wallpaper when it was over.

With topflight studio technicians, solid professionals who knew their jobs and did them well, Garbo was on easy terms. There was no cheap temperament, no phony airs, and she was always there on time. Clarence Bull, the still photographer, remembered the time one of his assistants, nervous at working around Garbo, dropped a lamp on her shoulder. She immediately put him at ease by making a light remark—always the true test of the real lady. But, then, he may have been goodlooking, for she continued to twit him each time she saw him.

The average studio hand she disregarded altogether, unless an accident befell him that brought him to her attention. This occurred to a nervous father-to-be, who fell off a ladder. When she encountered the studio propman five years later, she stopped to chat. "The bay-bee must be five now, yes? Was it boy or girl? Boy! How nice!" She fluttered her long lashes, which someone said must have folded down like a pair of Venetian blinds when she went to sleep, and walked away, leaving the burly worker speechless and watery in the knees. A Garbo close-up—just for *him!* If he ever had it evaluated, it might be worth a small Rembrandt.

Some women are born goddesses, others achieve goddesshood, and still others have it thrust upon them. Garbo is a little of each. Today, when someone calls her for dinner, her answer is apt to be, "How do I know this afternoon how I'll be feeling tonight?" If she deigns to show up, she will, as likely as not, leave the table early and go out to the kitchen and have a long chat with the cook. Her diet is still Gaylord Hauser, with an occasional Chlorophyll Cocktail to change the pace. Her companions are either very, very rich or very, very beautiful or very, very talented. She has cruised the Mediterranean with Onassis, traveled the Riviera with Noel Coward, and walked around the Central Park reservoir with Cecil Beaton. She has dined with Mae West in Hollywood, broken bread with some choice Rothschilds in New York, and taken tea with Princess Margaret in London. Her moods are quixotic—she will show up, unexpectedly and uninvited, at the kind of upper-fringes-of-Bohemia soirée where the guests are Ned Rorem and Ming-Cho-Lee or at the rehearsal of a *New Faces* revue. No one knows how she got there, or why, and the conversation on these occasions is apt to run along the lines of: "My God! There's Greta Garbo!" . . . "Sandy, are you back on mescaline?" . . . "I'm telling you, that's Greta Garbo!" . . . "You really are insane, of course. Now, Sandy, I've heard of this wonderful new doctor." . . . "But, it

is Greta Garbo. Look, over there! Leaning against the bookcase."
. . . "Sandy, this doctor is just brilliant; what he did for Ernestine's delirium tremens—my God, it *is* Greta Garbo!"

Even Café Society takes note when Garbo hovers on their home territory. A world-famous maharanee once almost smothered to death in a fitting room, when she heard that Garbo had an appointment at her couturier's and, if she sat perfectly still, she might catch a glimpse of the Divine One as she walked by. Garbo never showed up and the maharanee was revived with smelling salts. Irene Dunne once sat transfixed in her car for two hours, when she was told that Garbo would emerge from a certain door, though at an unspecified time. Unlike the maharanee, Miss Dunne was rewarded with a glimpse of Garbo.

Not so blessed were the first-class passengers of a luxury liner who, learning that Garbo was on board, set up a day-and-night watch outside her cabin. Whoever saw her first would tip off the other passengers, according to an agreement that was reached by a Texas cattleman, a surgeon-general's wife, and an auto-parts-chain owner, among others. Miss Garbo never left her cabin during the entire trip.

Among the Manhattan peasants, looking for Garbo is also a sport, shared by men, women, children, and infants.

"Oook! Gaa-boo!" were the first words spoken by a baby who grew up in the East 50's, where Garbo lives. The baby's father swears that what his progeny meant was, "Look! Garbo!"; but then, father love being the overpowering emotion it is, you can't be sure.

Still, the baby may very well have wanted to "oook at Gaa-boo," along with everyone else in the world. Hollywood, which keeps its pulse on the desires of men, women, children, and infants, has tried many times to lure her back into pictures, offering her the sun and the stars in exchange.

But, like Catherine Sloper, the heroine of Henry James's *Washington Square,* she seems totally oblivious to the knocking on her door. They turned her out once, when she made a flop, and now they want her back. Well, let them knock. Greta Lorjissa Gustafsson, a rich woman now, stays seated in her parlor with "her morsel of needlework . . . for life, as it were."

Dissolve 5:

The Continental Enchanters
(*1920–45*)

If Garbo was the screen's all-time great enchantress, then Rudolph Valentino, an immigrant from Italy who had worked in New York as a waiter, a gardener, and a dancing instructor before invading Hollywood, was its all-time great enchanter.

He had a lithe, compact movie-body, a well-featured, distinctive movie-face, and a particular trademark—a sleek, pomaded hairdo, with long sideburns, which was widely copied as "the sheik cut," and has recently been revived. Whether he played an Indian rajah or a Parisian apache, he was altogether at ease in the *outré* costumes of the silent era, although he appeared less comfortable in his half-naked portraits (in one he is Big Chief Whitefeather, with only a thin loincloth to make it legal), which were sent out by the studio publicity department to doting fans.

Today, he is far more interesting as an important, but neglected, chapter in American sociology than he is as an actor—for Rudy, unlike Garbo, was no grand master of his art, although his dramatic ability can be described as par for the time. Far more fascinating than Rudy himself is the impact that this blandly handsome young man—you will see his like standing idly outside a café that is popular with tourists in Rome, his white shirt glistening clean, every hair of his head in place, his body scented with pine oil and musk, his well-tailored trousers subtly, very subtly, evoking the contours of his warm flesh, his feet shod delicately by Gucci—had on the predominantly middle-class WASP audiences of that day.

Did Valentino create Valentino, or did the American public create him to fill a void in their lives? Did he intentionally unlock that gushing tidal wave of popularity and ridicule that he inspired or is it something that just happened?

Who *was* Valentino?

For one thing, he was an exponent of a school of film acting that can be described as psyche-sexual and that includes Theda Bara, Mae West, Elvis Presley, and Marilyn Monroe. Except for Miss West, a good actress, its exponents are largely unskilled performers who project a heightened sexuality in vivid pop art colors. It's not what they do, it's how they do it.

Valentino, on the screen, didn't just walk—he slithered, with the well-muscled sensuality of a jungle cat, his hips moving in self-enchanted rhythm with his torso. Valentino didn't just look at his leading lady—with a casual glance he undressed her, laid her down on a couch, and made love to her. And when he kissed her—*mama mia!* Lights flashed, trumpets blew, rivers overflowed, the earth shook, the moon fell down.

Until his advent, only the very rich could afford a gigolo— and now, through the leveling medium of the screen, you could have him for a quarter, if you went in before the prices changed at six. And, with *The Four Horsemen of the Apocalypse*, his first starring role, they poured in at all hours to see him—and went back to see him in *The Sheik, The Son of the Sheik, The Eagle, Monsieur Beaucaire, Blood and Sand*—in almost anything. When he stayed off the screen in a foolhardy attempt to beat "the package system"—exhibitors were then forced to take films of inferior worth, along with one or two good ones—the customers stayed away from the pleasure domes until he came back. On a nationwide tour, his fans hid themselves behind the potted palms in hotel lobbies until he appeared, and then jumped at him, screaming, "Touch me! Oh, Rudy, *touch* me!"

Frayed rumors were unearthed—he was "a pink powder puff" who had lived for years on the kindness of strangers. A society woman in New York had put a bullet through her husband's head in the hope that Rudy would, afterward, marry her. His wives would have lived happily on the isle of Lesbos.

The caveats failed to detract from his popularity, which was at its height when, at the age of thirty-one, he died in a New York hospital after some routine surgery.

It was then that the Valentino cult erupted like one of the volcanoes of his native Italy. Some of his fans literally lost their minds. Others killed themselves. Most of them merely walked around in a state of terrible shock that lasted for days. *Rudy was dead!* Could life go on?

It did. It always does. But for years afterward, the date of his death, August 23rd, was observed in front parlors of Montana, rose gardens in Massachusetts, marble stoops in Maryland. Wreaths were hung, and tears were shed. In Hollywood a memorial service was held, with his old sheik costumes on display like papal robes. Revivals of his films were shown in theaters that hadn't run a silent movie in thirty years. Candles were lit. Masses were intoned.

Dry-eyed in Hollywood remained the moguls. They had pictures to make; theaters to fill. Valentino was dead, but there were hundreds to take his place—or so they thought. A New York actor named Jake Krantz was rechristened Ricardo Cortez and rushed into smoldering epics that had blood, sand, and Tippecanoe, too. No dice. Ricardo was Jake, no matter how much vaseline you put on his hair. Then there was Gilbert Roland, snatched from an extra line and rushed into the role of Armand, opposite the Camille of Norma Talmadge. *Nein.* Antonio Moreno, Ramon Novarro, and Tullio Carminati were then plucked, pruned, and presented to the Great American public. All honey-bunches, said the ladies with quarters, but not Rudy. A sigh from Antonio was just a sigh; a look from Novarro was just a look; a kiss from Tullio was just a kiss.

Well, as Samuel Goldwyn said once, "We have all passed a lot of water." Maybe it was time to try other types of foreign enchanters.

From Hungary, they brought in Paul Lukas; from Czechoslovakia, the bouncing and beautiful Francis Lederer; from Belgium, Fernand Gravey (they even, thoughtfully, changed the spelling of his name to Gravet); from Germany, Conrad Veidt; from Austria, Paul Henreid; from Sweden, Carl Brisson.

Nein!

Nej!

Non!

¡No!

And, in just plain English, N-O!

If they'd go for anything, it was for the Frenchies. Maurice Chevalier. Charles Boyer. Adolphe Menjou (he was born in Pittsburgh, but they thought he was French, and what they didn't know wouldn't hurt them).

Thus, a new generic school of continental enchanter was born —The French Lover. He was never the box-office landslide that Valentino was, but, anyway, they came in.

Chevalier was, of course, particularly blessed to have Ernst Lubitsch direct many of his films. The Frog and the Walrus, they called them, both operating from the same wavelengths and understanding one another perfectly. With other actors, Lubitsch had to plead, entreat, pray; he spent most of his time on the floor. With Chevalier, all he did was lift a finger, an eyebrow, at the most, a toe. And out it came—*tzcharm!*

Their films together, from *The Love Parade* in 1930 to *The Merry Widow* in 1937, have *tzcharm*—oh, how they have *tzcharm!* Even if Paramount kept trimming down their budgets, even if they insisted on Jeanette MacDonald (she went over big in Philadelphia, they told Lubitsch; "*Gott!* Philfadelfia!" replied Lubitsch), even if you ran them backward, sideways, upside down, they are among civilization's fairest flowers.

The ladies with quarters liked Maw-reece's protruding lower lip, his straw hat, his polka-dotted bow tie, and the fact that, unlike Rudy, he didn't send their husbands into convulsions. He was big in the early talkies.

This was not the story with Boyer: The only work he could find, while Chevalier was lining them up at the box office, was bit roles—he was the chauffeur in Jean Harlow's *Red-Headed*

Woman—or else they put him in French language remakes of such talkies as *The Trial of Mary Dugan* and *The Big House. Eh, bien! Au revoir! Au Paris!*

He made *Mayerling* and came back a star. A carriage-trade star, to be sure, but a star, nonetheless. As one theater manager recently said, Boyer in *Caravan* or Boyer in *Private Worlds* "brought out the goddamnedest collection of old limousines you ever saw. His pictures lost money, but I used to book them just to see those old Pierce-Arrows and Isotta-Fraschinis pull up. One old dame, ninety if she was a day, came in a MacFarlan. A MacFarlan! And her chauffeur was just as old as she was. I don't understand it. The only other time I saw them was when I played Garbo. Yeah, they always came out for Garbo."

The French Lover from Pittsburgh, Adolphe Menjou, had something of this appeal in the silent screen days. His was perhaps the most definitive career in movies—spanning as it did the one-reel Fort Lee, New Jersey, days (he began as a $5-a-day extra in 1913, borrowing dress suits from his old Cornell classmates to fill in his wardrobe), moving on to Hollywood after World War I (he made *A Woman of Paris* for Chaplin and *The Marriage Circle* for Lubitsch), and then working in the talkies in the days of the great directors—Lewis Milestone, Gregory LaCava, Leo McCarey, Josef von Sternberg, William Wellman, Frank Lloyd, Frank Capra, Sam Wood: Menjou had them all.

The later 20's were his Grand Boulevardier days, when in such silents as *The Grand Duchess and the Waiter, A Social Celebrity*, and Michael Arlen's *Ace of Cards* he lived in mink-lined overcoats or brocaded dressing gowns and dined on pheasant, pressed duck, Westphalian ham, and truffled *paté de foie gras* (he made sure that the food was real, since he was the son of a famed restaurateur), washed down with vintage champagne.

There were some drawbacks. As "Menjou, the Parisien," he was expected to give interviews that were cynically witty, so he had to bone up on Rabelais and Montaigne before greeting the press. Since he was the best-dressed man on the screen (a gentleman's annual expenditure for wardrobe should be $14,500, a publicity release quoted him as saying, although this amount included $50 for garters, which could be used the following year), he was forced to live up to his image offscreen. This required seasonal jaunts to Europe, where he had his clothes tailored by Sholte, Anderson, and Sheppard in London; by Caraceni in Italy; by Caraterro in Madrid; by Larson and Pile in Paris; by Knize in Berlin; and by Lillywhites in Scotland, among others.

To satisfy his fans, he played his first talkie, *Fashions in Love*, in a phony French accent; but, realizing that the dress-suit days were over, he transformed himself into that slovenly newspaper stiff, Walter Burns, in Milestone's great 1931 version of *The Front Page*. The Runyonesque bookmaker in *Little Miss Marker* (where he was almost, but not quite, upstaged by six-year-old Shirley Temple) added to the transformation.

Then, when the Merchant Tailors Association condemned him for his shabby wardrobe, Menjou knew that he had a career ahead of him in talkies.

The continental enchanter, he knew, was dead. Talkies and the depression had done him in. So, out with the old and on with the new!

Chapter 13

Marlene at War and Peace

By 1938, when she was called box-office poison by the
nation's exhibitors, Marlene Dietrich, the most intelligent woman
in Hollywood, also knew that the era of synthetic, sugar-coated
glamour had come to an end in Hollywood and suspected that
she might have gone down with it.

It had been a great time, and a good time, and from it had
emerged some genuine classics, including several of her own
films, but it was clear that the party was over. Bangles and beads
were going out of style; blue jeans were the coming thing.

A transitional period would lead, within a decade, to the postwar Italian neo-realism (*Open City*), to an unexpected Renaissance of good film-making from England (*The Red Shoes*),
and, eventually, with General DeGaulle's blessing and backing,
the French *nouvelle vague*. The emphasis would shift away from
Hollywood and to Rome, London, and Paris, which would become the new film capitals of the world.

In the late 30's, though, all roads still led to Hollywood, even
if they did not always lead to those two bastions of the star
system, Metro-Goldwyn-Mayer and Paramount. Many of the
best pictures of those recession years were made at little Columbia, under the aegis of a show-wise ogre, Harry Cohn; or at
RKO and Warner Brothers, who, because they felt the competition more keenly, had to stay that much smarter; or were
released through United Artists. When M-G-M did tackle a
subject of significance, as it did in the antiwar tirade, *Idiot's*

Delight, it tended to submerge the subject by spotlighting the stars (Clark Gable and Norma Shearer). On the other hand, *The Petrified Forest*, also based on a play by Robert E. Sherwood, was much more skillfully handled by Warner Brothers, who filmed it as a parable with melodramatic overtones. Audiences flocked to see it, just as they stayed away from *Idiot's Delight*. They may have been attracted by the sterling acting of Leslie Howard and Humphrey Bogart or by the high professionalism of Bette Davis; but, in any case, its message, that the American dream was turning into stone, had a sledge-hammer impact. So did Frank Capra's comedies for Columbia—*Mr. Deeds Goes to Town* and *Mr. Smith Goes to Washington*—which combined Brechtian bitterness with *Broken Blossoms* sentimentality. They were, for all their flaws, true works of art. Other popular movies of that day were the screen versions of Shaw's *Pygmalion* (a surprise hit) and *Major Barbara*; and Lillian Hellman's *The Children's Hour*, which as *These Three* had its lesbianism laundered, although its theme—the effect of slander on the innocent —was kept intact. Into this period, too, fall Chaplin's burlesque of fascism, *The Great Dictator*, and Orson Welles's two masterpieces, *Citizen Kane* and *The Magnificent Ambersons*, both of which make D. W. Griffith's attempts at Americana look like Grandma Moses gone wrong. Other abrasive looks at America's self-destructiveness included *The Ox-Bow Incident*, *Fury*, *The Grapes of Wrath*, and *Talk of the Town*—which cast a cold eye on mob violence, the Ku Klux Klan, the Okies, and the legal rights of a suspected criminal, in that order.

Lubitsch's *Angel*, which starred Dietrich, was a brilliant screen comedy that said important things about love, life, and the human condition—but how could it compete with films which tackled subjects of more immediate import—like these? But the death knell of old-style movie glamour was really sounded by two earlier Dietrich films, *The Garden of Allah* and *Knight without Armor*. They were radiantly and expensively done— *Allah* filmed in the Mojave Desert in the soft, washed-out colors of Georgia O'Keefe landscapes; *Knight without Armor* (for which Marlene collected $450,000, making her the highest-paid woman in the world) in a lavish Jacques Feyer production. No one, though, came in to see them, unless it was the old ladies in limousines who were drawn by the stylish co-stars, Charles Boyer and Robert Donat, and who as young girls had become addicted to desert/Cossack romances. Dietrich saw the writing on the wall, and removed herself to the Riviera to sit it out.

She might still be sitting there were it not for Joe Pasternak, a Berlin film-maker who had transplanted himself to Hollywood with remarkable success, notably in *100 Men and a Girl* (Stokowski, Menjou, Durbin, starving musicians, comeback concert, everyone up-to-their-ass in daisies). Universal, where this high-grade schmaltz was brewed, was on an economy spree, busily brushing off the filing cabinets to see if there might be any sparks of life left in them thar old scenarios. Among them was *Destry*, a classic Western novel that had made a classic silent film, which was turned over to Pasternak for a revamped version.

The only way to do it, decided Joe, was to cast it against the grain—for the strong, silent hero find a weak, shy actor; for the beribboned and calicoed heroine throw in a spangled and sexy dame. James Stewart would be right for Destry; and for "Frenchy" why not . . . Dietrich!

Dietrich in a Western—why, it was as revolutionary an idea as Minnie Mouse in *Electra*! Still, if she'd come down on her price—way, *way* down—maybe. Joe rushed to the phone— quick! the Riviera—and sounded out Marlene on the idea.

She hardly jumped up and down with joy. A businesswoman to her fingertips, the comedown in salary didn't sound appealing. And then, a *Western*? Were they sure they didn't want Tom Mix?

Pasternak used all his continental charm, of which he had plenty. It would mean a whole new career for her, he told her; it would put her back on the Hollywood map again. Dietrich, unconvinced, hung up. But the idea swam around in her head, and she got in touch with von Sternberg. Svengali Joe thought it a wonderful idea—yes, yes, the only thing for her to do.

Still uncertain, Marlene returned to Hollywood to discuss the matter further. Pasternak was charm itself—he would get her Frederick Hollander, who had done her songs in *The Blue Angel*, to do sultry ditties like *See What the Boys in the Backroom Will Have*, which she could croon in her whiskey baritone; he would surround her with one of those Lubitsch-like supporting casts, Brian Donlevy, Charles Winninger, Una Merkel, Mischa Auer. He would supervise the script and see that the photography was right: The entire production would revolve around *her*. She signed the contract.

Destry Rides Again, the title of the picture, opened up an entire new genre in Hollywood, that of the stylish Western— more Freud than William S. Hart; more sex than horses; more spoof than sagebrush. Lovers of the classic Western sometimes wish it had never happened, but anyway Dietrich was very good as the barroom girl with the heart of gold, and a hen-fight scene with Una Merkel was one of the high points in her career. Audiences believed her and bought the picture; it was one of the box-office hits of 1939.

She would never duplicate its success at Universal—although her subsequent films at Carl Laemmle's old lot were modest successes then and have often been revived since. They were: *Seven Sinners*, in which she warbled *I've Been in Love Before*; *The Flame of New Orleans*, directed by René Clair, whose French style did not transpose to the California sound stages; *The Spoilers*, in which she was "Cherry Malotte," a lady saloonkeeper; and *Pittsburgh*, in which she was "Hunky."

But Pasternak was right—they opened up a whole new career for her. Warners signed her to do *Manpower* with Edward G. Robinson and George Raft; Columbia tailored *The Lady Is Willing* to her specifications; and Metro took *Kismet* out of mothballs just for her. The old siren had been revamped along more flexible, contemporary lines; she was well on the way to becoming one of the Hollywood perennials, like Crawford and Stanwyck. But there was a war on, and the old Mother Courage that lurked beneath the vamp drew her to it.

And so Dietrich bade farewell to Ronald Colman, Randolph Scott, Cary Grant, and her other leading men, and went off to war. Being Dietrich, she played the role of "soldier" with enormous style, astounding even "Old Blood and Guts" General George Patton with her courage and endurance. No war theater was too dangerous; no front line too far. Dietrich was there, dressed trimly in khaki, with her trunk of costumes and her musical saw not far behind. While shells burst all around her, she slipped into something sexy, and *voilà!* Venus at the front lines began to belt out *Lili Marlene* to mesmerized G.I.s.

Only the daughter of a Prussian officer could have pulled it off—and therein lay the irony. But the G.I.s saw no irony in it: They saw only a gorgeous pair of gams (sonnets could be written to those legs: the slim ankles, the delicately muscled calves, the deftly dimpled knees, the firm thighs, carved as if from ebony). As their eyes moved upward—unwillingly, they moved upward; why tempt fate?—they saw this compact, curvy body, as perfect as a grown-up doll's, with ice-cream cones for breasts, and then this face ("the biggest thing in faces since the Mona Lisa," said *The Times* of London, a journal not usually given to superlatives). Holy Cow! Look at her face!

Although they did not know it, she was old enough to be their mother—that, too, was irony. But even if they did know it, they wouldn't have cared—Mom never looked like this, except maybe on her wedding day.

As if compelled by the drive that shoots spawning salmon northward, they rushed toward her *en masse*—here was a dame who was born to be kissed and they were going to kiss her! No camp follower in history has been kissed so often and so well as was Dietrich in those war years. From Labrador to North Africa she was kissed, kissed, and kissed. It may be coincidental, but when she got back home she had to have an operation on her jaw. Other battle scars included a nearly fatal case of pneumonia and some frozen fingers.

Not surprisingly, Marlene's wartime personal appearances paid off in increased box-office appeal after the war. Back to Paramount she went to make *Golden Earrings*, a sleazy yarn in which, her face smeared with grease and wearing a stringy black wig, she played a gypsy in love with Ray Milland. More happily, the Lola Frobisch of *The Blue Angel* was recalled in Billy Wilder's bitter tale of the flourishing Berlin black market, *A*

Foreign Affair, with John Lund as the involved army colonel. (This film so enraged some members of the audience that they stood up in the middle of it and shouted, "I can't stand *you!*" and stomped out of the theater.)

Marlene next voyaged to England to make a Hitchcock thriller, *Stage Fright*, in which she upstaged not only the top star, Jane Wyman, but The Old Master himself. In his dialogues with Truffault, Hitchcock keeps a discreet silence about the matter, although he was careful after that to hire pliable maidens like Tippi Hedren, who had never acted before.

Having picked the pocket of Hitchcock, the Grand Empress of the twentieth century moved southward to Italy, where she co-starred with Vittorio DeSica in *The Monte Carlo Story*, and then moved upward and onward in Mike Todd's *Around the World in Eighty Days*. One of her more convincing screen portrayals was that of the murderess in *Witness for the Prosecution*: It was the kind of one-dimensional, everything-on-the-surface role that she did masterfully.

Dietrich wasn't a Bernhardt, but she was a great beauty and was indisputably the best-dressed public figure of her time. She doesn't wear her Diors, as does Joan Crawford, as if she were all done up in her Sunday best; nor, as does Zsa Zsa Gabor, as if she were standing on a Flag Day float; nor, as does Lauren Bacall, as if she were to step before Hoyningen-Huene's camera any second now. She wears them casually, as if she were at home in them. It all seems absolutely effortless, but it isn't: Couturières alternately idolize her and want to strangle her, for they have never encountered a woman who wears their clothes so well or who demands so much from them in extra fittings.

The Yale-man-turned-dress-designer, Travis Banton, is usually credited with teaching her all she knows about clothes—just as the silent screen actress, Lilyan Tashman, is said to have shaped up the Garbo look. But Garbo had no interest in clothes, off the screen, and reverted to her dowdy self once she retired. With Dietrich, quite the reverse was true: She was an instance of the pupil outstripping the master, for soon it was *she* who was giving Banton a hard time.

Hedda Hopper recalled the occasion Dietrich decided to go

to one of Ouida and Basil Rathbone's costume parties as Leda the Swan. Banton designed an intricate costume for her that took days and weeks of work by the large staff of seamstresses at Paramount to complete. When it was delivered to her, on the eve of the party, Dietrich noticed that the eyes of the swan were blue, and matched her own. This would never do. The eyes would have to be changed to another color. But a swan's eyes are *blue*, she was told. Well, then, change them to *green*, commanded Dietrich. The blue embroidery had to be ripped out, and the green eyes were put in. She arrived at the party five hours late, and stole the show. Many eyes turned green that night, and they weren't the eyes of swans.

Edith Head, who has dressed all the big stars, still finds it a thrill to do Dietrich. A fitting with Marlene is not just a fitting —it's a *happening*. She arrives at the crack of dawn wearing black leather pants and carrying a huge hamper filled with thermos jugs of coffee and seven-layer cakes, which she has baked herself, for the staff of seamstresses. She shucks off her pants—no one but Dietrich and Roy Rogers should be allowed to wear them, says Miss Head—revealing that classic chassis clad in perfect French lingerie, with just a touch of lace. Bolt after bolt of cloth is then brought to Her Imperial Highness for inspection: That one is too coarse; this one is too beautiful. Finally, a cloth is selected and a fashion is designed. With a regiment of seamstresses trailing her, they now pick a hat. Hours later, they have created a new hat. Then come the shoes. Enough shoes for the population of Los Angeles are examined, but none of them will do. No, Edith must meet her at 8 a.m. tomorrow, and they will go and *buy* a pair of shoes.

And so it goes, and on—and on—and on—until the Dresden doll is at last fully clothed from head to toe in absolutely impeccable *couture*. Is it any wonder, then, that she wears Diors as if she were at home in them?

Dietrich's instinct for clothes would come into full bloom when in 1953 she entered the last, great phase of her fabled career—that of a nightclub chanteuse. She was by then twice a grandmother and already in her fifties, although she brushes that off by saying that she married very young, and just how old she is can be no one's concern but her own. A Berlin birth certificate, however, has unkindly established the date as December 27, 1901. Like cads, certificates kiss and tell.

However old she was, she had never looked more gorgeous in her life. She stood before the microphone in a transparent dress that revealed intimate details of her anatomy, including her handsomely cupped breasts, and in a sultry bedside voice she intoned "I'm the Laziest Gal in Town," "Falling in Love Again," "Miss Otis Regrets," "Taking a Chance on Love," "Here I Go Again," "La Vie en Rose," "Lazy Afternoon," "Look Me Over Closely" —in English, French, German, and Hebrew. The Hebrew may have been a bone tossed to please the coat-and-suit trade, and then again it just may have been Mother Courage's way of letting us know that we are all Her children.

Anyway, Josephine, it was a bash. It's not much fun living in the twentieth century, what with Doomsday Machines and the high cost of toothpaste and the Crimmins murder case and *everything*, but Dietrich made it fun again. Her screen career had spanned three decades and she had been called everything from box-office poison to von Sternberg's Trilby to von Hindenburg in drag—and Lillian Ross was once unkind enough to report that she stole towels from the Plaza Hotel—and Elizabeth Taylor swiped her favorite escort, Michael Wilding—and Erich Maria Remarque—well, she had been through it all, and she had come through, she had survived, just as we had, somehow, survived— so, it just wasn't Dietrich standing up there, it was *us*, the human race.

Her cabaret debut made headlines around the world. It was the entertainment news event of the century, and rightly so, for now the great Marlene Dietrich was unencumbered by a story to act out, a role to play—she was just herself, MARLENE DIETRICH, Venus in person, Venus versus the universe.

They all came to see her—Princess Margaret, Noel Coward, Jean Cocteau, Princess Grace, the Aga Khan, Prince Aly—and Mr. and Mrs. Babbitt, in Las Vegas on a two-week vacation.

"Oh, she's so Russian!" said Mrs. Babbitt.

"Now, Agnes, what do you know about Russia?" asked Mr. Babbitt.

"I read about it in John Gunther," said Mrs. Babbitt.

"Oh, that's all right, then," said Mr. Babbitt, as he turned his attention back to Marlene.

"She has so much beauty—within!" said Mrs. Babbitt.

"I hear she pulls a rubber mask over her face," said Mr. Babbitt.

"Jer-e-mi-ah Bab-bitt! If it weren't for Babs and Bob I would have divorced you years ago!"

A chilly silence enveloped the Babbitt table, and then Mrs. Babbitt said: "Do you think she really wears a rubber mask over her face?"

Dietrich's appearances in cabaret became an annual event, eagerly awaited not only in Las Vegas but in Europe's smartest clubs—among them the Casino de Paris in London, the Sporting Club in Monte Carlo, and L'Étoile in Paris. She appeared in Germany and Israel, reducing her audiences to nostalgic tears in both countries, and in Australia—where she made international headlines when the *hausfrau* in her insisted that the stage be scrubbed down or she would not go on.

Each year she would go to Jean Louis, the French-born couturier whose clients include Rita Hayworth, Loretta Young, and Irene Dunne, for a new gown.

As Louis, still youthful and blond and possessed of a Boyerish accent, recently recalled, "She is a perfectionist. She wears clothes exquisitely, of course, but this is no accident. Everything is planned; thought out. 'Move that spangle up a quarter of an inch,' she will say, and we will stop everything to do it for her. Her demands are so exacting that often on the very eve of her opening we are still working on her dress. Then it has to be flown to Las Vegas by special plane."

New York remained, until the 1967 season, the one city she would not play in—reportedly because she feared the Manhattan critics, the meanest hombres in the world. But she needn't have worried—they did flip-flops over Dietrich, just like the crowned heads of Europe. No wonder she was so good, quipped the wise-acres at Sardi's bar; she had kept the show touring on the road for fourteen years before she brought it in. It was, nonetheless, *good*, one of the few decent things that season. It often played to standing room, and its engagement was extended.

She was, at the end of the season, given a Tony (Broadway's equivalent to an Oscar), and those who saw her accept it will never forget it.

They delayed presenting it until the very end of a particularly tiresome televised show that included noisy stand-up comics and snippets from that season's vile musicals. The waiting may have tired her, or she may have been affected by the occasion—but, when she finally came on to accept the Tony, her glamour was gone. What remained was a mature woman, of enormous poise and distinction, who was receiving this recognition from her fellow professionals with astonishing dignity. This was the first award anyone had given her, she told the spellbound audience, and she was particularly glad it had come from Broadway.

As she slowly walked off the stage, while the tinny orchestra in the pit played "I've Been in Love Before," making it sound, for all the world, like the blowsy band in *The Blue Angel*, the Broadway theater had one of its few golden moments in recent years. Many in the audience wiped a tear—some of the younger actresses sobbed openly.

A living legend had appeared before their eyes, and they knew that they would never, in their lifetimes, see her like again.

Chapter 14

Ingrid Bergman; or, Venus at the Stake in Congress

There would be just one more great continental star of the stature of Garbo and Dietrich. She was, of course, Ingrid Bergman, a tall, wholesome-looking import from Sweden, who became a major box-office attraction of the 1940's. In terms of sustained earning power, if not in prestige, Bergman was the greatest import of them all: Eight of her films appear on *Variety*'s list of "All-Time Boxoffice Champs," determined on the basis of U.S.-Canadian rentals. They are:

The Bells of St. Mary's (45)	$8,000,000
For Whom the Bell Tolls (43)	7,100,000
The Yellow Rolls-Royce (65)	6,000,000
Anastasia (57)	5,000,000
Spellbound (46)	4,975,000
Notorious (46)	4,800,000
Inn of the Sixth Happiness (59)	4,400,000
Saratoga Trunk (46)	4,250,000

She never had the charisma of Garbo or Dietrich. She set few fashions. The intelligentsia never worshiped her as a cult. The limousine set stayed home unless her co-star was Cary Grant or her director was Hitchcock. But they loved her in Podunk—not since Mary Pickford did they admire any star so much and enshrine her along with the American flag, Old Dog Tray, and

Thanksgiving Dinner. What a relief it was in that day of sub-marginal cinema queens just to look at her—brimming over with vigorous health; playing baseball in her nun's costume; taking the snideness out of sex when she hit the sleeping-sack with Gary Cooper; mouthing such lines as, "Oh, Victor, please don't go to the underground meeting tonight!" with deadpan seriousness (as she did in *Casablanca*). An invisible halo perpetually surrounded her golden head.

She was America's newest Sweetheart.

If Lilian Harvey conjured up a chocolate soufflé, Vilma Banky Weiner Schnitzel à la Holstein, Pola Negri Baltic Sea caviar, Garbo kippered herring baked in lemon, Dietrich prosciutto wrapped around a slice of cantaloupe, then Bergman was a heaping bowl of Wheaties and strawberries, swimming in thick cream. Such a nice, healthy girl, and she spoke a softly accented English you could *understand*. (At Garbo pictures, a repeated whisper was, "What did she say? Oh, no, she didn't say 'Put these roses with the other flowers,' she couldn't have—what she said was, 'You have given me so many rousing hours,' I'm sure of it!") You always understood Ingrid, even when you didn't find her particularly convincing—as you didn't when you saw her play the prostitute in *Dr. Jekyll and Mr. Hyde*. Ingrid a prostitute—my goodness gracious, what could they be thinking of? Still, you found yourself rooting for her—as you would a friend in the St. Barnabas Church annual play. So she wasn't a prostitute the way Garbo was in *Anna Christie*; so what? No matter what role Ingrid played she always emerged as pure as Ivory Soap.

In actuality, Ingrid Bergman was a complex, romantic, and rather neurotic woman—much more fascinating off the screen than on. Hitchcock was the only director who got to the core of Bergman. In *Notorious* and *Spellbound*, particularly, he removes the sugar-coating and shows us the tart, tasty personality that lay beneath. Working with his scalpel, he touched some sensitive nerve that resulted in performances revealing the true Ingrid—she was, by far, the most interesting of his leading ladies, with only Madeleine Carroll (in *The 39 Steps*) a serious competitor.

Early childhood tragedy played a part in molding her unique personality. Her German-born mother died when she was two; and her father Justus, a fashionable Stockholm photographer, died when she was twelve. Enough money was left her in trust to send her to a good private school, and then enter her at the Royal Dramatic Theater School for further study. But, as Ingrid once said, "When my father died, I almost died *too*." According to intimate friends, she was a woman in search of a father—and she may have found one, at last, in Roberto Rossellini who, like Justus, was well-born, fine-nerved, mercurial, and fond of the color red. But her fans, who read *Movie Life* instead of *Vogue* and the *New Republic*, just couldn't understand how she ever fell in love with a man who, to them, resembled a balding Italian waiter; and the marriage was doomed. *They* and not Ingrid owned Ingrid Bergman, and only after she left him did they take her back.

It was producer David O. Selznick, one of Hollywood's great masterminds, who created the false image that would, eventually, do Ingrid in. When she arrived in Hollywood a gauche, awkward girl who blushed too much, he took her into his home and set about doing her over. He had unlimited resources—his *Gone with the Wind* was the box-office sensation of all time—and a great commercial instinct for understanding just what the American public wanted. What they wanted, he decided, was a Venus who was just plain folks, with only the merest whiff of an exotic perfume. He carefully set about creating her, introducing her to the American public in *Intermezzo: A Love Story*, which was nothing more than a long trailer to exhibit her before the Hollywood moguls. It had two of the finest British actors of the day, Leslie Howard and Edna Best, to give it respectability, but not even their finesse could fatten up the thin soup in which his golden girl was on show.

Having established the fact that she photographed well, and that she was a creditable actress, Selznick then farmed her out to the highest bidders. She made *Rage in Heaven*, which had a good Christopher Isherwood screenplay, and *Adam Had Four Sons*, an adaptation of a best-selling novel of that day, for other studios. They were only modestly successful, but meanwhile Selznick was setting the publicity machine into high gear.

No Detroit automobile, no Pittsburgh steel, no Washington politician ever got a better "product launching" than Ingrid Bergman. In an age of packaged thinking, Selznick offered one of the neatest bundles of them all. His campaign played up the facts that (1) Miss Bergman was the wife of a successful Stockholm dentist who had followed her to America to begin a study of medicine; (2) their union was blessed with a lovely blonde daughter, Pia; (3) his star had studied at the same dramatic school as Garbo, and not since the Divine One had any actress had so meteoric a rise—she was discovered by a Swedish film producer at the end of her first year of training, and immediately cast in an important role.

Carefully concealed in this grand public relations scheme— deftly executed by Joseph Henry Steele, who would later become one of her biographers—were certain other facts: that her films for Svensk Filmindustrie, in which she often played a young lady to-the-manor-born, were great favorites in Hitler's Germany, and that she had made a film for the Nazi-dominated German film industry. Also entirely excised from her public image was the fact that she was not an unsophisticated woman, and that her leading men and directors, naturally, found her highly attractive. So did the *Life* photographer, Bob Capa, whom she met very casually in Paris and often saw in New York. These were probably "puppy love" affairs, but Ingrid didn't always sit at home with her knitting needles when her husband, Dr. Peter Lindstrom, wasn't available to take her to dinner.

Ordinarily, such rumors were grist for the mills of Hedda and Louella, who made good livelihoods by smelling out a faltering movie marriage and then employing old *New York Graphic* methods to lock the story as an exclusive. But, through some private understanding, no hint that Ingrid's marriage to Dr. Lindstrom was dissolving ever appeared in the press. These were war years—Ingrid was a public goddess—and, anyway, maybe the whole thing would blow over.

When Ingrid went to Italy to make *Stromboli* for Rossellini, the first rumors of a love affair appeared in the European press. Ingrid's Hollywood friends knew they were probably true—the star had become infatuated with Rossellini and had written him a schoolgirlish note (the woman in search of a father) in which she told him she would abandon Hollywood to make films of artistic merit with him. Later, in Hollywood, this regard for the artist would develop into one of her classic "near-affairs," which only an inner circle knew about. In Rome, under the malevolent eyes of the *paparazzi*, though, it blossomed into a full-time scandal, with pictures of Ingrid and Roberto strolling hand-in-hand appearing in the daily press.

Still, American newspapers tended to play down the stories. So carefully drawn had been Ingrid's public image that the fact that this handsome woman could have a love affair seemed inconceivable. This could not be true of *their* Ingrid, who had played the nun in *The Bells of St. Mary's*; who had *been* the very spirit of Saint Joan, both on the stage in *Joan of Lorraine* and in the movies; whose virginal beauty and purity dimmed the issues of the Spanish Civil War in *For Whom the Bell Tolls*.

But when *Stromboli* was finished and Ingrid moved into Rossellini's apartment in Rome rather than return to Hollywood, the rumors became a furious press scandal. And then Louella Parsons broke the story that she said got more space over a longer period of time than any other story ever to emanate from Hollywood—the story that Ingrid was pregnant with Rossellini's child. It was headlined in the *Los Angeles Examiner* in two bold lines of type that pushed almost everything else off the front page. The headline, a classic in American journalism, read:

INGRID BERGMAN BABY DUE
IN THREE MONTHS IN ROME.

The American people reacted as if they had been struck in the face. Among them was the senior senator from Colorado, Edward C. Johnson, who stood up on the floor of Congress and for one entire impassioned hour let flow his fury and his rage. This event, which took place on March 14, 1950, was one that shook Hollywood to its core, for, according to the senator, not only Miss Bergman but the entire film industry was evil incarnate.

On that memorable day Senator Johnson proclaimed Ingrid Bergman "one of the most powerful women on the earth today —I regret to say a powerful influence of evil." To prevent any recurrence of such witches, the senator proposed federal licensing of actors and actresses, as well as producers and distributors. These licenses, according to the senator, "could be revoked when a holder was convicted of a crime involving moral turpitude or admitted conduct of such a nature."

As the tirade, a true classic of the hell-and-brimstone school, continued, the senator went on to call Ingrid "Hollywood's apostle of degradation," "a free-love cultist," "a common mistress," and it ended with a screech, "Out of her ashes may come a better Hollywood!"

Who was this Rossellini, anyway? Americans of more restraint wondered. They could not accept Senator Johnson's conclusion that he was "a treacherous viper," and since the American press was dead set against him it would be some years before they found out. Today, American women who encounter him in business say they can quite understand Ingrid's infatuation: He is one of the most attractive men in the world—something of a spoiled darling (he was a rich man's son who squandered an inheritance on racing cars before he went into film-making) and a genius (he single-handedly lifted the Italian film industry from its Mussolini period of mangy epics, which celebrated the great days of Ancient Rome, into the glorious postwar neo-realism that led to Fellini, Visconti, and Antonioni).

Interviewing such ladies, however, will gain you little specific information, for the ladies aren't telling. *Is he handsome?* Who cares? *What does he look like?* Well, nothing very much, really. A bit too round at the waist, maybe. Balding. But, oh those eyes! The most expressive I've ever seen. *What color are they?* I never really noticed. *Is he tall or short?* Who cares? *Why do you find him so attractive?* I can't put my finger on it. His lovely, lovely manners, maybe. He is so gentle; so sweet. The way he makes you feel as if you are the *only* woman in the world—the only woman since Eve, although all he's doing is asking you for an eraser. And once, when he kissed my hand before he went back to Rome and said "avy rederssy" (*this particular lady is from the South*) I almost left *my* husband. *How well does he talk English?* Who cares?

We can see then why romantic Ingrid, orphaned at twelve and married to a solid Swede while still a young girl, found Roberto devastating. Not since the Duke and Duchess of Windsor had there been so world-shaking a love affair. It would end in marriage, eventually, with the most famous lovers in the world festively sipping champagne in the stylishly Bohemian Rossellini apartment on Rome's Bruno Buozzi while they were being married by proxy in Juarez—a lawyer, Javier Alvarez, representing Roberto, and another lawyer, Arturo Gomez Trevino, standing for Ingrid. More trials, more tribulations: Dr. Lindstrom refused to recognize the divorce. The custody of Pia became a world-celebrated issue. But finally the air was cleared and sanity restored. They were Mr. and Mrs. Roberto Rossellini at last.

All would have been well that ends well if *Stromboli* had been a success. But, though Ingrid Bergman and Roberto Rossellini were two of the most striking cinematic talents of their day, they did not make beautiful music together. Ingrid's nineteenth-century German romanticism did not fuse well with Roberto's essentially quizzical and cynical twentieth-century mind. It was the marriage of a latter-day Lotte of Weimar to a new, jazzed-up Machiavelli.

Ingrid's old fans, cut to the quick, stayed away from *Stromboli* in droves; the critics jeered it; the box office, after a play from the curiosity seekers, took a sharp nose dive. This would be the pattern of their subsequent films, which should be re-released some day in less frantic circumstances for an impartial look.

Meanwhile, more babies arrived—an adorable Botticelli-like set of female twins followed the handsome first-born son, Robertino —but all was not well at the ducal Rossellini household. Told that the larder was almost bare, Ingrid brightly suggested that they partition their villa and rent out half of it. Roberto just groaned; he was hopelessly in debt and could find no new backers for his films.

Ingrid appeared on the stage in Paris, in *Tea and Sympathy*, and toured Europe in Honegger's opera-oratorio, *Joan at the Stake*. Among the cities she visited was Stockholm, where she got some idea of what it must have been really like to be Joan: On opening night the audience hooted. She dared not return to the United States but, when 20th Century-Fox offered her the leading role in *Anastasia*, to be filmed in London, she accepted it, despite Rossellini's protests. It was the beginning of her new career, which would bloom again, and the end of her marriage.

But, Ed Sullivan, of all people, would open up the old wounds when on his Sunday evening broadcast of July 18, 1956, he announced that he would like to book Ingrid on his show, in connection with her return to the screen in *Anastasia*, but he felt he should poll his audience for their feelings on the matter first. Hadn't they felt she had suffered enough; wouldn't they like to see her on his show? The letters poured in: 6,433 against Bergman; 5,826 for her. But Ed's lack of taste—as well as just plain good sense—backfired on him. It was his big blooper that year.

Years later he admitted, "Ingrid never forgave me for what I had done—and she was right." But the harm had *been* done—although *Anastasia* turned out to a major success and Ingrid got an Academy Award for it (accepted for her by Cary Grant, a friend who stood by through even the kinkiest episodes of the Rossellini entanglements). It would be twenty years before she returned to Hollywood to make films again, and the years between were filled with remembered bitterness. Recently, though, she returned to star in two pictures—*Cactus Flower* and *A Walk in the Spring Rain*; and in her interviews she appears philosophical about her days at the stake. "The wind blows this way and that," she has said, "and in life you have to take what it gives you."

Her calmer acceptance of the fickleness of fortune may be the influence of her third husband, a handsome, wealthy Swede, Lars Schmidt, who seems to combine the more appealing qualities of both Lindstrom and Rossellini. Schmidt was the traditional rich man's son, infatuated with the theater, who turned his hobby into a lucrative career. Today he is a producer on an international scale, with a solid commercial instinct that leads him to acquire foreign rights to such properties as the hit Broadway thriller, *Wait until Dark*. He also oversees Ingrid's increasing appearances on the stages of the world: In New York, she recently appeared in O'Neill's *More Stately Mansions* and, in London, in a revival of *A Month in the Country*. Together, they manage to spend a part of each year in an estate in the Chevreuse Valley of France—like another celebrated pair, Elizabeth and Richard Burton, surrounded with their children from previous marriages, their pets, and their entourage. Unlike the raffish Burtons, though, Queen Ingrid and Prince Lars look comfortable in ermine.

She is the last of them—the old-style continental enchantresses of the Garbo-Dietrich school. While she still reigns, a new kind of Venus—slangy, contemporary, and often naked—stands by and looks longingly at her throne. Ingrid Bergman views the contenders with royal calm as she enters a new phase of her career—that of the mature beauty, poised, elegant, and patinaed. The old romanticism is still there—romanticism dies hard—but its patterns are more richly brocaded and darkly shaded. When she smiles, her lips curve with a rueful knowledge of the ways of the world.

Gothic—Swedish Gothic—and on her it looks good.

Fade-out 2:

Gott, *Ernst! Heaven Could Have Waited*

In one of his German-made films, he cast himself as a juggler who returns from a scene of wholesale slaughter to dance and joke again—"for the public wants to laugh."

This might have served as the epitaph for Ernst Lubitsch, who died in 1947, thus bringing to a close a Hollywood era that S. N. Behrman has called "a kind of Athens . . . as crowded with artists as Renaissance Florence." Many of them were refugees from Hitler's Germany: Max Reinhardt, Thomas Mann, Bruno Walter, Otto Klemperer, and Arnold Schoenberg. Garbo, and to a lesser extent, Dietrich, were a part of this circle, but it was Lubitsch who was its center—finding jobs, pulling strings, and seeking commissions for these displaced artists. He was the last of the Renaissance princes, holding together a court in exile in the new St. Helena—Hollywood.

It finished him off at fifty-five. His last few films had shown a noticeable decline in vitality: *That Uncertain Feeling, Heaven Can Wait,* and *Cluny Brown.* Even *To Be or Not to Be,* a satire on the Nazis which should have been a major *oeuvre,* didn't quite come off. The pesky fly in the ointment may have been the casting, which he no longer controlled. As with another great director of the period, Alfred Hitchcock, Lubitsch required a very polished, highly professional kind of actor or his films went off the track. He no longer had Herbert Marshall, Edward Everett Horton, Miriam Hopkins, Laura Hope Crews, Frank Morgan, and Fredric March to work with; instead he had Don

Ameche, Gene Tierney, Jennifer Jones, and Jack Benny, none of whom caught the Lubitsch beat. Something of the old Lubitsch returned in his very last picture, *That Lady in Ermine*, in which he worked with actors who understood him: Douglas Fairbanks, Jr., Reginald Gardiner, Cesar Romero, and, surprisingly, Betty Grable. Or maybe that was not so surprising—pretty girls always loved Ernst.

Ernst Lubitsch!

Gott!

The name above the title of a picture was a signature of quality for three decades. It meant a film that was a genuine pearl among the usual dime-store beads, a film that was carefully thought out, imaginatively structured, and wittily edited. You could be sure if it was Lubitsch.

It didn't really concern him whether the picture made money or not—although it is one of the Hollywood hallucinations to *think* they did not. Among the top-grossing pictures of all time, if one takes into account the erosion of the dollar, were such silents as *Old Heidelberg* (*The Student Prince*), in which he drew radiant performances from Ramon Novarro and Norma Shearer, and the Chevalier talkies. Lubitsch was, after all, the son of a Berlin shopkeeper, and he knew that, ultimately, art was just another form of commerce. Yet, his standards were the old-fashioned European ones—he gave you *quality*, even if it was just a Betty Grable musical. If he was not one of the great cinematic artists, he was the next best thing—a master artisan.

In appearance he was small, dark, merry, and brown—with a huge cigar planted dead center in his crooked, sardonic, gorgeously non-Aryan kisser. He looked like a gnome who was trying to look like a producer, but never quite made it. He was impeccably groomed, in the slightly too sharp continental manner—always creating the impression that he had just returned from a Beverly Hills *bar mitzvah*. Only, with Ernst, it might have been he who had just been *bar mitzvahed*.

If Dietrich was a Dresden doll, then Lubitsch was a kewpie doll, his patent-leather hair parted smoothly down the side, his eyes bulging with mischief, his postures bursting with wit.

Miriam Hopkins remembers him acting out *all* the roles in *Design for Living*, sometimes the girl, sometimes the boy, sometimes both at once. Pola Negri rapturously described him as "bee-*oot*-i-ful! Just so bee-*oot*-i-ful! How can any man be so bee-*oot*-i-ful?"

He, too, got his start with Reinhardt, but soon gravitated to the movie studios, which in Germany in 1915 were producing only war propaganda pictures. He made a series of one-reel comedy shorts—with titles like *My Wife, the Movie Star*—in which he sometimes starred. The comedy was broad but it was also human—based on the foibles of man. There was never a villain in a Lubitsch comedy unless that villain was pomposity. Man's greatest enemy is his own exaggerated sense of self-importance, Lubitsch told his audiences. He was the first to proclaim: MAKE LOVE, NOT WAR.

He might have gradually evolved into a German Charlie Chaplin were it not for the first of the great enchantresses— who else but the spellbinding Pola? Ufa had this volatile star under contract, but didn't want to unleash her before the public unless she was in the hands of a master. They begged Lubitsch, happily producing his own comedies, to direct her first picture, *Carmen*. After much persuasion, he agreed—and thus Ernst Lubitsch became the true perpetuator of the cinematic Venus. He would work with many of the great ones later in Hollywood —through the good times and the bad, through the fat years and the lean. His home was always open to them: "*Gott!* It's Greta! What a blezzing you are to these eyes, *mein* Greta! Come in! Come in! *Gott!* Come in and zit down, in a chair this time, Greta, not on the floor! *Gott!*" Then, he would pull out a chair for Garbo, sit down in it himself while The Divine One curled up on the floor, hold up his chin with his hands while his eyes danced, his cigar danced, the floor danced, the ceiling danced, the world danced.

It was that way with Lubitsch.
Gott!

His arrival in Hollywood was a calamity. He had been summoned by none other than Mary Pickford, who had seen *Carmen*, the first German film to be shown in the United States, as well as his subsequent historical spectacles, *Madame DuBarry* and *Anne Boleyn*—all of which were distinguished by a particular twist: After the crowd scene, one single solitary figure, with whom the audience could empathize, was left on the screen, forlornly surveying the havoc that man had brought on himself. Little Mary sensed that this was one of the great talents of her time, but she had grown accustomed to directors who let her direct herself (which she did most competently) and Lubitsch had other thoughts on the matter. They fought bitterly throughout the production of *Rosita,* two small bundles of energy poisoning one another with their rays. In later years, she could never bring herself to see a Lubitsch-made picture. It recalled the unbridled terror of producing *Rosita,* with a director who insisted on directing the picture.

Rosita was in the style of his German-made pageants, but, inspired by Chaplin's *A Woman of Paris,* Lubitsch began to evolve an entirely new form of cinema. On the surface, it was a variation of the French bedroom farce, with much opening and closing of doors; but, like the comedies of Oscar Wilde, it made some sardonic comment on the vagaries of *l'amour.* Love, to Lubitsch, was a kind of prison in which the loved one was the jailer. Just when you thought you were free and slammed a door (doors, in Lubitsch pictures, were as important as actors), you found yourself locked up in a new room that was even more of a prison than the old one. So, you went back to the old room—this time closing the door behind you softly, with resignation, with defeat, with sorrow. *The Marriage Circle, Forbidden Paradise, So This Is Paris,* his major silent comedies, all employed variations of this theme—but it was in the great Dietrich talkie, *Angel,* that it achieved its ultimate refinement. *Angel* is to Lubitsch what *The Tempest* was to Shakespeare—the final, calm retelling of recurrent themes that run through his work.

Beginning with his silent films, Lubitsch evolved new camera techniques—he shot from above, shot from below, swirled the camera as if it were a partner in a waltz, photographed shadows, did entire sequences in silhouette—thereby achieving startling juxtapositions in mood, place, and time. Fast rat-tat-tat-tat cutting contributed to his over-all design, which would, eventually, be advertised as "the Lubitsch touch." The slogan has been perpetuated over the years but, since his style is very similar to that of Pointillism in art, it might very well be called Lubitschism. Lubitschism did not only signify rhythmic camera angles and diamond-hard cutting; it was many other things besides. For example, you knew you were watching a Lubitsch picture even before the title flashed on the screen. In *The Merry Widow*, you first see a map of Europe, with a geographer frantically trying to locate the Graustark where the story takes place. Finally, he gives up, and the title flashes on the screen. Lubitschism could be a Cubistic way of filming a love scene: in *Trouble in Paradise* we first see the lovers embracing, next see their reflection in a mirror, and, finally, their shadows on a bed cover. Lubitschism could be droll characterization, such as that of the Commissars Razinin, Iranoff, and Buljanoff, in *Ninotchka*. Lubitschism could be a manner of conveying an idea cinematically, without dialogue, as in *Forbidden Paradise*, when he establishes that the ruler has great power by having a caller pass through countless doors, opened by innumerable flunkies. Lubitschism can be a sardonic turn of dialogue, as in *A Royal Scandal*, when Catherine the Great calls her Treasurer to the carpet for stealing from the state treasury. She doesn't mind his stealing small amounts, she tells him, but "Take it easy! Take it easy!"

Every movie buff has a favorite list of Lubitschisms—they could fill an entire volume—but a note here on how they were achieved.

By, in a word, *tyranny*.

Lubitsch dominated every facet of every picture he made. He sat over the set designs of Hans Drier, for example, to see that he got the Mondrianish white-on-white effect that he wanted, down to the tiniest detail. He prodded dress designer Travis Banton until his costumes—white satin against a dull white wall —were exactly perfect down to the last bow, the final hemline. He made writers like Ben Hecht write and rewrite until the final script was more Lubitsch than Hecht (or Noel Coward, from whose play *Design for Living* only a few snatches of dialogue were retained). He sat over the cutter, Carl Ruggiero, until each frame glistened with Lubitschism. He was, perhaps, the screen's supreme *auteur*.

Pola Negri was only the first of the many film stars whose entire careers he shaped. He can also be said to have created Chevalier when he cast him as a prince in the first large-scale operetta ever written especially for the movies, the classic *Love Parade*.

"The hero is a prince?" said Chevalier uncertainly. "You see *me* as a prince?"

"*Ja, ja*, Mauritz. Of course you are a printz," said Lubitsch, and, putting the French *boulevardier* into elegant combinations of uniforms and boots, and feathered headgear, transformed him into the world's dream prince.

Lubitsch's transformations of Dietrich and Garbo, at critical points in their careers, were equally masterful, but he could be wonderful with American actresses as well. Margaret Sullavan has never been more appealing on the screen than in his *The Shop around the Corner* (an underestimated jewel, which Lubitsch himself considered one of his major talkies), and Betty Grable comes through as highly polished brass in *That Lady in Ermine*. Other favorite Lubitsch blondes were Miriam Hopkins and Carole Lombard.

There is one final anecdote that tells us something more about Lubitsch, the man. At a Hollywood party, someone made a snide remark about the Warner Brothers's signing of Max Reinhardt to do *A Midsummer Night's Dream*. The berater did not know that Lubitsch himself was one of the powers behind the throne in arranging this assignment for the great director, whose property had been confiscated by the Nazis and who was living on slim rations in Hollywood. Nor could he know, the slob, that Hollywood would never have been Hollywood without Reinhardt, who first gave employment to many of its major stars, its directors, and its technicians. From the atelier of the great Reinhardt had sprung the geniuses of the theater, and now this clown thought it was hilarious that Warner Brothers was going "highbrow" and making *A Midsummer Night's Dream*.

Lubitsch listened to him, growing redder and redder in the face, and puffing longer and longer on his cigar. Finally, dramatically surrounded by clouds of smoke, his face crimson, his puppetlike body tense with rage, he spoke. If Hollywood, with all its money, could not afford to take a chance on the greatest director in the world, and have him film a production that had already been acclaimed one of the most beautiful examples of modern theater craft in the twentieth century—if Hollywood could not afford to do this for Max Reinhardt, who had given it so much—then it should just fold up its tents and go away. The clown was silenced.

As S. N. Behrman said, it was a terrible day for very many people when Ernst Lubitsch died.

Gott, Ernst!

Heaven could have waited.

Part III

Venus Goes Back to Europe

Chapter 15

The Rise of the Art Theaters

It was in 1950 that David Selznick told Ben Hecht, "Holly-wood's like Egypt, full of crumbling pyramids. It'll just keep on crumbling until finally the wind blows the last studio prop across the sands."

For all its *Gone with the Wind*ish melodrama, Selznick's prophecy seemed, on the surface, at le⸱⸱⸱, the shape of things to come. Audiences in the movie palaces had dropped to thirty million a week, almost half of what they were a decade earlier. Princely M-G-M was reporting losses for the first time in its history (in 1948 the deficit was $6.5 million), and 20th Century-Fox, sometimes called the studio with the nickelodeon mind, veered from its familiar musical and biography genres into the realm of historical spectacle—a course of action that would, in the *Cleopatra* year of 1962, result in a loss of $39 million.

The studios began to consider offers from industry for pur-chase of their lush green acres, as retrenchment became the order of the day. A sale to the Aluminum Company of America saved 20th-Fox from bankruptcy and, with the growth of Sperry Rand, gradually Lotus Land became known as the Electronic Brain of America, rather than its Movie Capital. As the population ex-plosion popped, klieg lights were the signal of the opening of a new supermarket rather than an old-style "pre-meer." Neon signs advertised funerals at discount rates instead of "Motion Pictures Are Your Best Entertainment." An aura of defeat, the creeping paralysis of fear, overtook the once fat and sassy "fourth largest industry in America."

Hollywood would spring back—bigger and maybe better than ever—but a decade of lean times had begun. Discarded were the bulk of the "B" pictures, which served as a training ground for young directors and film technicians; so, too, were the studio dramatic schools, where young contract players like Robert Taylor and Marilyn Monroe learned to walk and talk. A whole new contingent of foreign imports was brought in, in the fond hope that one of them might be a new Garbo, but none of them really seized the imagination as did Brigitte Bardot, who was making films in France, or Sophia Loren, who was based in Italy. The big Hollywood draws were the male stars—"Coop" and "Bogey" and Cary—and, a throwback to the heyday of Little Mary, *Miss* Doris Day. Like Pickford, Day dispensed sweetness and light and virtue, but there was an undertone of coy carnality in the lush ice cream soda décor of her wry comedies. Pursued by Rock Hudson, a cleverer actor than most people think—he used his Irish-American football-hero body with the same sensual effect as did the Italianate Valentino—Doris was really doing *Daddy Long-Legs* in a new Eisenhower Era guise. But the intellectuals, who went to see Pickford and Valentino, although they quietly smiled, recognized the Day-Hudson comedies as the vulgarization of a great popular American art form. They were the beginning of the end, for all their expert Technicolor and injections of *je m'en fous* Thelma Ritter dialogue.

Was it really the picture tube that caused Hollywood's decline? Actually, television with its hungry mouth (there were eighteen hours of programming to feed every day) saved Hollywood from extinction. Any old can of film that was lying around its shelves was converted into ready cash as it made its way to the Late, Late Show. The growing legion of old film buffs could see an entire survey of talkies, from the early 30's on down, in any given week. A flick of the wrist would bring you a Preston Sturges classic, *Sullivan's Travels* (1941); a Dietrich opus, *Shanghai Express* (1935); a Will Rogers masterpiece of Americana, *Steamboat Round the Bend* (1935); or even one of the all-time greats, Orson Welles's *The Magnificent Ambersons* (1942), as fresh as a daisy and just as rewarding to the eye. The rentals from these films helped Hollywood on its comeback trail—until, by 1965, it had become the bank for the entire foreign film industry.

No, one must probe more deeply to get at the root of illness that caused annual movie production to drop from six hundred pictures a year to a meager one hundred and fifty. More valid reasons may be higher taxes; higher production costs. In the early 30's a major film like Hepburn's *Morning Glory* was shot in seventeen days for a mere $217,000; two decades later, its shooting time would have tripled and its production costs would have increased tenfold. Furthermore, for all its superficial glitter, this imaginary 1952 version (actually *Morning Glory* was re-made, as were many of the hits of the 30's, in the 50's) would be a much inferior production. There was no young George Cukor around to direct it; no new Hepburn to star in it. The eagle-eyed, show-wise old moguls were dying out; the Golden Age was drawing to a close.

Then, too, congressional investigations had turned the once self-possessed and graceful débutante that Hollywood had be-come in the late 1920's into a shrieking, sniveling ingenue from a *Dracula* picture. Hollywood was scared shitless. An unattrac-tive portrait of a banker would cause a producer to shelve a scenario and fire the writer; war was portrayed as a manly art, practiced by an elite group of aging young men of predominantly WASP persuasion (although there might be a comic Italian or a studious Jew or a "nice nigger," for a bit of leavening); even the mention of the color "red," was suspect. As Sheilah Graham recounts in *The Rest of the Story*, "To be accused of being a Communist in that period of frightening hysteria was a one-way ticket to oblivion." In one of her gossip columns, Miss Graham mentioned that Peter Lawford was wearing bright red socks and Elizabeth Taylor "a flaming red sweater." One of the leading West Coast papers immediately took this as a clue that Miss Graham herself had turned red.

This was comic, of course, but also destructive to good picture making. Who could you trust? What red might be lurking in

the woodpile? And, if it wasn't a red, it might be someone with
"moral turpitude," a disease more deadly than leprosy. At the
height of this madness, a quite fascinating Swedish actress, Anita
Bjork, who had made a sensation in a foreign film, *Miss Julie*,
and might very well have had the magnetism of the great super-
stars, was brought to America by Hitchcock to appear in *I
Confess*. When it was learned that she was traveling with an
illegitimate child *and* a lover, she was sent right back to depraved
Sweden. An unsullied American star, Anne Baxter, was given her
role, and ruined the picture. (It might very well have been the
greatest that Hitchcock ever made, a serious probing of the
limits of Catholicism, giving it a philosophical depth that was far
beyond the usual cops-and-robbers chase that Old Hitch was
handcuffed to, but no one will ever know.)

It is small wonder that Hollywood turned increasingly to
"the trite and the true"—or to the sure bet, a movie version of
a hit Broadway play or musical. "The play's the thing" became
one of the war cries of that embattled era—as the price of a hit
rose to astronomical figures. This trend had started in the 30's,
when *Lady in the Dark* fetched $285,000 and *The Man Who
Came to Dinner*, $250,000. In the 40's the price had boomed to
$1 million, Harry Cohn's payment for the rights to film *Born
Yesterday*, and now it would keep going onward and upward
until it reached the stratospheric heights of *My Fair Lady*, which
the fair Brothers Warner acquired for $5.5 million, plus a per-
centage of the profits. That may stand as the all-time record,
until some Broadway *savant* makes a musical comedy of *Lincoln's
Doctor's Dog*.

The movie theaters that suffered the most in this transitional
era were, inevitably, the large pleasure domes, situated on high-
taxed prime real estate sites, right in the center of the metropolis.
In the 1940's they were filled by a Hoboken, New Jersey,
wunderkind, Frank Sinatra, who became the No. 1 "in person"
attraction of the decade. His headquarters in New York was the
Paramount on Times Square, the scene of the celebrated Colum-
bus Day Riot of 1944. On this eventful day Sinatra's bobby-
soxed fans began to queue up at 4:30 a.m., each armed with a

hamper of peanut-butter sandwiches and an extra supply of panties. When they were admitted, some hours later, they dashed down the aisles of the still-darkened theater to get ringside seats for a close-up view of their idol. Since they dared not leave their seats, the extra panties came in handy, as did the peanut-butter sandwiches. They were there for the day.

And what a day! Those who could not get in demonstrated outside by smashing windows. Traffic on the world's busiest thoroughfare came to a dead halt. The screeching of ambulances could be heard as they arrived to cart away the wounded and the fainting. It was the biggest thing of its kind since The Children's Crusade, reaching its grand climax when the bow-tied crooner, he of the lean and hungry look, arrived on stage. In a mass, these depression-begot and war-reared Lolitas rose and screamed and waved dampened panties. Up there was their Saviour, a man who understood the hellish indignity of being born female and cursed with a love that forever remained unrequited. *All or nothing at all,* he crooned into the microphone, as they writhed and screamed in ecstasy. The handsome old crystal chandeliers shook; Adolphe Zukor shook; Caruso, in his grave, shook.

Also shaking were the fifty extra ushers, fortified with bands of tough, broken-nosed New York policemen. None of them could do a damned thing about it until, after eight weeks, Sinatra finally left town to tour pleasure domes across the land. To Philadelphia, to Boston, to St. Louis traveled the *wunderkind,* leaving a trail of desolated theater seats and strep throats behind him.

It seems, in retrospect, a publicity scheme that just got out of hand, but it was the last time the great movie palaces would be jam-packed. By 1950, declining attendance forced their managers to drop stage shows entirely, concentrating instead on highly promotable pictures. But even carnylike exploitation didn't help. Audiences preferred to see movies in their neighborhood theaters, in the new drive-ins or, in larger cities, "on the movie strips"— entire city blocks of third- and fourth-run theaters offering double and triple features around the clock. In New York, "the strip" was situated on West 42nd Street, in what was once a block of elegant showplaces whose very names conjured up the great days of the American stage—the New Amsterdam, the Lyric, the Apollo, and the Selwyn. These architectural jewels were modeled after London's West End playhouses, and even today retain dim echoes of their former glory. Particularly notable is the New Amsterdam, where the greatest of the Ziegfeld *Follies* were staged. Time cannot fade the Joseph Urban-like curve of its staircases, or the lobby friezes of J. Hinton Perry, which portray scenes from *Faust*, *A Midsummer Night's Dream*, and *Tristan and Isolde*. The New Amsterdam was a great favorite of Edmund Wilson, who pleasantly recalled its green peacocks, gilded panels, and luxurious haze, as well as the photos of *Follies* girls that once hung above the staircase, "where they gave the effect of a gallery of the more illustrious graduates of some rather smart college."

But television, the drive-ins, and higher taxes were not the only villains in the decline and fall of the great pleasure domes. A more subtle, but probably equally important, factor was the coming into maturity of millions of Babs and Bob Babbitts during World War II and the postwar years. They had been to college; they had emigrated to the large cities to find jobs on magazines, as junior executives in industry, or in fashionable interior decorating offices, where they hobnobbed with Mrs. Henry Ford; and they thought most of the Hollywood product strictly low-grade camp, except for Busby Berkeley and Bogey, who were high-grade camp. They were attractive, restless, bored— and searching for something, they didn't quite know what. For some, the answers might be found in psychoanalysis; others would explore wilder shores of love, withdrawing into propriety when they found their feet getting wet; and it was not at all unusual to have the son of the vice president of a Pittsburgh steel company tell you over a martini at the King Cole Room that he had just joined the Communist Party.

Such interests were fleeting and fragmentary, for these post-Scott Fitzgeralds and pseudo-Thomas Wolfes and would-be Edna St. Vincent Millays were bourgeois to the bone, and they would put away their toys in time and go home to gingerbread mansions in Shaker Heights or Sewickley or Grosse Pointe, or variations thereof. But meanwhile they weren't buying Joan Crawford, although they'd walk a mile for Anna Magnani. And they would no more think of going to the Roxy than they would visit Grant's Tomb. The theaters they went to were small, select "art houses," situated in New York in the East and West 50's, and, in other cities, in the areas adjacent to a college or art museum.

These theaters coincided, of course, with the popularity of the new foreign films, for it was here that Bob fell in love with Jeanne Moreau and Babs was thrilled to pieces by Jean-Paul Belmondo. The admission prices were high, but this was a locked audience, with money. The décor was subdued, almost Spartan, but it gave these small theaters an intimate clublike feeling. If you were a foreign film buff, you recognized one another at sight; you read James Agee and, later, Andrew Sarris; and you knew, inside you, that if you lived long enough you would inherit the earth and that it would become a better place.

The rate growth of these new art theaters spiraled upward— from a hundred a year in the 1950's to four times that number by 1965—while eight thousand or so "regular theaters" became supermarkets or boarded up their doors. As they grew in number, so did their audiences become more diversified. Everyone— everyone who was old enough to be admitted, that is—went to see Brigitte Bardot, who became the queen of the art theaters, just as Vilma Banky had been the queen of the pleasure domes. Everyone went to see Marcello Mastroianni—who was to Babs what John Gilbert had been to Mrs. Babbitt. Everyone went to see Sophia Loren, just for the sheer pleasure of looking at a beautiful woman, a pleasure denied movie-goers since the heyday of Hedy Lamarr.

So rapid was the growth of these new art theaters that they seemed to spring up overnight like mushrooms. One of the most famous ones in New York was in such a rush to open that its entrepreneur did not discover until the morning of its premiere (before a select audience that included the mayor) that the architect had neglected to specify sufficient electrical current for the film to be projected. While elaborate makeshift cables were being strung in the lobby, the world-famous artist who had been commissioned to paint the murals quietly put finishing touches on his impressionistic nymphs and satyrs. By 8 p.m., when the limousines began to arrive with international celebrities, they were still wondering if there was enough juice to feed the projector. A host of lovely ladies was rushed to the lobby with glasses of vintage champagne and instructions to "get 'em drunk . . . feel 'em . . . fool 'em . . . do anything to keep 'em up out of the theater until we get enough juice to run the &4??u947c.s% projector!" At 9:30 a tipsy audience sat down to watch an exquisite *pastorale* which had won some kind of prize at Cannes, blissfully unaware that they had been waylaid.

In New York this theater, which shall remain forever nameless, was joined by hundreds of others that stretched the length of Manhattan Island, and spilled out into the surrounding boroughs and suburbs, at the very time the great pleasure domes were closing down. Some of them were "double-deckers" (twin theaters, on alternate floors), an architectural design first explored in the 30's, but which lay dormant until the great new art theater building boom of the 50's and 60's. These were built not only by chains like Rugoff and Walter Reade, but by Loew's, who converted one of their old Broadway showplaces, the State, into Loew's State I and II. Also in the Broadway area is the city's first triplex theater, the Orleans/Penthouse/Cinerama, carved out of the innards of the old Mark Strand, where talking pictures were first introduced. More recent conversions include the Ciné Lido, a 575-seat theater which occupies the site of a once famed night club, the Latin Quarter, and the very handsome Cinemas I and II, which have won designing awards for their open façades, eye-level movie screens and continental seating arrangements. (There is no center aisle, but the rows of seats are set far enough apart so that no one has to stand up to let a latecomer pass through.)

These theaters, for all their ultra-modern, severely contemporary décor, are often costly—even more costly than the most grandiose of the pleasure domes, where the effects were achieved with plaster of Paris, as often as not. Almost all of them are inspired by the auditorium of the Museum of Modern Art, opened on May 10, 1939, and are indebted to the designs of its architects,

Philip L. Goodwin and Edward D. Stone. In this superb theater, actually little more than a shoebox in the Museum's cellar, but giving the feeling of so much light and space and air that it might as well be suspended from the moon, the Museum pioneered its daily film showings of film classics. It is still filled with intense young cinéasts, playing hooky from their duties so they can catch rare showings of Noel Coward's *Cavalcade*, Lubitsch's *Ninotchka*, King Vidor's *Hallelujah!*, or Kenneth Anger's *Fireworks*.

Fortunately, though, not all the pleasure domes were doomed as the art theaters flourished. Every major city has retained a handful, which play road-show attractions like *Camelot* and *Star!* on a reserved-seat basis. Others have been restored to their original 1920's glory, and are used as legitimate theaters or concert halls—notably the St. Louis, an extravaganza of the silent screen days, which has become Powell Symphony Hall, one of the glories of Missouri. Designed by Rapp & Rapp of Chicago, a firm that also did New York's Paramount, it was one of the great buildings of 1925 and its preservation and second life as a concert hall have made old pleasure-dome lovers ecstatic. Its magnificent seventy-foot central ceiling dome looks handsomer than ever as it glitters with gold and crystal. In New York, another happy restoration was that of the Palace on Broadway. This house, originally the shrine of vaudeville, became a movie theater in the 1930's, and remained one until the 1960's, when the Nederlanders, a Detroit theatrical family, restored it to its original baroque design. Uncovered by renovator Ralph Alswang, as he stripped away the "Ruby Keeler moderne" façade that was installed when it became a movie theater, were some ornate ironwork, an elaborately sculpted ceiling, marble balustrades, and crystal chandeliers. Today it plays musicals like *Sweet Charity* and *George M!* as well as movies.

The trend toward preservation and restoration continues, with Pittsburgh's Loew's Penn currently being talked about as the new home for the Pittsburgh Symphony. Pleasure dome buffs, elated at such developments, now even have their own magazine, *Marquee*, published by the Theatre Historical Society in Washington, D.C., and filled with illustrations of the San Francisco Fox and other movie palaces. Leafing through its pages is a sure way to shed a nostalgic tear—particularly for those who are not quite at home with the "Swedish Gymnasium" school of theater architecture.

But the intimate "art theater" will undoubtedly remain the cinematic shape of things to come, for the next generation at least.

Movies are a strong life force, and they create the showplaces that are just right for them. As the century turned, these were the nickelodeons, functional and simple, and just the right setting for the first of the Essanay one-reelers. Next came the renovated vaudeville houses, where for a dime you saw the Griffith two-reelers plus a stage show. These evolved, as films evolved, into the magnificent era of the movie cathedrals, with elaborate stage presentations surrounding the silent classics of Banky and Valentino and Negri and Pickford and Chaplin and Fairbanks. Then, as the film industry geared itself for smaller, more discriminating audiences, came the art theaters—just the right habitat for the Venus of today—and of tomorrow.

Chapter 16

Zsa-Zsa-Zsa-Zsa-Zsa—and Others

There would be a new wave of foreign imports in that brackish Hollywood period which followed World War II and led to the crumbling of the pyramids.

These lovely ladies, like the post-World War I enchantress immigration, came from Germany and Austria (Hildegarde Neff, Maria Schell, and Romy Schneider); from France (Leslie Caron, Corinne Calvet, Denise Darcel, Capucine, Juliette Greco, and Christine Carere); from Sweden (May Britt and Signe Hasso); from Italy (Pier Angeli and Anna Maria Alberghetti); from Poland (Bella Darvi); and, last but not least, from Hungary (Zsa-Zsa-Zsa-Zsa-Zsa).

By *no* means least.

Everyone had a special name for her. To Conrad Hilton she was Georgia; to George Sanders she was Cokaline; to some television colleagues she was Gabby. The world at large knew her as Zsa Zsa Gabor, and they came to know her quite well— for she was the last of the red-hot continental mamas, the Pola Negri variety, who were in the headlines as often as not. As a matter of fact, those days when you pick up the morning paper and don't find Zsa-Zsa-Zsa-Zsa-Zsa embroiled in some exploit or other are apt to be distinct letdowns—you might as well phone the office, fake a sore throat, and stay home and have another cup of coffee. Tomorrow will be better.

Thanks to Zsa Zsa, the dreary 50's and the depressing 60's had a kind of *Merry Widow* lilt—or should one call it a tilt?

Her life and times reached a kind of crescendo when Representative Wayne Hays of the United States Congress—it sounds, sometimes, as if those boys just don't have enough to do—stood up on the floor and called Zsa Zsa "the most expensive courtesan since Madame de Pompadour." Having spoken his mind, the Ohio congressman sat right down again—while the pressroom broke out in pandemonium. Ohio had declared war on Zsa Zsa—which was equivalent to shooting paper wads at a solid gold jeep.

This impregnable fortress was one of three beautiful daughters —Eva and Magda are the other two—born into a solid Budapest household. (Jewelry, darlings.) She always thought Eva was prettier; but it was Zsa Zsa who was discovered by tenor Richard Tauber when, at the budding age of sixteen, she was vacationing in Vienna. Tauber had just composed an operetta, *The Singing Dream*, and was searching Vienna for a *jeune fille* to play his daughter, when he spotted Zsa Zsa at an ice-skating rink. (An ice-skating rink, darlings.) But, though everyone agreed that she was a beauty, it soon became evident at the rehearsals that Zsa Zsa could neither sing nor dance, and they were about to throw her out of the show—silly boys, *anyone* can sing and dance!—when Mama Jolie Gabor came to the rescue.

Mama Jolie has a way of turning up at the *nth* hour, when all seems lost, and rescuing her gorgeous daughters from flood, famine, and fire—not to mention stingy financiers, about to discard one of her loved ones without making a just settlement.

Anyway, Mama Jolie would have none of it. They had plucked Zsa Zsa from the ice-skating rink, and put her in *The Singing Dream*, and in *The Singing Dream* she would stay! Backed with such fierce mother love, Zsa Zsa stayed—and, of course, almost walked off with the show. Vienna, which knows a beautiful woman when it sees one, came and was conquered. So what if she wasn't really a professional?

It is this quality—perhaps in later years a put-on—that has made Zsa Zsa Gabor so appealing to a vast public. She remains the talented amateur, dazzling you with her charm rather than her expertise, and letting you know that she knows it. She shares a joke with her audience—they are helping her pull one over;

they are her partners in crime. It is a very human and warm quality that few really have; Zsa Zsa can get under your skin.

Audiences felt like this about her from the beginning—including a composer, old enough to be not only her father but her grandfather, who fell into the habit of sitting in the first row and making moon-eyes at Zsa Zsa. She fell in love with him, but he was married, of course, and had an "invalid wife," so she went back to Budapest and proposed to a gentleman in the Turkish Embassy. Zsa Zsa was not the kind of girl who waited to be proposed to; if a gentleman interested her, she let him know it. Later this approach would net her two other husbands— hotelman Conrad Hilton and actor George Sanders—who never quite knew what hit them until it was all over.

These three marriages all had their moments—Zsa Zsa had a unique way of remaining on speaking terms with her ex-spouses—but a *quelque chose* was missing from her life until she met Porfirio Rubirosa, better known as "Rubi" to newspaper readers.

The Dominican Republic's foremost export, next to sugar, had sufficient time left after winning trophies at polo to devote to Jet Set Amour—Barbara Hutton being just one in a long list of ladies who succumbed to his manly scent of good horses, good leather, and good cologne. But, as Zsa Zsa was to learn, such a man was often an incurable romantic and could fall deeply, even tragically, in love. (My God, he really *believed* it, darlings!) She was to learn the ferocity of Rubi's passion when he blackened her eye on the eve of her debut in Las Vegas (a picture of Zsa Zsa in a black eye-patch surely appeared in every newspaper in the world) and later, when he flew a $200,000 plane that Miss Hutton had given him as a wedding present to be at her side (well, that was that, said the practical Miss Hutton, and promptly divorced him).

The Zsa Zsa-Rubi affair was rivaled only by the Ingrid-Roberto affair in newspaper coverage, and may have garnered more space than any of the recent wars. Day after day, week after week, month after month bulletins were issued recording each lovers' spat, each reconciliation, each hint of marriage, each threat of final separation.

When, finally, Representative Hays got into the act by comparing our Zsa Zsa to Madame Pompadour, no one was very surprised—after all, her public image was light years removed from Rebecca of Sunnybrook Farm. Still, it seems to have been an ungentlemanly thing to do—all Zsa Zsa did was accept a Mercedes Benz and a chinchilla coat from General Trujillo at the time the Dominican Republic was given a loan of $1.3 million by the United States government. (Don't be so uptight, darlings!)

Anyway, her ·doting fans would remain true to Zsa Zsa, although she never again found so good a role as that of Jane Avril in John Huston's *Moulin Rouge*. That was the film in which the color photography, supervised by Vertès, caught her at the height of her beauty—all peaches and cream and glints of gold—and in which she sang the title song in what became the high point of the picture. And John Huston, that old meanie, thought she would ruin the picture.

Hah!

None of the other of the new crop of enchantresses would bring back the good old glamour days as did Zsa Zsa. She was the last of the Movie Queens—just as Leslie Caron, with her windswept hair and her Little Orphan Annie eyes, pointed to a new trend.

It was director Vincente Minnelli who first saw the movie possibilities in this Parisian ballerina—whose mother, by the way, was born in Kansas. She was whisked from the Ballets Champs Elysées into *An American in Paris*, a musical with a Gershwin score in which she sang and danced *Our Love Is Here to Stay* with Gene Kelly. The title roles of *Lili* and *Fanny* followed, but she may have been at her best in a sensitive British soap opera, *The L-Shaped Room*, in which she played, accurately and with compassion, an unwed mother.

But fine acting and good dancing don't make a Venus—Leslie didn't have the Dietrich *pizzazz*, nor did a quartet of other French beauties. Denise Darcel, a soubrettish type, and Corinne Calvet, a tall, statuesque beauty, appeared in a number of films of the late 40's and 50's—Denise in *To the Victor*, *Westward the Women*, and *Vera Cruz*; Corinne in *On the*

Riviera and *Peking Express*, an unsuccessful remake of *Shanghai Express*, one of the high points of the Dietrich era. The bravura of the *prima donna assoluta* was missing, however, as it was in Christine Carere, who played a fictionized Françoise Sagan in Françoise Sagan's *A Certain Smile*, and in Capucine (Germaine Lefebvre), who starred in a screen treatment of Nelson Algren's *A Walk on the Wild Side.*

Two Darryl F. Zanuck protegées, Bella Darvi (Bella Wegier) and Juliette Greco, also failed to shine brightly enough to win a permanent perch in the high Hollywood heavens. Miss Darvi, introduced with P. T. Barnum fanfare in the first Cinemascope film, *The Robe*, got lost among the camels in this kitchen-calendarlike Biblical spectacle, and Miss Greco, likewise hooplaed in *The Sun Also Rises* and *Roots of Heaven*, failed to register a movie personality, although you sensed there was a real someone there somewhere. They were costly litmus papers which didn't turn rosy pink when dipped in the acid of popular taste, despite all Darryl's Horsemen and all Darryl's Men.

A failure to come through as a recognizable cinematic entity also marred the careers of two Swedish ladies—May Britt (Maybritt Wilkens) and Signe Hasso. Miss Hasso, a most versatile and talented actress, appeared in *The Seventh Cross*, *The House on 92nd Street*, and *A Double Life*, and Miss Britt starred in a remake of another Dietrich classic, *The Blue Angel* (this time Dietrich threatened to sue), but they never stopped traffic on Main Street. The lovely May, however, did create a movie milestone when she married Sammy Davis, Jr.—it was the first interracial marriage among stellar performers in Hollywood history, and it sold a lot of tabloids, if not movie tickets.

The Italian entries fared better—at least Anna Maria Alberghetti was *someone*, even if you didn't like her, as was M-G-M's Pier Angeli. But compared to the magnetic Magnani, the luscious Lollobrigida, the super-luscious Sophia Loren—the *real* Italians—they were just so much sweetness and light.

The German-Austrians—Hildegarde Neff, Maria Schell, and Romy Schneider—were just as delectable; just as talented (Miss Schell's Gruschenka in *The Brothers Karamazov* was a good one); although they proved to be not so evanescent.

But, why didn't one or two of these lovely and gifted ladies take fire, as had Garbo? Anyone who has seen Denise Darcel sweep into P. J. Clarke's Third Avenue saloon, with old ladies selling flowers and a convoy of escorts trailing her like ducks, can testify that among these imports were some authentic sirens. As actresses, they may have been better trained than their predecessors—Romy Schneider, for example, comes from a famous European theatrical family, and is highly skillful. Their publicity build-ups were often just as costly as Garbo's—Zanuck left no kopeck unspent to promote Darvi—but he might as well have dumped the money in the Pacific.

The answer is that, as often as not, these beauties reflected the genteel mannerisms that had become commonplace in Hollywood with the passing of the old guard. And the relentless and probing camera demolished their sugary façades, just as it does any untruth. A synthetic cinema queen has the same relationship to a real one as applesauce has to a McIntosh apple. The bite, the flavor, the zest are gone. The public just stopped caring about them, and stayed home and watched Milton Berle.

When Brigitte Bardot burst on the scene, they started coming back. They went back to see Signoret and Mercouri and Loren.

Suddenly, everything that was happening in the movies was happening in Europe. Hollywood, cut off from the brilliant and controversial talents of its time, went into decline. The witch hunters had won a Pyrrhic victory.

Chapter 17

The Night They Invented Brigitte Bardot

Back in the 1930's, Paris had become the movie capital of Europe—its cinematic Maginot Line held by several dozen directors and stars whose films proved highly exportable— among the directors: Jean Cocteau (*The Blood of the Poet*), Marcel Pagnol (the *Marius* trilogy), René Clair (*Under the Roofs of Paris*), Jean Renoir (*Grand Illusion*), Julien Duvivier (*Un Carnet de Bal*), Sacha Guitry (*Pearls of the Crown*), Marcel Carné (*Port of Shadows*), and Jacques Feyder (*Carnival in Flanders*); among the actors: Louis Jouvet, Raimu, Jean Gabin, Françoise Rosay, Arletty, Pierre Fresnay, Jean-Louis Barrault, and Danièlle Darrieux.

Paris's rise in preeminence coincided with the fall of the great Ufa studios in Berlin, but, with the Occupation, French film production came to a standstill.

After the war, the French cinema, like the Maginot Line, found itself riddled with holes. Gabin and Renoir and Clair were among those who had sought refuge in Hollywood. Others, like Guitry, had the stigma of collaboration attached to their names. The rest were silenced by the Armageddon. France's greatest export, next to champagne, was in a state of shock.

France could endure the humiliation of being a second-class world power—but a second-class cultural power—never! Some-how, government funds were found to put the industry back on its feet. With typical French foresight, a part of these funds were allocated to a new generation of cinéastes, many of them critics on intellectual weeklies, who were encouraged to make their own films. Thus, the celebrated *nouvelle vague* came into being.

A revived French film industry would soon be making pictures —erudite, complex, stylistic, contemporary—that ranked with those of Italy's Fellini, Rossellini, and De Sica in world prestige. Italy's postwar supremacy in the foreign film market would thus be challenged and, with the invention of Brigitte Bardot, so, too, would Magnani, the first postwar enchantress.

Yes, Virginia, Brigitte Bardot was invented, just as Chanel No. 5 was invented and Dior's New Look was invented. But, then, every great star was. Garbo was invented by Stiller; Dietrich by von Sternberg; and even Anna Sten by Sam Goldwyn. Brigitte Bardot was invented by Roger Vadim, but was taken up by the *nouvelle vague* when Vadim passed on to other inventions, including her own sister, Mijanou, and, later, Jane Fonda. Everyone was condescending about it, but there is no question that her opalescent *derrière*, photographed in radiant Technicolor and projected in Cinemascope, put French films back on the map. Her supremacy was rather short-lived, a bottom being, *au fond*, a bottom, but she was marvelous fun—even if it was preordained that she would go out of fashion like the hoola-hoop.

Her story, like that of all the great enchantresses, has a quality of fiction about it—indeed, she sometimes appears in the slim, fashionable novels of Sagan, thinly disguised; and Simone de Beauvoir has written about her directly and openly. She was born Brigitte Bardot, the daughter of Louis Bardot, an industrialist, and Anne-Marie Bardot, a society lady who ran a dress shop for her own amusement. The types are familiar (Louis B. Mayer's "beautiful people in beautiful pictures"), as is the locale, the handsome Passy district of Paris. Brigitte had the obligatory governess, the obligatory lessons in ballet, and the obligatory annual vacations in St. Tropèz. She would soon have made the obligatory well-connected marriage of her class, and would never have been heard from again, were it not for one thing: The random hand of God sometimes pauses to create a beautiful mortal, a perfect specimen, to remind us of what He had in mind when He fashioned the human race. God's hand paused with Brigitte. At fifteen she was so strikingly pretty that her mother's fashion acquaintances begged her to allow Brigitte to model, to pose for a fashion layout, to appear on the cover of a magazine. Madame Bardot, unbeknownst to Monsieur Bardot, busy back at Bardot et Cie (chemicals), consented. After all, Brigitte would be among friends.

Then one day at a director's studio she met The Young Man Who Would Take Her from Heaven and Plunge Her into Hell. (Note to Casting Director: a twenty-two-year-old Anthony Quinn, if they come like that any more.) His name was Roger Vadim Plemiannikov, the son of Russian emigrés, and he was just getting established in the movies. The attraction between the Blonde Pedigreed Kitten and the Mixed-Pedigree Cat was instant and intense, to the horror of the Bardots, who finally said she would have to wait until she was eighteen. (If she had been eighteen, they would have said twenty-one: The Bardots of the world are like that.)

Young Vadim (he soon dropped the Plemiannikov in deference to billing) set about remaking this impressionable but very proper upper-middle-class girl into the cinema's first Baby Beatnik. Concluding that Dietrich-style glamour was dead and Michèle Morgan-like decorum was on its way out, he foresaw the teeny-bopper (indeed, with Bardot he *styled* her) as the new sex symbol. Off went her lovely *jeune fille de Passy* frocks; on went blue jeans. Her coiffure was reshaped into a studiedly tangled sailor's knot, and her *Elle*-ish cover-girl smile was replaced with a perpetual *Partisan Review* pout. As Françoise Sagan has noted, the effect was electrifying on the Left Bank, but film producers —the voluptuous Martine Carole was the big star of that day— were wary. Why would movie-goers pay money to look at a teen-ager who was unkempt and unhappy when they could see the smiling Martine's breasts bobbing up and down in her bath like apples?

When she was eighteen, Brigitte married Vadim, but there would be more bit roles and lean pantries ahead of them. The

new postwar Sex Kitten was ahead of her time. But her time
would come, in 1956, with *And God Created Woman*, which
established Vadim as the most commercially successful of the
young French directors and Brigitte as the top-ranking Venus
of the late 1950's.

Simone de Beauvoir, in her celebrated essay, "Brigitte Bardot
and the Lolita Syndrome," admitted that God may have created
woman but she made it clear that Vadim created Bardot. In her
first starring picture, Vadim posed his wife in a series of provocative sex tableaux that included a near-rape and an explicit
wedding-night scene, and ended with a voluptuous solo dance.
But the scene that had them gasping at the neighborhood Bijou
was pure Rabelais: Brigitte keeps her shy, blushing young husband (Jean-Louis Trintignant) occupied in the bedroom while
his parents are celebrating at the wedding party downstairs. When
hunger overtakes them, it is Brigitte, dressed in a bathrobe, who
marches downstairs and calmly fills a plate with food. Then
silently, contemptuously, she marches back upstairs, where
the bedroom athletics are resumed. It is a classical bit of ribaldry,
deftly done, which also depicted the current generation gap
on the screen for the first time.

That it would shock a generation that grew up on Valentino
and Clara Bow and *Our Dancing Daughters* seemed improbable,
but it did. *And God Created Woman*, which grossed $4 million
in the United States alone, was forever being protested by the
women's clubs, seized by the police, or banned by a court order.
When it reopened, the lines around the Bijou only grew longer
—and longer. It would be good to report that this little French-
made quickie (it was financed by Columbia Pictures only because
Curt Jurgens agreed to appear in it for fifteen shooting days;
it was scripted in four days) was only the beginning of a brilliant career. But the truth of the matter is that, though her subsequent films were better scripted, better directed, and more
carefully produced, Bardot was never again so convincing. *And
God Created Woman* was one of those good-bad pictures that
for all their flaws hit some vital nerve. It remains, in its naïve way,
a testament of youth.

Bardot divorced Vadim when the picture was over, and her rather sensational press coverage began. A headline-making affair with Trintignant was followed by other affairs, other marriages, as well as two pathetic attempts at suicide. These events followed one another so fast and furiously that soon everything got a little blurred. All her husbands and all her lovers somehow fused into a single image: They were uniformly handsome, uniformly broad-shouldered, and uniformly shaggy-haired. They looked quite nice in their bikinis, but it was impossible to tell them apart.

Her pictures, too, suffered from a lack of individuality. Although they were made by the best directors—Julien Duvivier, Henri-Georges Cluzot, Claude Autant-Lara, and Jean-Luc Godard—in recollection they fuse into a *Guernica*-like montage: a bit of thigh here, a leg there, a disjointed breast there. Like her love affairs, this may be because they were so frequent: At the height of her popularity, in the late 50's, it was not unusual for three Bardot pictures to be showing in one city at the same time. You had a choice; you went to see Bardot or you stayed home and watched *I Love Lucy*.

Certain episodes do linger in the mind—in *A Woman Like Satan* she did a flamenco dance in the nude; in *The Truth* she danced under a sheet to a jazz record; in—what was it?—she walked blissfully naked to the bathroom. These scenes were interjections that frequently stopped the flow of the narrative. Like the early 30's musicals, when everything came to a halt so that Dick Powell could sing, in a Bardot movie everything stopped for the obligatory nude scenes. Future film historians should enjoy tabulating them.

Bardot was closer to Dietrich than any of the other sirens of the previous generation, in that she was more of a personality and a fashion influence than she was an actress. Brigitte hairdos sent the hairdressers into higher income brackets, and high-fashion houses came out with Brigitte blue jeans. "B.B." also popularized the man's button-down shirt, worn as a blouse, and ballet-slipper pumps. When she went barefoot in one picture, a hit Broadway play of the following season was *Barefoot in the Park*. *Mademoiselle*, *Seventeen*, and *Glamour* no longer featured smiling young ladies on their covers, but pouty *gamines*.

Hundreds of Hollywood starlets simulated the beatnik look or point of view, among them Piper Laurie and Tuesday Weld. It became the fashion to be interviewed by Rex Reed dressed in torn jeans with a shaggy-haired lover lying at your elbow. Any Greenwich Village sidewalk café was filled with at least a dozen startling duplicates of Brigitte, and the Brigitte Bardot look even was slowly worming itself into the better finishing schools.

"B.B." watchers reckon 1958 as the big Bardot year, when her popularity was at its peak. That was the year that the *New York Times* called her "a phenomenon that has to be seen to be believed" and that her photos began to sell on the Black Market in Moscow.

By 1963, though, almost everyone was staying home and watching *Gunsmoke*. That was the year that Andrew Sarris, a critic who adopts unsuccessful pictures as if they were stray kittens, went to bat for *Contempt*. In his influential column in the *Village Voice* he urged Manhattan exhibitors to book this neglected film—but the rub was that he was concerned about it not because of Bardot but because it was directed by Jean-Luc Godard. That looked like the kiss of death for B.B., as far as being a popular enchantress went. Then, as if this were not enough, Frank Sinatra, who had talked for years of co-starring in a film with Brigitte, suddenly stopped talking about it. Bardot is still around, of course—long may she live—but she is no longer lining them up at the Bijou—or even the Art!

In addition to Dietrich, there was, at the height of her fame, a bit of Negri in Bardot. This came out in the droll interviews she gave to the press: "Sex and marriage are two different things," she reminded a reporter on the *Police Gazette*, who had presumably confused them. When a French reporter asked her what she liked most about a man, she paused for a moment, pouted prettily, and said: "His teeth." To a Milanese journalist who asked her why she appeared in the nude so often, she replied, "But, after all, I'm so beautiful!"

Yes, Bardot had style, and temperament, and carried her movie personality into her personal life—or was it the other way around?

As in Pirandello's *Six Characters in Search of an Author*, no one quite knew.

It made her fascinating for a time, but then the original Venus de Milo managed to preserve her allure for one hundred and twenty generations. *Or*, a romp in the nude may be quite continental, but a tunic is still a Venus's best friend.

Dissolve 6:

The New Directors

Roger Vadim was only one of a number of clever young men who put the director to the forefront of the star as "the art film" began to reach larger and larger audiences. So popular did some of these films become that, in English-dubbed versions, many of them played the pleasure domes and drive-ins, after running a year or more at the art houses. Federico Fellini's *La Dolce Vita* is, to date, the one that leads them in box-office returns—taking in $7.5 million in domestic rentals, and now flourishing on television. Trailing it is Michelangelo Antonioni's *Blow-Up* ($6 million), and Jules Dassin's Greek-made *Never on Sunday* ($4 million). In 1968, Vadim's *Barbarella* ($2.5 million) and the Swedish-made *Elvira Madigan* ($2 million plus) were listed among *Variety*'s "Big Rental Films." More recently, *I Am Curious—Yellow*, a variation on a traditional Swedish recipe for meatballs, outgrossed the picture at the Radio City Music Hall (the only remaining movie palace that has a stage show). The crowning blow was that the Music Hall has 6,200 seats; the little Cinema 57 Rendezvous, where *Curious* was playing, 587 seats. By the end of 1969, it ranked twelfth among the year's box-office favorites—having taken in $6,600,000 in U.S.-Canadian rentals to that date.

As the art film becomes big business, more and more focus is placed on the directors. Fellini, for example, was the subject of an NBC-TV "Sunday Night Special," and the first stills of his

new production, *Satyricon*, were proudly announced on the
cover of *Life*. Antonioni has been interviewed by Rex Reed, who
didn't like him, and *Playboy*, who did. Jean-Luc Godard and
François Truffault, once the *enfants terribles* of French cinema,
are regularly profiled in *Esquire* and the Sunday *Times* Magazine,
and may be valentined in *The Ladies' Home Journal* any day
now. Generally overlooked by the U.S. press is Luchino Visconti,
according to some pundits the master of them all, but the 1970
success of *The Damned* may change all that. Luchino has noted
that, when the box office sags, his type of pure art film succeeds—
an interesting variant of Hobson's choice.

Much of this hoopla was unheard of a generation ago, when it
was assumed that foreign films appealed only to highbrows, and
invariably lost money. That may be part of a myth that Hollywood once fostered to protect its native product; but since it
began investing heavily in European films, the picture has
changed. Today, the studios accept the fact that foreign film
directors travel badly, and that the new generation prefers to
stay home. The era when Lubitsch came to Mohammed is gone.
These days, a French director finds it easier to make films in
Paris with Jeanne Moreau as his star, and a crew that he can
control right on hand. In this way he avoids Lana Turner, and
other California tribal customs, and the picture has his stamp,
for better or worse. The foreign director solicits Hollywood
backing, however. Too often he has found that a film that he
has financed himself has tough sledding when it reaches New
York—it is often lucky to end up at a six o'clock screening
during the Lincoln Center Film Festival. In this rather sublime
way, Hollywood continues to control the world picture market.

Even if his picture is only a critical success, and does just
moderately well at the box office, the new director can find
himself famous overnight. This happened recently to Pier Paolo
Pasolini, long recognized by cinéastes as a major talent. With
Teorama, however, he found himself on the map for the first
time. The same thing happened earlier with Roman Polanski.
His *A Knife in the Water* and *Repulsion* were connoisseur's films,
but with *Rosemary's Baby* he became almost as famous as Mia

Farrow. Since new faces in directors appear almost daily, the reverse can also take place: Today's bright young man can wake up to find himself a grand old master by the morning. The new directors are graded like actresses: starlet, star, has-been. Sometimes, as with Luis Buñuel, a "has-been" makes a "comeback," and is greeted with the same adoration that plain old-fashioned moviegoers once showered on Bette Davis when she returned to the screen in *Whatever Happened to Baby Jane?*

Whatever happened to a director like King Vidor, who worked quietly and almost anonymously for years, until his style was set and his reputation was secure? Then he allowed the adulation and the fame to pour in. Standing in the glare of the spotlight as he does, it occurs to the more cautious director that he may be swimming in the same shark-infested waters that once destroyed Jack Gilbert, Marilyn Monroe, and a host of other superstars.

Sweden's Ingmar Bergman is of the cautious school. He manages to elude most requests for interviews as he continues to make films that grow more and more introspective. Even Fellini, no shrinking violet, dramatized the plight of today's celebrity-director in *8½*, an autobiographical film in which he portrayed himself as spiritually, emotionally, and physically exhausted—although he took care to cast Marcello Mastroianni, a real glamour boy, in the role of the director.

As the attention given to directors accelerates, those once-revolutionary young movie-bugs who formed the *nouvelle vague* —François Truffault, Claude Chabrol, Jean-Luc Godard, Alan Resnais, and others—find themselves almost academicians—horrified at the thought that if there were a Nobel Prize for film-makers they would have won it by now. Just a few years ago they were penniless bums. Now they find themselves in museums, like impressionist painters, hanging right next to the classicists. Just as embarrassing is the adulation they receive from college students, who bestow on them the hero worship they once reserved for Ernest Hemingway or Red Grange. Today, any college man worth his salt dreams of making a film that will win

First Prize at Cannes. Writing the great American novel has become pretty square.

A number of younger American directors have already modeled themselves after the *nouvelle vague*, with some disconcerting results, since *Hiroshima, Mon Amour* and *The Lovers* are as inimitably French as Pernod. What they come up with instead of the real stuff is lime soda pop or green-tinted corn whiskey—it's either too sticky sweet or too coldly cruddy. Much more astute is Andy Warhol, who has found a style of his own. His films are primitive, poorly photographed, repetitious, boring, just downright awful, simply preposterous—but they are original. Like drawings left in caves, they are designed as communications for posterity.

How Warhol and his European brethren will fare as we enter the Age of Big Brother remains to be seen. It may be that twenty years from now each stage of a masterpiece's development will be photographed and discussed—from incubation period to the finished product. The old-style director—that sweaty little man who worked on a closed set, communicating with his God and fighting off the Devil—may have gone out of style. If this is so, there will be no more films like *Wild Strawberries*.

Chapter 18

Brava, *Sophia!* Brava, *Gina!* Brava, *Claudia!*

More durable than Bardot, and in many ways closer to the sex siren in the old-fashioned glass apothecary jar, is Sophia Loren—Italy's gift to the tired businessman. Unlike B.B., who has remained slangy and *today*, even as middle age approaches, Loren has passed through a number of evolutionary stages, growing more sedate and respectable with the years. Of all the Venuses, she is probably the most likable: A down-to-earth quality keeps her on terra firma no matter how sequined or gilded her gown. There is none of the hauteur of Dietrich or the aloofness of Garbo about Loren. She herself has said that she is everyone's kid sister—the slightly wild one, who became a nice old married lady right before your eyes.

In actuality, she is an astute professional, one of today's highly paid performers in the arts—including opera singers, symphony conductors, harpsichordists, ballerinas—who spend much of their time traveling by plane to keep commitments that have been made as far as two years in advance. They are the solid core of reliables who can be counted on to show up on time, in good condition, and ready to perform. Sophia has circled the globe to make her films—to Russia for *Sunflower,* to Spain for *The Pride and the Passion,* to Greece for *Boy on a Dolphin,* to Libya for *Legend of the Lost,* to England for *The Key.* When the cameras stop, she whisks off again—to Italy to see her new son, to Hollywood to do a retake, to New York

to do a television special. The Flyingest Venus, someone has
called her.

A personality of this caliber—a Birgit Nilsson, an Isaac
Stern, a Dame Margot Fonteyn—is much too busy to show
any cheap temperament. Not that Sophia couldn't. A movie star
has a hundred different ways in which she can sow the seeds of
dissension on a set: She can pit her cameraman against her
director by wooing him outrageously (he will then light her
so that she will dominate every scene, particularly those with
her leading man); she can, in the middle of the picture, complain
that the dialogue is too stiff and not her style, thus necessitating
costly rewriting; she can arrive on the set looking blue and
bruised; she can just not show up at all; she can make herself
look increasingly pretty while the picture is in production,
when the script calls for her to look more and more haggard—
infinite are her methods of sabotage, and varied.

But with Sophia there is none of this. Although a personal
crisis in which she is involved may be making headlines, she
is serene and calm on the set—bursting out in rich, Neapolitan
laughter during emergencies (as when the gilt from her dress
kept peeling off on Cary Grant's dinner jacket, holding up
production on *Houseboat* for half a day).

This evenness in her nature sometimes results in one-dimensional performances. Often, too, she is cast beyond her depth
in prestige films—Jean Paul Sartre's *The Condemned of Altona*,
Eugene O'Neill's *Desire under the Elms*, George Bernard Shaw's
The Millionairess—into which she has been shoehorned for
purely commercial reasons. On the other hand, she can be
absolutely magnificent on the screen—one of the truly exciting
film personalities of our day—as she was in "The Raffle" sequence
in *Boccaccio '70*, in *Marriage—Italian Style*, in *Yesterday, Today
and Tomorrow*, and in *Two Women*, for which she won an
Academy Award. From this, one can conclude that she runs
through the extremities of comedy and drama easily; it's in the
middle range that she's not too sure of herself.

Sophia, who literally glows on camera, no matter how convincing she may or may not be, started her career as a beauty
contest winner in Naples, where she was named "The Princess

of the Sea." She was then Sophia Scicolone, but she journeyed to Rome to compete for Miss Italy under a new name, Sophia Lozzaro. She didn't win, although she was given the token title of Miss Eleganza, but she came to the attention of one of the important producers in the world today—Carlo Ponti. He fell in love with her, almost on sight, and changed her name again, to Sophia Loren. Then her career, under his personal supervision, really began.

American audiences first noticed her in *Aida*, in which she appeared on the screen while Renata Tebaldi's brilliant soprano was heard on the sound track. This did not exactly endear her to opera lovers, who see nothing at all wrong with the way Miss Tebaldi looks; but Sophia's natural beauty, even in that preposterous camouflage, caught the attention of producers around the world. Stanley Kramer cast her in her first United States production, *The Pride and the Passion*, co-starring her with Frank Sinatra. Sophia's English, which had an Oxford cadence under the tutelage of Ponti, thus took on a touch of Hobokenese. She told Frankie that he was "a gasser" and later announced to a reporter, "I am not just another cheesecake pot."

Sophia now began to appear regularly in the headlines—her frustrated marriage to the intellectual Mr. Ponti garnering nearly as much coverage as Zsa Zsa's affair with Rubi. Its twists, turns, and curves, steeped in the logarithms of ancient laws, were difficult enough to solve at the time. In retrospect, they seem even more formidable—but essentially the facts are these: The first Mrs. Ponti had given Mr. Ponti a divorce so that he could marry Miss Loren. The Catholic Church refused to recognize the legality of the divorce, so Carlo and Sophia decided to be married in Mexico without the Church's consent. Mr. Ponti was then declared a bigamist—with both him and Sophia liable to prison terms of five years if they set foot in Italy. Only by their becoming French citizens, and by marrying again, was the beauteous Sophia spared a sojourn in an Italian Sing-Sing and made respectable at last.

This thorny problem out of the way, Sophia announced to the world that she wanted a baby. Since Ponti had two children from his first marriage, a baby did not assume the mystical significance for him that it did for Sophia, but he was very game about it. The progress of Sophia's baby—it was preceded by two headline-making miscarriages—became the most discussed topic in Italy, causing one disenchanted observer to say: "If I hear anything more about Loren's Fallopian tubes, I'll spit!" When Carlo, Jr., a most handsome child, with Sophia's hazel eyes, finally entered the world, it became an unofficial Italian holiday. Tarantellas were danced in the streets of Naples, and in New York's Little Italy women opened their windows and screamed to their neighbors: "*É arrivato!*" Just as hysterical were the nation's women's magazines, who devoted page after page to Sophia's baby, chronicling its progress with day-to-day reports. The entire world went berserk about Sophia's baby, including the *New York Times*. The *Times*, in its haste to report the details, erroneously stated that Mrs. Ponti had *three* miscarriages, prior to Carlo's birth, and that she was immobilized for nine months prior to the great event. (Sophia got up to switch television channels.)

Carlo, Jr., has lived up to his publicity by proving to be a most telegenic infant. He is, says Sophia, being brought up according to Dr. Spock—with some Neapolitan variations. He dwells, as a prince should, in four Ponti residences situated around the world—including an ex-cardinal's castle in the south of Rome, which is an Italian historical shrine. His mother has announced just recently that she wants her son to have a little sister.

Sophia Loren is one of three *bellissimas* who are constantly jockeying for No. 1 position in the Italian popularity polls, although in the United States Sophia wins hands down (she is, as a matter of fact, the *last* remaining enchantress in the *Motion Picture Herald*'s survey of exhibitors' favorites).

In Italy, however, Gina Lollobrigida sometimes ranks ahead of Loren. She has been around a bit longer, and Italians are loyal. Also she is much more typical of the piquant Mediterranean beauty than Loren, who is as tall as a Swede.

Lollo, as she's often called, started her career via the same beauty contest route as Loren, also competing for the title of

Miss Italy and losing. For a time she changed her name to Diana Loris, and posed for the photographed romances (very popular in Italy), which are equivalent to our comic strips. She was soon playing small roles at Cinecitta, however, and in no time at all got the lead in *Fanfan, the Tulip*, opposite Gérard Phillipe. A much less flamboyant personality than Sophia, she remained quietly married to Dr. Milko Skofic, a Yugoslav, for twenty years, divorcing him only recently.

Her career, too, proceeded along a steady, workmanlike path —with one quite untypical *cause célèbre*. That involved her appearance in *La Bambole*, in which, naked to the waist, she seduces Jean Sorel, who is cast as the nephew of a cardinal. This would be bad enough, but in the movie the seduction scene takes place during an ecumenical council.

This aroused the Christian Democratic Party to introduce a bill in the Italian Chamber of Deputies to permit the censorship of a film that can be construed as slandering the Church. Gina was arrested. In the United States that would be equivalent to arresting Doris Day—but nothing very much seems to have come of it, except worldwide publicity.

Gina divides her picture-making into three locales—Rome, Hollywood, and Paris, in about that order of importance. In Hollywood she once indulged in a celebrated feud with director George Cukor over her make-up—each is a perfectionist, each had differing ideas, each was obstinate—which resulted in her withdrawing from his picture. On the other hand, she has worked very peaceably with many of Europe's front-rank directors— with René Clair (*Beauties of the Night*), with Jean Dellanoy (*Imperial Venus*), with Mario Soldati (*The Provincials*), and for a time shared Vittorio De Sica (*Bread, Love and Dreams*) with her arch-rival, Sophia. The most celebrated of her American directors was John Huston, who, while filming his potpourri, *Beat the Devil*, noted how precise and businesslike she was. "She's like a modern apartment building with outside balconies," he said of her. Opinions among her co-stars vary: On the negative side, Humphrey Bogart once dubbed her "Miss Frigidaire," while Bob Hope enthusiastically called her Italy's second most popular dish, next to pizza. As for Marcello Mastroianni, who has had the good fortune to co-star with both Gina and Sophia, he leans, decidedly, toward Sophia.

Lollo, like Loren, has learned to mature gracefully on the screen, and recently was perfectly cast in *Buona Sera, Mrs. Campbell* as the mother of a grown-up daughter (actually, she has a grown-up son). "You're as beautiful as you feel," she told a reporter recently, "and I've never felt more beautiful."

The last of this trio of contemporary Mona Lisas is Claudia Cardinale, an ex-schoolteacher from Tunis (she is a by-product of one of Mussolini's global expansions), who has found her knowledge of languages most useful in making films.

She is, in fact, the first trilingual actress since Lilian Harvey, the soubrette of the 30's who made her films in three versions— German, English, and French—using different leading men— Conrad Veidt, Laurence Olivier, and Charles Boyer—each time. In Claudia's instance, the languages in which she is fluent are English, French, and Italian. Dubbing has eliminated the need for making three separate versions of the same picture, but Claudia is capable of using her own voice on the different sound tracks.

Her mastery of languages—she speaks all three perfectly— allows her to move from Italy (*Rocco and His Brothers*), to France (*Cartouche*), to America (*The Professionals*), without a dictionary in her luggage. Since she is also a highly finished actress, producers regard her as a true jewel and she is very much in demand in the film centers of the world.

Like Loren, however, her best pictures are made in Europe, and two of them are among the masterpieces of the 60's. In Mauro Bolognini's *La Viaccia*, an adaptation of a Zola novel, she portrays the star attraction of a Parisian brothel who lures a country boy (Jean Paul Belmondo) to his doom. She avoids all the platitudes of playing a prostitute in this remarkable film, whose every *mises-en-scène* is an evocation of a French impressionist painting, and she and Belmondo are among the most impassioned screen lovers in recent memory.

Cardinale's greatest triumph, though, was in Luchino Visconti's transcription of Di Lampedusa's novel, *The Leopard*. If

Soldati evokes Renoir and Pissarro, Visconti sets many scenes as if they are Manets, and a more Manet-like beauty than Claudia Cardinale can hardly be imagined. As the newly rich Sicilian heiress who marries into the great old aristocracy, Cardinale seems to actually *understand* the role, a rarity in cinema actresses who walk through everything as if they were playing *Peg O' My Heart*. It is one of the many pleasures in a generally underrated film, a film that ranks with *Citizen Kane* in its epical sweep and its recreation of an entire society through a central figure (even if that figure is played by Burt Lancaster).

Even in more conventional roles, Claudia has a delicate luminosity that brings to mind Luise Rainer. If she lacks anything as an actress, it is mystique. In her gentle way, she looks as if she has the situation well in hand—fatal in a Venus, who must always give the impression of being a lady in distress.

Her competence is such, as a matter of fact, that one just overlooks the more sensational aspects of her personal life. No one cares very much that she is the mother of a son born out of wedlock (the rumor is that the child's father was a French pilot whom she met in Tunis) or that her marriage to film director Franco Cristaldi is on the same shaky theological grounds as the Pontis'. Claudia is such a lady that everyone pretends not to notice.

If Loren is the Flyingest Venus, Lollobrigida the most Mediterranean of Venuses, then the exquisite Cardinale is the Venus with the highest I.Q.

Brava!

Bravi, tutti!

Dissolve 7:

The Continental Enchanters
(1945–70)

Paul Henreid, Conrad Veidt, and Francis Lederer proved very serviceable in Nazi roles during the war—when any idea of developing them into romantic stars was quickly dropped. The end of World War II, though, saw the studios once again searching for that elusive replacement for Valentino—this time they tried with a young Turkish actor, Turhan Bey, who, in such sand epics as *Sudan* and pastel-tinted fantasies as *A Night in Paradise,* didn't prove to have the star power. A handsome young Austrian, Helmut Dantine, was cast in romantic leads, but he also soon found himself playing heavies and retired from the screen. Then, a matinee idol from France, Jean-Pierre Aumont, was featured in prominent films like *Lili,* but they walked rather than ran to see him at the Bijou. This was the case, too, with Jacques Bergerac (*Les Girls*), Horst Bucholtz (*Fanny*), and Vittorio Gassman (*Sombrero*).

Two continental actors did enjoy substantial success in postwar Hollywood. They were the Italian Rossano Brazzi and the French Louis Jourdan. Brazzi, who had something of Boyer's appeal with the blue-haired ladies, co-starred with Katharine Hepburn in *Summertime,* with Joan Crawford in *The Story of Esther Costello,* with Joan Fontaine in *A Certain Smile,* and Olivia de Havilland in *The Light in the Piazza*—and also played the Ezio Pinza role in the screen version of *South Pacific.* No matter what role he played, he remained the same character—

wise in the ways of the world and of women, a Henry James kind of Italian, decorative but untrustworthy.

Louis Jourdan was given a wider range of roles to play— *The Paradine Case*, an unsuccessful Hitchcock thriller in which he co-starred with Alida Valli; *Gigi*, in which Maurice Chevalier, inevitably, walked off with the picture; the interesting Vincente Minnelli version of *Madame Bovary* (he was, of course, the young lover who leads Jennifer Jones to suicide); and the romantic leads in *The Swan*, opposite Grace Kelly, and *Can-Can*, with Shirley MacLaine. He has admitted, though, that he was only "a modest success in that era of the two-gun hero," and that he arrived in Hollywood two decades too late.

Or, perhaps two decades too early—for late in the 60's an enchanter from Egypt would appear on the Hollywood scene and steal the hearts of the ladies, even the hard heart of the critic Pauline Kael. He is, of course, Omar Sharif, who in *Doctor Zhivago* and *Funny Girl* gives the distaff side their money's worth (the money has gone up from a quarter to four dollars, in the interim) by glowering at them in close-ups with dark, insolent eyes. It's a throwback to the good old days of *The Sheik*, and, somehow, it works.

Until Sharif appeared on the screen, the ladies kept themselves busy during the afternoon by going to see Alain Délon—an ex-butcher boy from Paris, who after fighting in the Indochina war was spotted by a talent scout at the Cannes Film Festival. He immediately became a star in *Plein Soleil*, in which he vividly projected a kind of Saint-Germain-des-Pres, kept-boy charm ("the heel you'd love to mother"). This was something new in matinée idols, but we were undergoing a sexual revolution, and it worked. Like Bardot, Délon transposed his movie personality into his personal life—with scandalous results. He was vaguely implicated in a trio of Hollywood-Paris murders which tantalized Europe for many months, since it involved orgies with top-ranking DeGaullists. *Der Spiegel* and *L'Express* gloried in the details, for Délon's intimate circle of friends included the Rothschilds, the Pompidous, Bernard Buffet, and Françoise Sagan —who never wrote a novel that could match Délon's life for interest. After days and nights of interrogation, however, Délon was released by the French police. He remains a figure that recalls the Renaissance with his undeniable glamour, good looks, and air of intrigue. Just what the screen needs.

When he's away, the ladies can console themselves with two other brilliant charmers who, unlike Délon, happen to be among the great actors of their generation. They are Jean Paul Belmondo and Marcello Mastroianni, and the ladies never had it so good. For, in addition to being masters of their profession and enormously magnetic to boot, these two actors have qualities that have never appeared among boudoir favorites before—intelligence and wit. These are characteristics that one associates with classical actors like Louis Jouvet, in roles like *Volpone*, but to find them at the neighborhood Bijou any old day of the week is a stunning bonus.

Both of these enchanters have an extraordinary range—Belmondo running the gamut from slapstick (*That Man from Rio*) to parody (*Male Hunt*) to tragedy (*La Viaccia*). He is best known in the United States for his role in *Breathless*, that perhaps overestimated new wave melodrama "dedicated to Monogram Pictures," but it served the purpose of making him an immediate sensation on the art-house circuit. As Truffault said in an interview recently, Belmondo can change himself from a plugugly to a romantic leading man by turning a light on inside. "Oh, you want it *sad!*" he will tell a director who has complained that he is playing a love scene for laughs. He will then play the same role in an altogether different key, giving it new meanings by shading it with his eyes. On a superficial level he is very much like the young James Cagney—the Cagney of the early 30's—with the same bounce to his step, sardonic smile around his lips, and "rough trade" appeal. But he has a depth Cagney never had, and he could do the great classic roles in the French theater, if he doesn't wear himself out. That could so easily happen—Belmondo's name on a picture means quick backing from the Hollywood studios, now serving mainly as financiers. His fans are legion, and have raised his price from $4,000 a picture (for *Breathless*) to the six-figure level. But this Nijinsky of contemporary actors (not known to most Americans is the fact that his father is a famed sculptor) should, maybe, stop and, like an English confrère, Albert Finney, do nothing for a year.

Marcello Mastroianni's range and flexibility are perhaps even more remarkable. This ex-Italian law clerk turned actor has done everything from black comedy (*Divorce—Italian Style*), to farce (*Marriage—Italian Style*), to tragedy (*Il Bel Antonio*), to social drama (*The Organizer*), to science fiction (*The Tenth Man*)— reaching the peaks of his career under Antonioni (*La Notte*) and Fellini (*La Dolce Vita*; *8½*). *Weltschmertz*, *Angst*, and pratfalls—Marcello does them all. And, in addition, he has the kind of sex appeal that lines them up three-deep at the Bijou. As Pamela Tiffin, one of his leading ladies, has said, "He's romantic, he's elegant, he's sensual, he's a Latin lover, and yet he's a teddy bear, too." Claudia, as well as Gina and Sophia, has played with him, as have Jeanne Moreau, Ursula Andress, Anita Ekberg, Monica Vitti, Anouk Aimée, Virna Lisi, and Faye Dunaway. We can see why Marcello could never be induced to take a sabbatical.

He did, however, pause long enough to stage a musical, based on the life of Valentino, in which he sang, tangoed, and acted. He said at the time that Valentino was never properly understood by any of his biographers, and that there was more to the man than met the eye. The musical, *Ciao, Rudy*, an expressionistic evocation of Hollywood's Age of the Baroque, did not please the Roman theater critics, and was soon withdrawn. He threatens to return to it.

Meanwhile, his films have grossed a cool billion cash around the world. He is the biggest international star since Greta Garbo, with an important body of work to his credit that insures Marcello Mastroianni Film Festivals in years to come. As Dwight MacDonald noted recently, the cinema never dies; it fades and then comes back again—better than ever. It may even be heading into a new Golden Age, just as it could so easily plunge into a deep, dark pit. Stars like Mastroianni and Belmondo are among the delicate balances.

Chapter 19

Ladies of a Certain Age

Mr. and Mrs. Babbitt preferred to stay at home and "watch TV" as the new wave accelerated and B.B. continued to perform her cinematic stripteases. The Babbitts were not so much shocked as they were disinterested—Mrs. Babbitt, in raising two children, had learned all there was to know about nudity; Mr. Babbitt had seen enough of it when he was a young 'un, yessiree. On the occasions when they made sorties to the Bijou, it was to take the grandchildren—yes, both Babs and Bob, those two Main Street revolutionaries, were married and alive and well, thank you—but they didn't particularly care for the new photoplays.

The truth of the matter is that movies were no longer being made for them; they were made for a new generation, with a median age of sixteen. On the most primitive level, these films had titles like *Beach Party Bingo* and featured bikinied lads and lasses, of a distinctly southern California cast, throwing beach balls at one another. Then there was *Tammy*, a mentally retarded post-adolescent, who uttered Shirley Temple-ish homilies while languorously twitching her butt. These films alternated with dramas of morbid violence, like *The Vikings*, in which eyes were gouged and great waves of technicolored blood filled the screen between close-ups of Kirk Douglas's two hundred and fifty-three perfectly even white teeth. This was the era when John O'Hara was thought "sophisticated," and somewhat leaden WASPS, who had no relationship to anyone living or dead, paraded decoratively from the terrace. Troy Donahue was its hero; Sandra Dee its heroine. Bits of adolescent fat clung to their bleached and well-bathed bodies. It is remembered by some as The Arrid Age.

But while this somewhat surrealistic concept of the American dream was being shown at the Bijou, films of a mature level were playing at the newly opened Artmart down the street. They were usually European, although good American ones and 30's revivals were also shown. Their leading ladies, unlike Brigitte Bardot, were not always young, but often were highly trained actresses, like Simone Signoret, who had become international film favorites rather late in life. They were the ladies of a certain age who brought a new kind of distinction to the screen.

Anna Magnani ushered in this new vogue with *Open City*, the first successful postwar import, and continued to appear on the screen intermittently over the next twenty-five years. She was thirty-seven when she made that Rossellini document, but behind her was an extensive Roman stage and screen career. Born in Egypt—her mother was Italian, her father of Egyptian background (which explains that Nefertiti look)—she made her stage debut at eighteen in *Anna Christie*. Roles in other O'Neill and Pirandello classics followed, as well as in movies (she made her screen debut in 1934 in *Blind Women of Sorrento*; between 1942 and 1943 alone, she appeared in six films). *Open City*, of course, brought her to the attention of the world, but not long afterward Ingrid Bergman disestablished Magnani's relationship with Rossellini and she stayed off the screen for a few years. In the late 40's she began to make films with other great European directors—*The Golden Coach* with Jean Renoir and *Bellissima* with Visconti, in which she added some dimensions of her own to a one-dimensional portrait of a Cinecitta stage mother—and then came to Hollywood, a bit reluctantly.

Tennessee Williams had written *The Rose Tattoo* a few years earlier especially for her. At the last moment, she decided not to appear in it on Broadway, but when the film rights were acquired by Paramount she agreed to co-star with Burt Lancaster in the movie. Her arrival is an eruption that is still remembered by a co-worker: "Anna appeared on the set, her thick, lustrous, black hair pouring over her eyes like an unkempt spaniel's, dressed in a black turtleneck sweater and black slacks, and speaking not one word of English. She was surrounded with an entourage of translators, admirers, and just plain hangers-on, creating tension and excitement wherever she appeared. Everyone on the set seemed to reflect her mood—if she was happy, even the taciturn propmen bubbled with joy; if she was *triste*, the script girl began to cry, too. What a woman!"

She was particularly difficult with make-up and costume people, fearing that they would try to change "the Magnani look" into something that was conventionally Hollywood. With Edith Head she kept up a running battle for weeks—the slip she wore must be made of poor material; it must not *fit;* her blouse must be a tattered and unkempt old print, not some glamorous Hollywood creation. When she was finally convinced that Edith was on her side, they became friends. Miss Head recollects that Magnani could understand English very well, *when* she wanted to, and that she could transform herself into a woman of great beauty and high fashion, in her black-silk European way, *when* she wanted to. "A human Vesuvius," she calls Magnani in *The Dress Doctor.*

More than any other actress since Garbo, Anna enslaved her fans into hyperbole. The editors of *Harper's Bazaar* announced that her beauty was so great it diminished that of every other beauty in the world; Tennessee Williams called her the greatest actress in the world; and James Agee, after recovering from the shock of seeing her in *Open City*, said, "She is the nearest thing to an absolute I have seen in films since the silent Garbo movies."

Hollywood kudoed her in the only way it knew how—it gave her an Academy Award for *The Rose Tattoo* and made her many film offers. She accepted only two—*Wild Is the Wind,* directed by Cukor, and *The Fugitive Kind,* in which she co-starred with Marlon Brando (it looked good on paper, but it was a combination that didn't take; Magnani's fluorescent intensity made the mumbling boy sound like an idiot). She continues to make films, and will until she dies, although she has announced that she is in retirement. That's like saying there will be no more thunder.

Simone Signoret was thirty-five when *Room at the Top* made her a big star, but behind her, too, there was an extensive acting background, largely in films. She was born Simone Kaminker, of French parents, in Wiesbaden, Germany, but grew up in Paris. When her father went off to fight with the Free French, she was left to support two younger brothers in Nazi-occupied Paris, an experience that embittered her and may account for her profoundly leftist opinions. Actresses are essentially self-centered and nonpolitical, and Signoret's opinions, expressed forcibly and dramatically, utilizing her considerable skills as an actress, made her the talk of the Paris film studios, which she began to frequent after the war.

Signoret's quite stylish beauty got her the leads in three of the important postwar French films—*Casque d'Or*, a film of the Paris underworld admired by cinéastes; *Diaboliques*, a popular import on the art-house circuit; and *The Maids of Salem*, Arthur Miller's commentary on the McCarthy era, transported to an earlier period of American history. She was superb in all of them —she has, in contrast to Magnani, an almost offhand way of acting that is nonetheless based on sharp observation of human character. She builds her roles slowly, looking bored and tired and a little distempered, and then they explode—POP! BOOM! —before your startled eyes. Of all screen actresses, she is the most like Laurette Taylor and even resembles her in an odd kind of way.

These were but preludes to *Room at the Top*, which was to Signoret what *The Glass Menagerie* was to Taylor. Suddenly the banked fire of her art lit up and singed the helpless fools in the audience, too mesmerized by the gold and silver flames to move. It even mesmerized the United States Justice Department—they had earlier banned her from immigrating to the United States (with her husband Yves Montand) but now they lifted the ban and allowed her to come to Hollywood to collect her Academy Award. In recent interviews, she has put them down: her attitude being that she is, after all, an artist, and who, pray, are *they?* Coming from Signoret, it seems, somehow, a welcome corrective.

She would never again find a role like *Room at the Top*, although she did *The Sea Gull* in England for Sidney Lumet and was one of the all-star cast in Stanley Kramer's *Ship of Fools*, a film that was poorly reviewed at its release but has come to have some kind of charisma among movie historians. As the drug-addicted contessa, Signoret almost outshines her co-player, Oskar Werner, and—let's see, who else was in it?

There were many other ladies who might be termed Mature Venuses, even though at eighty they will be younger than Sandra Dee ever was. Melina Mercouri, a volatile blonde from Athens (her father was once its deputy-mayor), hit the screen hard in *Never on Sunday*, and has been around ever since—even making history among the Venuses by transposing her movie into a musical on Broadway. It closed after a modest run, but Melina never will. Others of note are: Giulietta Massina (Mrs. Federico Fellini), whose films, made with her husband, include *La Strada*, *Nights of Cabiria* (musicalized on Broadway, but without Giulietta, as *Sweet Charity*), and the partially biographical and flamboyantly hued *Juliet of the Spirits*; Alida Valli, who returned to Italy after an unsuccessful career in Hollywood, and appeared in a number of first-class Italian films, notably Visconti's *Senso*; Ingrid Thulin, one of several striking Ingmar Bergman blondes —she was the lesbian sister in *The Silence*—who also failed in Hollywood (in the remake of *Four Horsemen of the Apocalypse*, another voice was dubbed on the English sound track); Anouk Aimée, who had been playing in French and Italian pictures for years until she scored a solid success in *A Man and a Woman*, and upped her salary to $150,000 a picture; and then there is Lilli Palmer (really Lilli Peiser), the very model of the European woman of the world, who often appeared with her ex-husband, Rex Harrison, the very model of the European man of the world. There are others, many others, but three must be at least mentioned—the superb Greek actress, Katina Paxinou, who appeared in *For Whom the Bell Tolls* and *Mourning Becomes Electra*; Lea Padovani (*The Naked Maja*); and Lila Kedrova, the Academy Award winner of *Zorba, the Greek*.

And then there is Jeanne Moreau, the Dark Lady of the Sonnets among cinema stars, a legend in her lifetime, the Tiffany among actresses. She is the Venus with the most snob appeal—today's "in" Venus.

Her fans say she is the biggest thing since Garbo; *she* says she has modeled her career after Bette Davis's; there are those who say she is more like Dietrich. If all this seems to be derivative, then, let's face it, Jeanne Moreau is a bit derivative. Only Antonioni cut through the bric-a-brac to show us a real woman, a *mal-de-siècle* Venus, thoroughly disenchanted with it all, clutching at the cinema dolls of yesterday to capture an identity, a focus.

But, in any event, she is the most interesting woman on the screen today. She is as enigmatic as a Paul Klee and as much fun to live with. You never grow tired of Jeanne Moreau; no one ever says, "What! *Another* Jeanne Moreau picture!" because you never know what you will find.

You may find her, as in the *The Lovers* of Louis Malle, doing an existentialist bit of eroticism as she tumbles in the hay with Jean-Marc Bory, for no apparent reason at all. In Joseph Losey's *Eva* she is a 1920's vamp, a cigarette in her Joan Crawfordish mouth, always unlit. In *Jules et Jim* she is an evocation of Elisabeth Bergner as she flirts first with Jules (Oskar Werner) and then with Jim (Henri Serre) and sings *Le Tourbillon*. In Max Ophuls's *Banana Skin* she is Bette Davis in *Fog over Frisco* neatly reincarnated.

Moreau is always neat. There are no sloppy edges to her impersonations and she knows when to stop—a rarity among mimics. This has made her the director's darling—they go wild over her, for she acts as a well-tuned Stradivarius performs—always in perfect pitch. She has another rare quality—restraint, which she may have acquired during her training at the Comédie-Française. No matter how erotic the picture (and *The Lovers* got pretty erotic) she purifies it with her presence.

Definitely one for the connoisseur is Jeanne Moreau. It is unlikely she ever will win an Academy Award for one of her performances, but then neither did Garbo or Dietrich. She has not, like Sophia Loren, appeared on the cover of *Life* ten times. Nor, like Bardot, has she been named The Girl I'd Most Like to Go to the Moon With. *Playboy*'s Hugh Hefner, a specialist in these matters, has said her sex appeal is zero.

She's someone very special, though, and, if you're doing the dinner party circuit this season, you'll just have to bone up.

Fade-Out 3:

The Sirens Keep On Singing

Ho-yo-to-ho! Ho-yo-to-ho!
Hi-ya-ha! Hi-ya-ha!
—Richard Wagner: *Die Walküre*

Babs and Bob Babbitt, when they were growing up, could walk into any movie—even the sulphurous old Dietrichs and Garbos—provided they had the jingle in their jeans. Their offspring, however, were often stopped at the Bijou by those ominous black letters—M, R, X—which meant the picture was "adult" and not intended for their eyes. Sometimes they managed to get through on an M picture (Suggested for Mature Audiences —Parental Discretion Advised) or they could coax a passing lady into pretending she was a parent and get them into an R picture (Persons Under 17 Not Admitted Unless Accompanied by Parent or Adult Guardian), but they reached a stalemate with pictures marked X (No One Under 17 Admitted).

These symbols were evolved by the Motion Picture Association of America (MPAA), following drastic revisions of the old Hays Code in 1966. Admitting that "censorship is an odious enterprise" and that "it destroys the freedom of choice," the restrictions of the old MPAA Code were modified "to keep in closer harmony with the mores, the culture, moral sense and the expectations of our society." Under the new, more intelligent code, nudity was permitted provided it was not "indecent or undue" and such American institutions as double beds were al-

224

lowed to be shown on the screen. A prostitute was a prostitute, and not "a hostess," as in *Destry Rides Again*, and other Hays Age double-talk was clarified and expressed in English that, if not basic, was at least clear. Everyone was more or less pleased, except Babs, Jr., and Bob, Jr., who felt sort of left out of things.

The guessing game of "will be it M, R, or X?" was played by producers who had anything more controversial than a G picture on their hands—G did *not* stand for Goody-Good but for General Audiences. A close-up of a nipple might change a rating from M to R, and if the nipple twitched it was X. Nipples were, however, the least of it, as films like *I Am Curious—Yellow* and *Blue Movie* came along to provide frequently funny variations on medieval debates like "How many angels can dance on the point of a pin?" Still, a 1970 poll discloses that 58 percent of all movie-goers find the ratings "useful," although many of them were often as confused as Babs and Bob. To make things simpler, M pictures overnight became GP pictures (all ages admitted, parental guidance suggested). The admission age to R and X films continued to shift from state to state, county to county, and even hamlet to hamlet—but seventeen was established as the minimum age.

The new freedom ushered in a new wave of sirens to meet the formidable "expectations of our society." Not the least of them was a clear skin, something that surprisingly few young actresses seemed to possess as the cruel color cameras caught every pimple, scratch, and blotch on their exposed derrières. How did the leading lady get those red spots? one wondered when the picture got dull. Had she, inadvertently, sat down on a waffle iron? Was she coming down with the measles? Had some butter-fingered assistant director splattered her with cherry jam? Renata Adler, a short-lived movie critic on the *New York Times*, matter-of-factly reported the condition of the ladies' skins along with a film's other qualities. It was a real consumer service, while it lasted.

Instead of searching for faces, producers now spent most of their time searching for derrières—a Swiftian state of affairs that soon began to bug the actors' unions. On Broadway, Actors' Equity now insisted that each nude audition be supervised by a representative of the union, and in Hollywood similar precautions were considered. The notation "she will" or "she won't," indicating an actress's willingness to disrobe, now appeared in many a casting director's notebook. Not only actresses but actors protested—a red-faced Stephen Boyd once told a press conference that he would never take off his clothes on camera again. He was, at the time, protesting nudity in European films, but shortly after that Paul Newman and Charlton Heston gave everything for their art in American-made films that even played the Music Hall. They were outdone, though, by Mario Montez, the first screen female impersonator since Julian Eltinge. In *More Milk, Yvette*, an underground film, Mario puts on and takes off a dozen Lana Turner sweaters, and in *M.M.* (for Marilyn Monroe) his big scene is a transvestite bubble bath. Somebody, it seems, was always coming up with a new angle.

The nude Venuses did not always, like Brigitte Bardot, enjoy their art. Catherine Deneuve, a really very pretty French girl who ranks high among them, admitted that she often had to down a few strong drinks before disrobing on camera in films like *Belle du Jour*. Essy Persson (*I, a Woman* and *Thérèse and Isabelle*) had few such qualms and neither did Lena Nyman of *Curious*, who in that Squirmy Sixties parable performed ferocious sexual acrobatics (perched on a balustrade, hanging from the trunk of a tree) that brought to mind Pearl White in *The Perils of Pauline*. It seemed a long time since Garbo made everyone gasp by *really* kissing John Gilbert in *Flesh and the Devil*.

Miss Persson and Miss Nyman were both Scandinavian, but the new wave was also represented by Austria (Marissa Mell), Italy (Sylvia Koscina), and Germany (Elke Sommer). The queen bee among them was, however, an American—whoever called this a nation of Puritans?—Jane Fonda, now making films mostly in France, under the direction of her new husband, the omnipotent Roger Vadim. Mr. Vadim had been scheduled to marry Catherine Deneuve, who had borne him a son, Christian, out of wedlock following his divorce from Annette Stroyberg, who had borne him a daughter, Nathalie, out of wedlock before he married *her*—etc. Well, anyway, it was our Jane who finally got Vadim this time around.

In one of their films together, Miss Fonda portrays the bored young wife of an aging very rich man (*Ecstasy*, move over), who is sexually awakened by her husband's young son (someone is always coming up with a new angle). Vadim left out the horse in this epic, which is called *The Game Is Over*, but reaches new heights in nudity as Miss Fonda unties, unbuttons, and unzips her co-star (young Peter McEnery) before, after, and during wiggling out of her own clothes, in a number of imaginative locales that include a gym, a sunken bathtub, and a hothouse, as well as a dreary old-fashioned bed. It is quite possible that Miss Fonda has been joshing us all along—for the movie seems suspiciously like a parody of *Stella Dallas* at the end, as Miss Fonda stands outside a picture window and watches her young lover marry a rich girl to save his once-rich father from bankruptcy, while . . . , etc.—but then one remembers that Miss Fonda was in the early days of her career named by the *Harvard Lampoon* the worst actress of the year, and, finally, you can't quite be *sure*.

These were the Venuses of the 60's Anything Goes generation, when one out of six brides was pregnant; when, at college, coeds joined the Sexual Freedom League instead of the Glee Club; when vacation agencies for singles used the slogan, "Togetherness while you travel." It is unlikely, after all, that this generation would buy the artificial cherry blossoms of *Random Harvest*, one of the epics of L.B.'s Empire days, or would listen to one of Judge Hardy's homilies—much as sentimentalists and traditionalists and exponents of law-and-order would want them to. Not, anyway, when the new "crotchies" were around—the crotchies being a new type of Venus vehicle with nude male homosexuals instead of old-style cinema queens, titles like *STUDy Farm*, and plots that harked back to *Susan Lennox: Her Fall and Rise*. The admission was now a well-rounded $5, instead of the nickel of the old nickelodeon days, but that too was progress.

Ho-yo-to-ho! Ho-yo-to-ho!
Hi-ya-ha! Hi-ya-ha!

Appendix A

Venus—Her Ten Best Films

GARBO: *The Story of Gosta Berling* (1923)

This Swedish film became, by accident rather than design, the first great star vehicle created to display a young actress at the peak of her beauty and allure. Its director, Mauritz Stiller, had intended a more serious Ibsenlike study of a defrocked country pastor at war with conventions—a favorite Swedish theme retold in contemporary terms by Ingmar Bergman in *Winter Light* and Vilgot Sjoman in *I Am Curious—Yellow*. In the minor role of Countess Dohna, Stiller cast an unknown actress, Greta Garbo, then seventeen.

Selma Lagerloff's classic story then proceeded to run off the track the moment Garbo came on screen. The ensemble style of playing was dealt a stunning blow by the unknown enchantress, unintentionally, of course, for she could not have known how beautiful she was. Only Stiller knew, and he was keeping it a secret. Garbo was the ace up his sleeve.

The Story of Gosta Berling established definitively (as Little Mary indicated it would) that the future design of film-making would revolve around a personality with superhuman powers of projection before the camera. The personality need not be pretty —Will Rogers, Marie Dressler, and Emil Jannings were plain; Garbo herself was not conventionally pretty—but it would come across in a way that would jolt audiences. In this context, the great star is a variation on Prince Charming, who awakens the Sleeping Audience with a kiss and brings it the gift of life. In this age of science or pseudo-science, the great cinema star is the vestigial reminder of the myths of the gods. She or he becomes our sole link to divinity.

NEGRI: *Hotel Imperial* (1926)

Shrewd Adolph Zukor understood the power of the star, perhaps more than any other producer—even Louis B. Mayer. His studio, which eventually became Paramount, was built around the star system from its beginnings, when he introduced Sarah Bernhardt to American audiences in *Queen Elizabeth* and *Camille* (1913). Pola Negri was the first great international cinema queen, preceding Garbo by five years. Zukor saw her potential immediately, and began negotiations to bring her to America. Despite her failure to catch on as he had hoped, she became one of the brightest stars on the Paramount lot—whose list of luminaries includes Dietrich, Chevalier, Jannings, Swanson, William S. Hart, Mae West, the Marx Brothers, Colbert, Lombard, Cooper, Crosby, Hope (who became a star, he says, when he learned to act with his eyes), Madeleine Carroll, and Paulette Goddard. The transition from Negri to Mae West to Paulette Goddard is the story of Hollywood's rise and fall in a nutshell.

Hotel Imperial is a dazzling display of some of the great Ufa and Svenskfilm talents at work in Hollywood—the star was Negri and the director was Mauritz Stiller but the *régisseur-général* was Erich Pommer, who transformed a little spy story into a cinematic *tour de force*. It bewildered the reviewers at the time of its release, for they just did not know what to make of it. It really wasn't too much of a photoplay, they finally decided. They were so right. It was only a masterpiece.

DIETRICH: *The Blue Angel* (1929)

It is not too original a story—Somerset Maugham's *Rain* being another variation on its theme of the uptight moralist stripped of his rose-tinted glasses by a low-down dame. And it was not, von Sternberg assures us, intended as an allegory on the rise of Hitlerism, although some film historians persist in interpreting it this way. It was made in an atmosphere of tension and mistrust—

Jannings came to regret his choice of von Sternberg as a director —and it shows it in many small ways.

There would be better German talkies—the remarkable *Mädchen in Uniform* and *M*, for two—but quibbling over *The Blue Angel* is like finding fault with a sunset—for this was, despite its sound track, the sunset of the "poetic silent film," which told a simple story in clear, pictorial images that everyone could understand.

It might not be remembered today, except by film historians, were it not for that "Dutch babe" who played Lola Frobisch— Marlene Dietrich. It was a gutsy portrayal, drawn from life, and it demonstrates what a great actress Dietrich might have been in another time, in another place. She would never reach this level of excellence again; her Lola is one of the screen's great portrayals.

GARBO: *Camille* (1936)

Charles Jackson, in *The Lost Weekend*, had the final word to say on this one:

> On the mantel over the bar, tilted against the mirror, was a yellow card advertising the double-feature at the Select next door. Greta Garbo in *Camille*, and some other movie. It was like a summons, for God's sake. He had seen the picture three times during the week it opened on Broadway, a month or so ago. All of a sudden (but no, it was too early, it would have to wait) he had to see again that strange fabled face, hear the voice that sent shivers down his spine when it uttered even the inconsequential little sentence (the fingertips suddenly raised to the mouth as if to cover the rueful smile): "It's my birthday." Or the rapid impatient way, half-defiant, half-regretful, it ran off the words about money: "And I've never been very particular where it came from, as you very well know." And oh the scene where the Baron was leaving for Russia—how she said "Goodbye . . . goodbye" like a little song. ("Come with me!" The shake of the head and the smile, then; and the answer: "But Russia is so co-o-old—you wouldn't want me to get ill again, would

you," not meaning this was the reason she couldn't go, not even pretending to mean it.) He knew the performance by heart, as one knows a loved piece of music: every inflexion, every stress and emphasis, every faultless phrase, every small revelation of satisfying but provocative beauty. There was a way to spend the afternoon!—The bartender slid the bottle across the counter and this time he poured the drink himself.*

RAINER: *The Good Earth* (1937)

It is a stagy performance, in the style of Nazimova, and somehow you get to thinking you're watching it from the first row of a legitimate theater rather than at a movie.

It coordinates beautifully with Muni's acting style—the entire film is a Thalberg triumph, the ultimate in Hollywood sound-stage movie-making.

If Luise Rainer's O-lan makes us uncomfortable—and it does —it isn't because it's not great—it is great, very great—but because in this fairyland movie palace, under those twinkling electric stars, springing at us from a proscenium that is done up to look like a castle in a not quite first-class book of children's tales—it does not belong. Such acting as this—the shoulders stooped artistically, as in a painting by Millet; the hands held with such infinite grace, born of centuries of resignation and years of sorrow, as in a study by David; the face tilted at just that precise angle, as if in one of those studies of demented peasants by Géricault, larger than life that face, grabbing and ripping out the heart of the spectator—such acting as this belongs in one of the amphitheaters of Greece, under real stars, in a true temple of tragedy.

It has, then, exceeded the limits of cinema art, just as Garbo stayed within them—Garbo, as Jackson tells us, was a polisher; it has looked back and then gone forward toward some new frontier. It is unique. When Katharine Hepburn, some years later, tried to duplicate it in *Dragon Seed*, she managed to look like a Bryn Mawr girl at a costume party—one of the milestones in disastrous cinema acting: why, the poor girl went up in flames like the papier-mâché decorations in the old Coconut Grove. It makes Rainer seem all the more remarkable to have really pulled off the stunt—even if a stunt it remains.

Rainer as O-lan in *The Good Earth*! It is one to tell the grandchildren about. To have seen it was to have visited a museum.

LAMARR: *Algiers* (1938)

This prize piece of late 30's schmaltz is machine-tooled Hollywood at its best. The problem was: how to introduce Hedy Lamarr, a continental sensation, to American audiences. The assets were: a face of almost indescribable loveliness; the rights to remake *Pepe LeMoko,* a good French film which had starred Jean Gabin; and Charles Boyer. The liabilities were: Hedy Lamarr's limited skill as an actress; a limited recession budget. The solution was: Dazzle the viewer with close-up after close-up of Hedy Lamarr, until the schnook feels as if he were high on wedding-party champagne; leave the acting to Boyer; concentrate on atmosphere rather than spectacle, since atmosphere was cheaper.

The result was: *Algiers,* a trompe l'oeil so magnificent that audiences poured out of the pleasure domes into the streets of Pittsburgh or Providence or Perth Amboy and went searching for the Casbah. Not since Banky and Colman had there been love scenes of such ripe, purple passion; not since *Morocco* had an exotic locale so fascinated a generation that had to count every penny and hoard every dime.

Algiers was, and is, elegant escapism.

BERGMAN: *Casablanca* (1943)

The Michael Curtiz melodrama, fast-paced, atmospheric, well-cast, neatly packaged, was one of the American art forms of the 30's and 40's. The true-blue movie buff knows there were better ones than *Casablanca*—who can forget Kay Francis as "Spot White," a notorious whore, in *Mandalay*; or Bette Davis doing a striptease to "Minnie the Moocher" before the innocent eyes of Richard Barthelmess in *Cabin in the Cotton*? But *Casablanca* combined Curtiz's remarkable dynamism (he was as bouncy as a tennis ball) with a syrupy coating of Warner Brothers' social consciousness (it came in a Shocking Pink dressmaker bottle) into a fine piece of Hollywood Pop Art with something for everyone.

For most audiences in the early 40's, this was Ingrid Bergman: Curtiz manages to take the edge off her well-scrubbed young matron's patina, although she does look as if she's slumming. For latter-day audiences, the something was Humphrey Bogart, in a fairly decent picture at last and tight-lipping it up to a farethee-well. For a special few, the particular charm of this picture was its trio of villains—Conrad Veidt, Peter Lorre, and Sydney Greenstreet, and not since Iago has villainy ever had it so good.

And then there is Dooley Wilson (Sam), who plays "As Time Goes By" again—and again. As Curtiz slyly knew, he was the real star of the picture.

MAGNANI: *Open City* (1946)

Audiences who had survived World War II wanted something more substantial than a Bergman-Bogart-Curtiz-Warner Brothers banana split by the time it was over. They got it in Roberto Rossellini's *Open City*, a fairly realistic study of the operations of the Italian underground when Rome was occupied by the Germans. At last, thought the first wave of postwar college intellectuals, someone is telling us the truth. This may not be exactly how it was, but, on the other hand, it's light years ahead of *God Is My Co-Pilot*.

But even if *Open City* were an Italian version of *East Lynne*, they would have flocked to see it in the first of the nation's art houses, dingy theaters that alternated epics like *Birth of a Baby* and *Illicit Traffic* with the first great European postwar films. For *Open City* had Anna Magnani, and she was well worth the flea bites, or even the crabs, that one picked up in the leatherette seats that had the stuffing pouring out of them.

If you haven't seen *Open City* in some years, it comes as a surprise to learn that Magnani played only a small role in it. She is killed by the time the picture is half over, and the picture is never the same after she's gone. But while she's there, the audience is given a feast—real acting which, after a surfeit of gumdrops and vanilla wafers, comes on with the impact of the taste of the first fresh fruit of late spring. Or a rare steak after a diet of chicken croquettes. Or the taste of real maple syrup after the imitation kind that comes in a can.

One uses food analogies because, truly, we are starved for acting like this—so fresh, so simple, so direct, so *pure*. Watch Magnani in a church: She has been touched with the new radicalism, but the church is still a church. As she genuflects before the altar, she becomes the peasant again; she wants to cry and *we* begin to cry, and everyone in that theater, from the projectionist to the usher, is crying, and, well, suddenly she has telescoped Spengler's *The Decline of the West* and Toynbee's *A Study of History* into three seconds. And that, we realize with a start, is what art *is*.

SIGNORET: *Room at the Top* (1958)

Simone Signoret won an Academy Award for her portrayal of a middle-class wife who sacrifices herself for a young man on the make (Laurence Harvey, lethally convincing in the role), in this English-made romance with a touch of Flaubertian realism.

Flaubert may have inspired Signoret's concept of the role—think of how it would have been flattened out by Lana Turner, and shudder—which catches fine shadings and nuances, down to the smallest details of costume and cosmetics. She is a provincial Venus, a bit too plump, a bit too run-down, but a Venus nonetheless.

The woman she has created is so universal that one thinks of her American counterpart as one watches the film—one sees her alone at the opera on Saturday afternoons or shopping on Fifth Avenue, with a look of boredom and mild contempt on her face. One sees her at a sidewalk cafe in Greenwich Village hungrily feeding on the young men with beards or the girls in their minidresses, as if by osmosis she will capture a bit of their youth. One sees her at a dinner party, where she is seated far down the table, away from the center of things, where the guest of honor, a shabby poet, is holding forth.

Begin with a type and you create nothing, someone said.

Begin with a character, and you create a type. Simone Signoret began with a character and created one of the few living portrayals on the screen.

LOREN: *Yesterday, Today and Tomorrow* (1964)

The love teams of the 1930's had run downhill by the 1960's. Just when everyone was giving up hope, along came Sophia Loren and Marcello Mastroianni in a series of well-made comedy-dramas from Italy. They were often scripted by Cesare Zavattini, photographed by Giuseppe Rotunno, and directed with a kind of left-handed skill by Vittorio De Sica.

The best of these have the sparkling zest of Italian comic opera —*The Barber of Seville* or *Don Pasquale*—and may very well prove as durable. Certainly *Yesterday, Today and Tomorrow* is a film that one can see once a year, just as one can hear *The Elixir of Love* once a year over a period of twenty years, and never grow tired of it. It's a tonic, and cheaper than Carlsbad.

Yesterday, Today and Tomorrow has our Roman Venus and our Milanese Adonis delineating three separate love stories which allow them to display a wide range of acting styles, from wry comedy to broad farce. Keeping up with Marcello, the best farceur of our day, is no easy task but Sophia pulls it off—she rarely lets him get away with anything, although he tries. It's a bit like watching Alfred Lunt and Lynn Fontanne in their heyday, but Sophia is more generously endowed than Lynn ever was.

In the long line of movie Venuses, she is the first with a broad sense of humor, and may well be parodying a type that began with Negri but has just about run its love-locked course. And her carnality is frank, direct, and unaffected; she doesn't smother it in irony, as did Dietrich, nor does she pat it absent-mindedly on the head, as did Ingrid Bergman.

Love . . . love . . . love . . . may have had it in the cinema; sex . . . sex . . . sex . . . may be the coming thing. Sophia, with one shapely leg in each puddle, may be a transitional figure, pointing the way to a new cinema frontier.

Appendix B

The Old Motion Picture Production Code

(*Note:* The Production Code was first drafted in 1930, and underwent many revisions throughout the years, until it was replaced by a drastically revised new code which became effective in September, 1966. The text that follows is that of the 1956 code of regulations, which remained in effect until the more liberal and flexible present code was adopted.)

General Principles:

1. No picture shall be produced which will lower the moral standards of those who see it. Hence the sympathy of the audience shall never be thrown to the side of crime, wrong-doing, evil or sin.

2. Correct standards of life, subject only to the requirements of drama and entertainment, shall be presented.

3. Law—divine, natural or human—shall not be ridiculed, nor shall sympathy be created for its violation.

Particular Applications

I. Crime

1. Crime shall never be presented in such a way as to throw sympathy with the crime as against law and justice, or to inspire others with the desire for imitation.

2. Methods of crime shall not be explicitly presented or detailed in a manner calculated to glamourize crime or inspire imitation.

3. Action showing the taking of human life is to be held to the minimum. Its frequent presentation tends to lessen regard for the sacredness of life.

4. Suicide, as a solution to problems occurring in the development of screen drama, is to be discouraged unless absolutely necessary for the development of the plot, and shall never be justified, or glorified, or used specifically to defeat the ends of justice.

5. Excessive flaunting of weapons by criminals shall not be permitted.

6. There shall be no scenes of law-enforcing officers dying at the hands of criminals, unless such scenes are absolutely necessary to the plot.

7. Pictures dealing with criminal activities in which minors participate, or to which minors are related, shall not be approved if they tend to incite demoralizing imitation on the part of youth.

8. Murder:
   (a) The technique of murder must not be presented in a way that will inspire imitation.
   (b) Brutal killings are not to be presented in detail.
   (c) Revenge in modern times shall not be justified.
   (d) Mercy killings shall never be made to seem right or permissible.

9. Drug addiction or the illicit traffic in addiction-producing drugs shall not be shown if the portrayal:
   (a) Tends in any manner to encourage, stimulate or justify the use of such drugs; or
   (b) Stresses, visually or by dialogue, their temporarily attractive effects; or
   (c) Suggests that the drug habit may be quickly or easily broken; or
   (d) Shows details of drug procurement or of the taking of drugs in any manner; or
   (e) Emphasizes the profits of the drug traffic; or

(f) Involves children who are shown knowingly to use or traffic in drugs.

10. Stories on the kidnapping or illegal abduction of children are acceptable under the Code only (1) when the subject is handled with restraint and discretion and avoids details of gruesomeness and undue horror, and (2) the child is returned unharmed.

II. Brutality

Excessive and inhumane acts of cruelty and brutality shall not be presented. This includes all detailed and protracted presentations of physical violence, torture and abuse.

III. Sex

The sanctity of the institution of marriage and the home shall be upheld. No film shall infer that casual or promiscuous sex relationships are the accepted or common thing.

1. Adultery and illicit sex, sometimes necessary plot material, shall not be explicitly treated, nor shall they be justified or made to seem right and permissible.

2. Scenes of passion:
    (a) These should not be introduced except where they are definitely essential to the plot.
    (b) Lustful and open-mouth kissing, lustful embraces, suggestive posture and gestures are not to be shown.
    (c) In general, passion should be treated in such a manner as not to stimulate the baser emotions.

3. Seduction or rape:
    (a) These should never be more than suggested, and then only when essential to the plot. They should never be shown explicitly.
    (b) They are never acceptable subject matter for comedy.
    (c) They should never be made to seem right and permissible.

4. The subject of abortion shall be discouraged, shall never be more than suggested, and when referred to shall be condemned. It must never be treated lightly or made the sub-

ject of comedy. Abortion shall never be shown explicitly or by inference, and a story must not indicate that an abortion has been performed. The word "abortion" shall not be used.

5. The methods and techniques of prostitution and white slavery shall never be presented in detail, nor shall the subjects be presented unless shown in contrast to right standards of behavior. Brothels in any clear identification as such may not be shown.
6. Sex perversion or any inference of it is forbidden.
7. Sex hygiene and venereal diseases are not acceptable subject matter for theatrical motion pictures.
8. Children's sex organs are never to be exposed. This provision shall not apply to infants.

IV. Vulgarity

Vulgar expressions and double meanings having the same effect are forbidden. The treatment of low, disgusting, unpleasant, though not necessarily evil, subjects should be guided always by dictates of good taste and a proper regard for the sensibilities of the audience.

V. Obscenity

1. Dances suggesting or representing sexual actions or emphasizing indecent movements are to be regarded as obscene.
2. Obscenity in words, gesture, reference, song, joke or by suggestion, even when likely to be understood by only part of the audience, is forbidden.

VI. Blasphemy and Profanity

1. Blasphemy is forbidden. Reference to the Deity, God, Lord, Jesus, Christ, shall not be irreverent.
2. Profanity is forbidden. The words "hell" and "damn," while sometimes dramatically valid, will if used without moderation be considered offensive by many members of the audience. Their use shall be governed by the discretion and prudent advice of the Code Administration.

VII. Costumes

1. Complete nudity, in fact or in silhouette, is never permitted, nor shall there be any licentious notice by characters in the film of suggested nudity.
2. Indecent or undue exposure is forbidden.
    (a) The foregoing shall not be interpreted to exclude actual scenes photographed in a foreign land of the natives of that land, showing native life, provided:
        (1) Such scenes are included in a documentary film or travelogue depicting exclusively such land, its customs and civilization; and
        (2) Such scenes are not in themselves intrinsically objectionable.

VIII. Religion

1. No film or episode shall throw ridicule on any religious faith.
2. Ministers of religion, or persons posing as such, shall not be portrayed as comic characters or as villains so as to cast disrespect on religion.
3. Ceremonies of any definite religion shall be carefully and respectfully handled.

IX. Special Subjects

The following subjects must be treated with discretion and restraint and within the careful limits of good taste:

1. Bedroom scenes.
2. Hangings and electrocutions.
3. Liquor and drinking.
4. Surgical operations and childbirth.
5. Third degree methods.

X. National Feelings

1. The use of the flag shall be consistently respectful.
2. The history, institutions, prominent people and citizenry of all nations shall be represented fairly.

3. No picture shall be produced that tends to incite bigotry or hatred among peoples of differing races, religions or national origins. The use of such offensive words as Chink, Dago, Frog, Greaser, Hunkie, Kike, Nigger, Spig, Wop, Yid, should be avoided.

XI. Titles

The following titles shall not be used:

1. Titles which are salacious, indecent, obscene, profane, or vulgar.
2. Titles which violate any other clause of this code.

XII. Cruelty to Animals

In the production of motion pictures involving animals, the producer shall consult with the authorized representative of the American Humane Association, and invite him to be present during the staging of such animal action. There shall be no use of any contrivance or apparatus for tripping or otherwise treating animals in any unacceptably harsh manner.

Appendix C

What's in a Name?

As the effect of the foreign film star was felt on Hollywood, a new language—Hollywood Esperanto—was created. Stars with Anglo-Saxon names acquired continental or "exotic" movie names, just as unpronounceable foreign ones were sanitized, shriveled, or shrunk. Although sometimes justifiable, there were other instances when such changes robbed a star of a definable personality—Cary Grant is more Archie Leach than he is Cary Grant, for example, just as Anne Bancroft is Anna Italiano. One star who held his ground was Lew Ayres; he was born Lew Ayres and promised his mother he would honor the name, so if they insisted on changing him into someone else they could just tear up the contract. It stayed Ayres; and he made his debut with Greta Garbo.

Most of the major film stars have undergone a name change at some point in their careers, but the following list shows the impact of the continental migration on movie star nomenclature:

ADOREE, Renee—Jeanne de la Fonte
ANNABELLA—Suzanne Georgette Carpentier
ARLETTY—Léonie Bathiat
AUMONT, Jean-Pierre—Jean-Pierre Salomons
BANKY, Vilma—Vilma Konesics/Vilma Loncit
BARA, Theda—Theodosia Goodman
BARTOK, Eva—Eva Sjöke
BELITA—Gladys Jepson-Turner

BRITT, May—Maybritt Wilkens
CALVET, Corinne—Corinne Dibos
CAPUCINE—Germaine Lefebvre
CHRISTIAN, Linda—Blanca Rosa Welter
COLBERT, Claudette—Claudette Chauchoin
CORTEZ, Ricardo—Jacob Krantz
DAMITA, Lili—Lillian Carré
DARCEL, Denise—Denise Billecard
DARVI, Bella—Bella Wegier
DIETRICH, Marlene—Maria Magdalene von Losch
DORN, Philip—Fritz van Dungen
GARBO—Greta Garbo/Greta Lorjissa Gustafsson (also calls
   herself Harriet Brown to avoid the press)
GERAY, Steve—Stefan Gyeryay
GILBERT, John—John Pringle
GISH, Lillian—Lilian de Guiche
GOLDWYN, Samuel—Samuel Goldfish
GRAVET, Fernand—Fernand Gravey/Fernand Martens
GRAY, Gilda—Marianne Michaelska
GRAY, Nadia—Nadia Kujnir-Herescu
GUÉTARY, Georges—George Guetary/Lambros Worloou
GURIE, Sigrid—Sigrid Haukelid
HAROLDE, Ralf—R. H. Wigger
HASSO, Signe—Signe Larrson
HELM, Brigitte—Gisele Schittenhelm
JANSSEN, David—David Meyer
JEANMAIRE—Zizi Jeanmaire/Renée Jeanmaire
JOLSON, Al—Asa Yoelson
JOURDAN, Louis—Louis Gendre
KARLOFF, Boris—William Pratt
LAMARR, Barbara—Reatha Watson
LAMARR, Hedy—Hedwig Eva Marie Kiesler/Hedy Kiesler
LAMOUR, Dorothy—Dorothy Kaumeyer
LISI, Virna—Virna Pierolsi
LOREN, Sophia—Sophia Scicolone/Sophia Lozzaro
LOY, Myrna—Myrna Williams
LUKAS, Paul—Paul Lukacs
MANNERS, David—Rauff Acklom

MARGO—Maria Marguerita Guadalupe Boldao y Castilla
MASSEY, Ilona—Ilona Hajmassy
MAZURKI, Mike—Michail Mazurwski
MONTEZ, MARIA—Maria de Santo Silas
MORGAN, Michèle—Simone Roussel
MUNI, Paul—Muni Weisenfreund
MURNAU, F. W.—Freidrich Plumpe
NEFF, Hildegarde—Hildegarde Knef
NEGRI, POLA—Barbara Apolonia Chalupez
OBERON, Merle—Estelle Thompson
PRESLE, Micheline—Micheline Prelle/Micheline Chassange
RALSTON, Vera—Vera Hruba Ralston/Vera Hruba
ROLAND, Gilbert—Luis De Alonso
TATI, Jacques—Jacques Tatischeff
STEN—Anna Sten/Anjuscha Stenski Sujakevitch/Anjuscha
    Stenski
STERNBERG, Josef von—Jo Sternberg/Joe Sternberg
STEVENS, Inger—Inger Stensland
VALENTINO, Rudolph—Rodolfo Alfonzo Raffaelo Pierre
    Filibert Guglielmi di Valentina d'Antonguolla/Rodolfo Gug-
    lielmi
VALLI—Alida Marie Altenburger/Alida Valli
VELEZ, Lupe—Guadalupe Velez de Villalobos
WALBROOK, Anton—Adolf Wohlbruck

Bibliography

Note: The material in this book is based on newly gathered reminiscences of the great continental stars, and of the movie pleasure dome era, wherever possible. This was supplemented with news clippings and memorabilia on file at the Library of the Lincoln Center of the Performing Arts and at the Museum of Modern Art Film Library. Books consulted either for historical backgrounds or to elucidate a fact or a sequence of facts include:

AGEE, JAMES: *Agee on Film* (McDowell, Obolensky, 1958)

ALLEN, FREDERICK LEWIS: *Only Yesterday* (Harper & Brothers, 1931)

ALLVINE, GLENDON: *The Greatest Fox of Them All* (Lyle Stuart, 1969)

AMORY, CLEVELAND: *The Last Resorts* (Harper & Brothers, 1952)

ANDERSON, JOHN MURRAY: *Out Without My Rubbers* (Library Publishers, 1954)

ARMES, ROY: *French Cinema* (A. Zwemmer Ltd., London, 1966)

ASTOR, MARY: *My Story* (Dell Books, 1960)

BAINBRIDGE, JOHN: *Garbo* (Doubleday, 1955)

BANKHEAD, TALLULAH: *Tallulah* (Harper & Brothers, 1952)

BARRYMORE, ETHEL: *Memories* (Harper & Brothers, 1955)

BARRYMORE, LIONEL: *We Barrymores* (Appleton-Century-Crofts, 1951)

BAUM, VICKI: *It Was All Quite Different* (Funk & Wagnalls, 1964)

BAXTER, JOHN: *Hollywood in the Thirties* (A. Zwemmer Ltd., London, 1968)

BICKFORD, CHARLES: *Bulls, Balls, Bicycles and Actors* (Paul S. Eriksson, 1965)

BILLQUIST, FRITIOF: *Garbo* (Putnam, 1960)

BLUM, DANIEL: *A Pictorial History of the Silent Screen* (Grosset & Dunlap) *A Pictorial History of the Talkies* (Grosset & Dunlap, 1958)

BOUSSINOT, ROGER: *L'Encyclopédie du Cinéma* (Bordas, France, 1967)

BROWN, JOHN MASON: *The Worlds of Robert E. Sherwood* (Harper and Row, 1962)

BROWNLOW, KEVIN: *The Parade's Gone By* (Alfred A. Knopf, 1968)

CALDER-MARSHALL, ARTHUR: *The Innocent Eye* (Harcourt, Brace and World, 1963)

CANTOR, EDDIE: *As I Remember Them* (Duell, Sloan and Pearce, 1963)

CARPOZI, GEORGE, JR.: *The Brigitte Bardot Story* (Belmont Books, 1961)

CASE, FRANK: *Tales of a Wayward Inn* (Frederick A. Stokes, 1928)

CHAPLIN, CHARLES: *My Autobiography* (Simon and Schuster, 1964)

CHAPLIN, LITA GREY: *My Life with Chaplin* (Bernard Geis Associates, 1966)

CHEVALIER, MAURICE: *With Love* (Little, Brown, 1960)

COBB, IRVIN S.: *Exit Laughing* (Bobbs-Merrill, 1941)

CONWAY, MICHAEL; MCGREGOR, DION; RICCI, MARK: *The Films of Greta Garbo* (Citadel Press, 1963)

CROWTHER, BOSLEY: *The Lion's Share* (Dutton, 1957) *Hollywood Rajah* (Holt, Rinehart and Winston, 1961)

CROY, HOMER: *Star Maker* (Duell, Sloan and Pearce, 1959)

DAVIDSON, BILL: *The Real and the Unreal* (Harper & Brothers, 1961)

DAVIS, BETTE: *The Lonely Life* (Lancer Books, 1963)

DAY, BETH: *This Was Hollywood* (Sidgwick and Jackson, London, 1960)

DEMILLE, AGNES: *Dance to the Piper* (Little, Brown, 1951)

DEMILLE, CECIL B.: *Autobiography of Cecil B. DeMille* (Prentice-Hall, 1959)

DESCHNER, DONALD: *The Films of Spencer Tracy* (Citadel Press, 1968)

DICKENS, HOMER: *The Films of Marlene Dietrich* (Citadel Press, 1968)

DIETRICH, MARLENE: *Marlene Dietrich's ABC* (Doubleday, 1962)

DRESSLER, MARIE: *My Own Story* (Little, Brown, 1934)

Essoe, Gabe: *Tarzan of the Movies* (Citadel Press, 1968)
Everson, William K.: *The Art of W. C. Fields* (Bobbs-Merrill, 1967)

Fowler, Gene: *Good Night, Sweet Prince* (Viking Press, 1944)
Franklin, Joe: *Classics of the Silent Screen* (Citadel Press, 1959)
Frewin, Leslie: *Dietrich* (Stein and Day, 1967)

Gabor, Zsa Zsa (with Gerold Frank): *My Story* (World, 1960)
Gassner, John, and Nichols, Dudley: *Twenty Best Film Plays* (Crown, 1943)
Godowsky, Dagmar: *First Person Plural* (Viking Press, 1958)
Goldwyn, Samuel: *Behind the Screen* (George H. Doran, 1923)
Goodman, Ezra: *Bogey: The Good-Bad Guy* (Lyle Stuart, 1965) *The Fifty-Year Decline and Fall of Hollywood* (Simon and Schuster, 1961)
Graham, Peter: *A Dictionary of the Cinema* (A. Zwemmer Ltd., London, 1968)
Green, Abel, and Laurie, Joe, Jr.: *Show Biz* (Henry Holt, 1957)
Griffith, Mrs. D. W.: *When the Movies Were Young* (Benjamin Blom, 1968)
Griffith, Richard: *Samuel Goldwyn* (Museum of Modern Art, 1956) *Marlene Dietrich* (Museum of Modern Art, 1959) with Arthur Mayer, *The Movies* (Simon and Schuster, 1957)

Hall, Ben: *The Best Remaining Seats* (Bramhall House, 1961)
Halliwell, Leslie: *The Filmgoer's Companion* (Hill and Wang, 1967)
Harris, Michael David: *Always on Sunday* (Meredith Press, 1968)
Hayden, Sterling: *Wanderer* (Bantam Books, 1962)
Hayes, Helen: *A Gift of Joy* (M. Evans and Co., 1965) *On Reflection* (M. Evans and Co., 1968)
Hays, Will H.: *Memoirs* (Doubleday, 1953)
Head, Edith: *The Dress Doctor* (Little, Brown, 1959)
Hecht, Ben: *A Child of the Century* (Simon and Schuster, 1954)
Hope, Bob: *Have Tux, Will Travel* (Pocket Books) *I Owe Russia $1200* (Doubleday, 1963)
Hopper, Hedda: *The Whole Truth and Nothing But* (Doubleday, 1963)
Hotchner, A. E.: *Papa Hemingway* (Random House, 1966)

JACKSON, CHARLES: *The Lost Weekend* (Farrar and Rinehart, 1944)
JACOBS, LEWIS: *The Rise of the American Film* (Harcourt, Brace, 1939) *Introduction to the Art of the Movies* (Noonday, 1960)
JESSEL, GEORGE: *So Help Me* (Random House, 1943)

KAEL, PAULINE: *Kiss Kiss Bang Bang* (Little, Brown, 1965)
KNIGHT, ARTHUR: *The Liveliest Art* (Macmillan, 1957)
KOBAL, JOHN: *Marlene Dietrich* (Dutton, 1968)
KOURY, PHIL: *Yes, Mr. DeMille* (Putnam, 1959)
KRACAUER, SIEGFRIED: *From Caligari to Hitler* (Princeton University Press, 1947)

LAING, E. E.: *Greta Garbo* (John Gifford, Ltd., London, 1946)
LAMARR, HEDY: *Ecstasy and Me* (Bartholomew House, 1966)
LASKY, JESSE L.: *I Blow My Own Horn* (Doubleday, 1957)
LIKENESS, GEORGE: *The Oscar People* (Wayside Press, 1965)
LOOS, ANITA: *A Girl Like I* (Viking Press, 1966)
LYND, ROBERT STAUGHTON, and LYND, HELEN: *Middletown* (Harcourt, Brace, 1937)
LUNDBERG, FERDINAND: *The Rich and the Super-Rich* (Lyle Stuart, 1968)
LYONS, EUGENE: *David Sarnoff* (Harper and Row, 1966)

MACGOWAN, KENNETH: *Behind the Screen* (Delacorte Press, 1965)
MAYER, ARTHUR: *Merely Colossal* (Simon and Schuster, 1953)
MAYER, MICHAEL: *Foreign Films on American Screens* (Arco, 1965)
McCABE, JOHN: *Mr. Laurel and Mr. Hardy* (Doubleday, 1961)
McVAY, DOUGLAS: *The Musical Film* (A. Zwemmer Ltd., London, 1968)
MENJOU, ADOLPHE (with M. M. MUSSELMAN): *It Took Nine Tailors* (McGraw-Hill, 1948)
MICHAEL, PAUL: *The Academy Awards* (Crown, 1968)
MONTAGU, IVOR: *Film World* (Penguin Books, 1964)
MOORE, COLLEEN: *Silent Star* (Doubleday, 1968)
MOREHOUSE, WARD: *Matinee Tomorrow* (Whittlesey House, 1949)
MORLEY, ROBERT: *Autobiography* (Simon and Schuster, 1968)

NEWQUIST, ROY: *A Special Kind of Magic* (Rand, McNally, 1967)
NOLAN, WILLIAM F.: *John Huston, King Rebel* (Sherbourne Press, 1965)
NOWELL-SMITH, GEOFFREY: *Visconti* (Doubleday, 1968)

NUGENT, ELLIOTT: *Events Leading up to the Comedy* (Trident Press, 1965)

OPPENHEIMER, GEORGE: *The View from the Sixties* (David McKay, 1966)

PALMBERG, RILLA PAGE: *The Private Life of Greta Garbo* (Doubleday, Doran, 1931)

PARSONS, LOUELLA: *Tell It to Louella* (Lancer Books, 1963)

PASTERNAK, JOE: *Easy the Hard Way* (Putnam, 1956)

PATTERSON, FRANCIS TAYLOR: *Cinema Craftsmanship* (Harcourt, Brace, 1921)

PEARSON, HESKETH: *The Marrying Americans* (Coward-McCann, 1962)

PICKFORD, MARY: *Sunshine and Shadow* (Doubleday, 1955)

POWDERMAKER, HORTENSE: *Hollywood, the Dream Factory* (Little, Brown, 1950)

QUIRK, LAWRENCE J.: *The Films of Joan Crawford* (Citadel Press, 1968)

RAMSAYE, TERRY: *A Million and One Nights* (Simon and Schuster, 1964)

RANDI, GIAN LUIGI: *Italian Cinema Today* (Hill and Wang, 1966)

RATHBONE, BASIL: *In and out of Character* (Doubleday, 1962)

REED, REX: *Do You Sleep in the Nude?* (New American Library, 1968)

ROSTEN, LEO: *Hollywood* (Harcourt, Brace, 1941)

ROTH, LILLIAN: *I'll Cry Tomorrow* (Frederick Fell, 1954)

ROTHA, PAUL, and GRIFFITH, RICHARD: *The Film Till Now* (Funk & Wagnalls, 1944)

SARRIS, ANDREW (ed.): *Interviews with Film Directors* (Bobbs-Merrill, 1967)

SCHICKEL, RICHARD: *The Disney Version* (Simon and Schuster, 1968)

SCHULMAN, IRVING: *Harlow* (Bernard Geis Associates, 1964) *Valentino* (Trident Press, 1967)

SELDES, GILBERT: *Seven Lively Arts* (Harper & Brothers, 1924)

SINCLAIR, UPTON: *Upton Sinclair Presents William Fox* (Sinclair, 1933)

STEELE, JOSEPH HENRY: *Ingrid Bergman* (David McKay, 1959)

STERNBERG, JOSEF VON: *Fun in a Chinese Laundry* (The Macmillan Company, 1965)

SWANBERG, W. A.: *Citizen Hearst* (Scribner, 1961)

TABORI, PAUL: *Alexander Korda* (Oldbourne Book Co., London, 1959)

TAYLOR, DEEMS; PETERSEN, MARCELENE; HALE, BRYANT: *A Pictorial History of the Movies* (Simon and Schuster, 1943)

TAYLOR, ROBERT LEWIS: *W. C. Fields* (Signet Books, 1967)

THOMAS, BOB: *King Cohn* (Putnam, 1967) *Thalberg* (Doubleday, 1969)

TYLER, PARKER: *Classics of the Foreign Films* (Citadel Press, 1962)

VALLEE, RUDY: *My Time Is Your Time* (Ivan Obolensky, 1962)

VIDOR, KING: *A Tree Is a Tree* (Harcourt, Brace, 1953)

WALKER, ALEXANDER: *The Celluloid Sacrifice* (Hawthorn Books, 1967)

WARNER, JACK L.: *My First Hundred Years in Hollywood* (Random House, 1964)

WEINBERG, HERMAN G.: *Josef von Sternberg* (Dutton, 1967)

WILSON, EDMUND: *The American Earthquake* (Doubleday, 1958)

ZIEROLD, NORMAN: *The Child Stars* (Coward-McCann, 1965)

ZOLOTOW, MAURICE: *Stagestruck* (Harcourt, Brace and World, 1964)

ZUKOR, ADOLPH: *The Public Is Never Wrong* (Putnam, 1953)

2. The Evolution of Movie Theaters

3. The Leading Personalities